# Mentoring from a Positive Psychology Perspective

Ann M. Brewer

# Mentoring from a Positive Psychology Perspective

## Learning for Mentors and Mentees

Springer

Ann M. Brewer
Academic Division
University of Newcastle
Sydney, NSW
Australia

ISBN 978-3-319-82233-4 ISBN 978-3-319-40983-2 (eBook)
DOI 10.1007/978-3-319-40983-2


Softcover reprint of the hardcover 1st edition 2016


Printed on acid-free paper

This Springer imprint is published by Springer Nature
The registered company is Springer International Publishing AG Switzerland

# Introduction

Just as there are countless mentoring relationships operating in every walk of life, so too there are numerous books on mentoring. No doubt, we have all read our fair share of them, with a lot of them focusing on the consequences of mentoring.

In the business and management literature, mentoring is viewed as an instrumental process used by managers, particularly human resource managers to assist either the assimilation of the new entrant into the enterprise or employees transitioning to new roles or a promotion so that they not only learn to "fit in" but also experience higher job satisfaction and self-esteem as a consequence of mentoring (Allen et al. 2004). Promotions and higher salaries are usually the proxy measurements for enhanced satisfaction and self-esteem (Eby and McManus 2004). Undoubtedly, such advantages of mentoring exist for the mentored employee, the mentor and the organisation (Allen et al. 2004; Eby et al. 2006). However, this is not the focus here.

The aim of this book is not to retrace old ground drawn from the management literature; rather, it is to discover some fresh insights from broader research into mentoring and cognate areas—to go inside the conversations as it were and to explore aspects, rarely communicated. The title of the book, *Mentoring Mindedness*, points to a fresh focus introducing readers and students into relevant research as well as a way of thinking about mentoring practice that they might not otherwise be acquainted with.

Why does anyone seek out mentoring? The reasons for seeking a mentor are vast, various and open to change as people develop throughout their life. Usually, mentees seek overall guidance and support or specific information about what they think they need to know (Parisi et al. 2009). Now and again, some mentees want to be advised about the "right way" to do things and that may be fine. However, a mentee's search while predictable may be limited due their experience. They may not be able to see beyond their current boundaries of work and life experience. Sometimes, mentees need to look at things differently, inside out as it were, or in ways that are unfamiliar to them to discover the real issues that they need to answer or are impeding their progress. Life for most of us follows a pattern that becomes predictable because we do not know another route to take. If we do take a different route, it is incidental and rarely life altering. Often, we are unaware of it. Some of us imagine a different route and wish to explore what this might mean. In other words, assess the risks of change. Mentors assist mentees in the process of reflection to lead them to venture outside their normal patterns of choices and actions.

Mentoring is rarely without difficulty and effort; in fact, it cannot be. For mentoring to become a positive relationship between two people, both parties have a responsibility to learn and benefit from it. When two people get together to talk, it takes effort for one to externalise their thoughts by explaining these to the other. A conversation is facilitated by its interrogative and inquisitive nature, asking why, what, how, when and where so each person understands the other's point of view. This process leads to the mentor and mentee not only listening to each other more carefully but also leads them to reflect, clarify, and adjust their thinking as they go. If so, this spry process leads to breakthrough insights, a more satisfying resolution of an issue, more rapidly than one person working on their own (Schwartz 1995).

Another reason for mentoring is found in the work of Angyal (1941), a little-known psychologist whose work influenced the renowned Rogers (1961). The concept of *homonomy*, which Angyal defined as "the tendency to conform to, unite with, participate in, and fit into super-individual wholes" (p. 182), is something that most people crave at some stage particularly when things are not working out as expected. Angyal viewed this need as "a source of profound motivation for human behaviour" (p. 182). It is this intense motivation that drives people to search for wisdom and learning, hence seeking out a mentor. Angyal believed that people have the propensity to transform themselves, develop or participate in a greater, life purpose. Mentoring assists people to take a long-term view, keeping in mind the effect of everyday decisions. This approach also serves to strengthen an underlying moral presence for mentees.

What is most important in mentoring is how the mentee's focus becomes increasingly multidimensional: not only focused on knowledge and skills but also building capacity to see beyond this. Mentoring is about being in the moment and seeing its relationship to a greater realm of experience and being; this is *mindedness* (Dreyfus 2007). Mindedness incorporates the dimensions of being mindful. It creates a crucial shift in our understanding of people and how they experience and relate to the world as well as their place in it.

Mentoring mindedness is what Noë (2009, p. 42) terms the "external correlates" of consciousness as well as the internal ones. The mentor assists the mentee to explore their experience as both an actor and an observer, aimed at moving towards an *immersed understanding* of what is going on. This understanding facilitates a more spontaneous approach to life which is less contrived and risk-averse. To use a prosaic example when we are driving a car, riding a bike and playing sport or a musical instrument, we are engaged in the spontaneous flow of decision-making, enacting and influencing others around us. Actions and decisions are best performed without the mentee having to deliberate on each one every time. The reason is that most of us have been shown how to do these things, engaged in practice and weighed up the risks of doing them or not. Years of practice allow us to drive or play in seamless sequences and interactions to suit the circumstances. Mentoring mindedness captures this process of artful consciousness and proficiency.

Mentoring also offers mentees a sense of optimism and anticipation through a process of goal-setting. Through their conversations, new strengths are gained by the mentee and they will feel a sense of optimism and confidence, peaking and sustained beyond mentoring. Hope is a wonderful gift for the mentee to gain from mentoring. It cannot be procured and develops over time through a trusting relationship that unfolds effortlessly throughout the time spent with a skilled mentor. However, as this book seeks to demonstrate, mentoring accelerates the mentee's development and capacity for reflection and integration of new thinking so as to sustain their learning beyond the mentoring relationship. This approach demonstrates the positivity of mentoring in a very real sense.

Although mentoring dates back at least to the Aristotelean era, it has attained renewed prominence in modern times, particularly over the last 30 years or so. About this time, empirical studies of mentoring appeared in scholarly journals. Allen and Johnston (1997) claimed that more than 500 articles on mentoring were published in management and education literature during the ten years leading up to 1997, although some publications by practitioners and theorists appeared earlier than that. There are still two frequently cited and more recent works, one by Allen and Eby's 2007, *The Blackwell Handbook of Mentoring*, which provides observations and advice as well as their much earlier publication, focusing on the phases of the mentoring relationship published in the *Academy of Management Journal* in 1983. Readers and students are encouraged to read this literature as either a companion or counterpoint to this book.

Suffice to say writing on mentoring continues. A research of multiple databases using similar parameters revealed that there are over 5500 articles published between 1998 and August 2014. So you might well ask, what could another book possibly add? Mentoring is about "swimming in the waters" with another person, alongside them as they seek to encounter the changing climactic conditions that challenge and, at times, impede their progress. What is meant by this is that a mentoring relationship assists mentees to develop, establish and sustain strategies for life, beyond mentoring.

The purpose of *Mentoring Mindedness* is to provide a holistic, multidisciplinary framework that assists mentors and mentees to take a more thoughtful approach to mentoring. The structure combines creative approaches with some conventional wisdom. It achieves this by drawing on perspectives from a range of complementary disciplines of knowledge to examine what will work for this mentee and, more importantly, what is realistically sustainable. The approach points to ideas and practices that hopefully inspire would-be mentors and mentees to look beyond the management and business literature where mentoring features widely.

The aim of this book is to *look inside* the mentoring relationship itself, how the conversation evolves and how the mentor potentiates hypothetical thinking by asking a serious of questions initiated by "what if?", followed by "why?" then "how?" and "when might you do that?". This form of questioning is realistic and organised and allows the mentee to see things differently. It seeks to challenge assumptions held by mentees so that they can participate more efficiently in an open-minded way and engage in creative exploration of the realm of possibilities for their future. It is also a simple means for applying it in everyday life. It replaces negative thinking with a more constructive approach through resolving issues and problems. The aim of mentoring is to facilitate thinking to enable the mentee to distinguish significant opportunities and assist in making informed decisions about the next step and formulating a pragmatic action plan that maintains commitment from the mentee beyond the mentoring experience.

Some mentors think that seeking breakthroughs in mentees' thinking is too grandiose and are content with satisfying the mentee's immediate needs by giving guidance. The latter is fine, although more is gained if a better understanding of mindedness is employed in mentoring. However, experience shows us that centring on short-term needs yields—"quick fixes," are usually untenable as they have not been bedded down. Having a stretch goal achieves not only short-term fixes but also facilitates significant professional and personal growth for mentees, which are continued given its powerful effect.

Themes such as diversity, blame, loyalty and silence are explored. *Mentoring Mindedness* takes the road less travelled in that it deals with emotions and process as well as content. It examines in a more intimate way how the mentee is challenged and how they fail to build or modify boundaries and to look beyond them.

*Mentoring Mindedness* is not characterised by commonplace advice or a Band-Aid approach. Instead, it spans a conversational passage of inquiry and actions—from reflection through to the detailed action plan that enable the mentee to experience confidence and optimism.

While chapter one touches on defining mentoring for readers coming fresh to the subject, the emphasis is on its potential goals, processes and impact. How mentoring is delivered and what form it takes are not as important as the value of the relationship. To demonstrate the point here, the *Five As* from Potter-Efron's positive interactions are useful and relevant for mentoring:

1. **Attention**: I have time for you.
2. **Approval**: I like what you do.
3. **Acceptance**: It is OK for you to be you.
4. **Admiration**: I can learn from you because you represent what I need to learn.
5. **Affirmation**: I acknowledge your cognitions, emotions and actions.

Anyone wanting to learn more about becoming an active mentor will find this book worthwhile. It is also important to have experienced mentoring as a mentee before one embarks on mentoring another person. Mentees will also find value in this book, for example how mentoring might benefit them, and if so, how to engage in it so as to make it worthwhile. Mentoring is what the mentee and mentor make of it, especially in conversation with each other. Whatever else mentoring is, there should be no disagreement about that the focus is on the mentee's experience and observations.

## References

Allen, T. D. (2004). Protégé selection by mentors: Contributing individual and organizational factors. *Journal of Vocational Behaviour, 65*, 469–483.
Allen, J., & Johnston, K. (1997). Mentoring. *Context, 14*(7), 15.
Allen, T. D., & Eby, L. T. (2003). Relationship effectiveness for mentors: Factors associated with learning and quality. *Journal of Management, 29*, 469–486.
Allen, T. D., & Eby, L. T. (Eds.). (2007). *The Blackwell handbook of mentoring: A multiple perspectives approach.* London: Wiley-Blackwell.
Allen, T. D., Eby, L. T., O'Brien, K. E., & Lentz, E. (2008). The state of mentoring research: A qualitative review of current research methods and future research implications. *Journal of Vocational Behaviour, 73*(3), 343–357.
Angyal, A. (1941). *Foundations for a Science of Personality*. New York: Commonwealth Fund.
Dreyfus, H. L. (2007). The return of myth of the mental. *Inquiry, 50*(4), 352–365.
Eby, L. T., & McManus, S. E. (2004). The protégé's role in negative mentoring experiences. *Journal of Vocational Behaviour, 65*, 255–275.
Noë, A. (2009). *Out of the head. Why you are not your brain.* Cambridge: MIT Press.
Parisi, J. M., Rebok, G. W., Carlson, M. C., et al. (2009). Can the wisdom of aging be activated and make a difference societally? *Educational Gerontology, 35*(10), 867–879.
Rogers, C. R. (1961). *On becoming a person: A therapist's view of psychotherapy*. London, England: Constable.
Schwartz, D. L. (1995). The emergence of abstract representations in dyad problem solving. *Journal of the Learning Sciences, 493*, 321–354.

# Contents

# Chapter 1
# Mentoring Mindedness

*It will be found that the ingenious are always fanciful,*
*and the truly imaginative never otherwise than analytic.*
Edgar Allen Poe.

**Abstract** The tradition of mentoring remains as active today as mentees seek to gain insight, practical knowledge and draw upon the experience of their 'mentors'. The latter is far less significant than gaining insight as the way each person experiences the world is different and cannot and ought not be replicated. Mentors are privileged in that they work with another person, the mentee, with the aim to assist them in whatever way is suitable and negotiated between them. How does this work? How do mentors deal with difficult issues? What if they are not able to assist the mentee? Both the mentee and mentor experience their relationship from inside mentoring. No one else experiences it, can observe it or by its very nature, understand what is going on or went on.

Mentoring is deeply personal and subtle. At times it can be confusing and complex in that inevitable contradictions present during the mentoring conversation and need to be noted and addressed. Sometimes a mentee may not be ready to deal with the issue or a mentor is incapable of dealing with the problem, although not always fully cognisant of this. Sometimes the problems need to be referred to an expert or reported to an authority. Mostly these require negotiation with the mentee. The mentee poses existential questions in conversation, crucial in shaping a choice, and may trigger in the mentor a discomforting response rather than one that they feel assured about. Suffice to say, the mentoring relationship is different to friendship or supervision, although the dynamics of both these relationships are present. However, neither the mentor nor the mentee should confuse their relationship with these bonds.

Mentors embrace a very special relationship with their mentees; however, mentoring does not provide a licence to control or direct them. In other words, mentoring is not about moralistically improving the mentee. A mentor does not seek to proselytise nor convert mentees to their way of thinking. Mentees may not



A.M. Brewer, *Mentoring from a Positive Psychology Perspective*,
DOI 10.1007/978-3-319-40983-2_1

share the same assumptions with the mentor about work and professional life and this may provide an important counterpoint. In fact, it may serve to strengthen the mentee in understanding disagreement within a positive relationship. Mentors are geared toward learning as much as possible about the mentee's world view. While there may be differences, both need to feel comfortable about the coexistence of diverse ideas, assumptions and values.

Mentoring is about how the mentor, usually an experienced person is invited into the world of the mentee, who may present as less knowledgeable although the converse may be true, to learn together as equal partners. The mentor does not derive power from the situation. If so, it defeats the purpose as this is often the issue that a mentee is struggling to deal with. Both the mentee and mentor learn more about this as the relationship unfolds in novel and challenging ways for each of them. Mentoring is a dynamic relationship whereby experienced people assist others by asking questions or, as some describe, posing choices (Lewis 2000). Posing choices is essentially a process of establishing hypothetical questions, which is exceedingly powerful in mentoring as it becomes more enterprising in that it is resourceful, adventurous and inventive. Like other relationships, mentoring is initiated around the interest of both parties, exploring viewpoints, sharing ideas, creating choices, problem-solving and evaluating these in preparation for application. Both mentees and mentors require agile thinking and a flexible approach.

Mentoring is based on a mentee-centred inquiry. The mentor assists the mentee in parsing issues that they bring forth for discussion. Initially, these are framed by the mentee which means that the mentee is privileged in regard to the mentor. This is often not the case in practice.

Mentees utilise the wisdom gained in mentoring to fathom whether they are making apt choices and decisions in their life. Coming to this realisation and acting upon it, is a salient aspect of a spirited life. As noted earlier, mentoring is durable, pan-cultural and universal. Its value extends beyond the experience. However, ideas and practices adjust as life, practices and expectations change. Mentoring assists in building and refining not only the development goals of the mentee but also their sensibilities towards achieving these.

In some situations, mentoring is cyclical and does not find closure. However usually it requires an end-date in mind to avoid one party becoming overly-dependent on the other for whatever reason. Just as in other relationships, mentors and mentees can become somewhat reliant upon one another depending on the conditions under which their relationship develops. Over reliance of one or the other is not the hallmark of a resilient life and is one of the warning signs to heed. However, more about this issue later.

Mentoring is relational as well as serving more than one purpose; often the purpose is clarified as the relationship evolves. Trying to define mentoring regarding how it is structured is perhaps the approach that attracts attention by many practitioners and management theorists alike. Structurally-speaking, mentoring is a relationship, whereby two people agree to work together instigated in the best circumstances for the mentee. From the outset, its duration should be specified so that goals and outcomes are planned. Mentoring in that sense, is formalised rather than formal in that there may be an assigned agreement between the parties, explicit or implicit.

Essentially mentoring, as previously stated, is creative and varies from one relationship to the next. Both parties create meaning together and this is continuously re-created throughout the span of the relationship. The mentor modifies their approach to assure that the mentee's perspectives are brought to the forefront and only influences the conversation, when appropriate and acceptable to the mentee's standpoint. The process is a toing and froing of each one's interpretations of events and the possible choices. Learning emerges through the interaction of the mentee with the mentor in a similar way to how an ensemble of musicians might tune their instruments or move between parts. It is done in unison. These insights are implicit especially regarding a mentor's predilections. Mentoring is different to other relationships in that mentors need to ensure that what they bring is inherent to the realm of the explicit. Specific training for mentors and mentees before the commencement of the relationship requires a more considered approach. See Sect. 2.8 of this book.

Creativity evolves through the contemplation by both the mentee and the mentor, focusing on outcomes rather than an explicitly defined purpose. An inward, reflective response from the mentee is induced while, at other times, it may be necessary to avert them from a self-focus to a more other-centred approach. The mentee presents with an "inner world", accessible only to them. Their "outer world" is open to others and forms the foundation of a seemingly objective reality (Dawis 2002). Section 3.5 focuses on how the mentor can utilise this perspective.

The purpose of mentoring is a process of gaining and implementing acumen as well as galvanising the mentee to continue with their new learning beyond mentoring. When the mentee commences executing actions formulated about the former, they often realise that it is not working out as expected and are required to modify (sometimes with the mentor's assistance) what they initially envisioned.

Assisting the development of emotional capability is another key purpose of mentoring. For example, a mentor works with mentees to support them regulate and hone not only their skills but also their attitudes, emotions—sometimes reassuring them while at other times attempting to energise them. Sometimes mentoring plays a central part for individuals in developing an identity-formation for and when taking on a new role.

The mentoring relationship is not an end in itself rather, as stated above, invigorating (or decisively taking no action) outcomes by the mentee. In other words, it is a means by which new learning is executed consciously by the mentee. The nature of the personal and professional opportunities (e.g. career promotion) arising from this relationship, rather than the quality of the relationship per se, speaks to its success. However, its outcomes are often inestimable.

Mentoring varies: from one-on-one pairings of seasoned experts with less experienced persons to peer mentoring where they exchange knowledge, skills and attitudes relevant to the workplace. Mentoring takes many forms. Examples of mentoring include teachers with students; male role models with boys, younger students with older ones, early career professionals with more experienced counterparts, youth workers with adolescents, and women seeking directorships on boards working with experienced board members, and leadership aspirants working with executives. Reverse mentoring is also prevalent; that is young people working with those more experienced than themselves, usually for the purposes of learning new forms of technology and communication media. All of these examples share a similar pattern of dynamic interactions of a mentoring relationship.

Over 35 years ago, an article in the Harvard Business Review (Roche 1979), instigated mentoring as a crucial concept for business attainment. This study reported an association between robust mentoring relationships and a variety of positive career outcomes, such as a greater likelihood of following initial career paths, higher earnings and educational achievement, and greater career satisfaction. A study of business school graduates a decade later revealed similar findings for those experiencing intensive mentoring relationships (Dreher and Ash 1990).

Whether the above is evidence of good mentoring is contentious. However whatever form mentoring takes, the nature of knowing varies: knowing how to do, knowing how to show someone else, knowing in theory and tacit knowing. It is important that these distinctions are made and understood by the mentee. This also helps people understand and accept ambiguity and uncertainty as it takes time to learn how to perform in a new context and is not too dissimilar to someone learning a new culture and language (Byram 2011).

Informal mentoring is just as valid as formal mentoring. These usually emerge and are either professional or psychosocial in nature, formed by the interpersonal dynamics between mentors and mentees, based on mutual interests and concerns.

Mentoring can be reciprocal: peer-to-peer or cohort-based as in co-mentoring, aimed at providing psychosocial support for participants. One or more of the members may have more knowledge and experience that they may use to "guide" the less experienced or new people, perhaps focusing on cultural and political issues.

Many have written that mentoring is about trying to achieve the best outcome for mentees (Schwille 2008; Radu Lefebvre and Redien-Collot 2013). The outcomes sought are specified by the mentee initially and negotiated as they change over time. In that way, mentoring relationships encourage mentees to become 'autonomous, self-aware, reflective and creative learners' (Yaghjian 2013, p. 225; Leck and Orser 2013).

The learnings and the process for mentoring are often ad hoc, unanticipated and rarely discussed. When wisdom surfaces in mentoring, such as how to cope with a complicated relationship mentees can initiate a process for dealing with it. Learning how to handle difficult relationships where there is a power differential is a critical issue for most of us. For example, dealing with dying patients, working with troubled clients; caring for the young and the elderly, teaching students and providing pastoral care are some of the tricky issues confronting mentees. Frequently a novice focuses on dealing with the technicalities of the role and is shocked by the psycho-social complexities that face them in their professional and personal relationships. Tackling the psycho-social aspects associated with work, although tacitly understood by experienced staff and experts, emerge as a surprise and often, unpredictably for the mentee. The novice is often ill-equipped to deal with these issues. While mentoring may convey technical knowledge and skills; its real focus needs to be about cultural and psycho-social aspects of the issue, "transferred" by the mentor to the mentee.[1]

Mentoring is now also conducted as a virtual relationship. Often social media is used for mentoring individuals or groups, especially those in remote locations. While virtual mentoring is a different relationship to an actual one, many of the attributes apply.

## 1.1 Searching for Greater Meaning

Mentoring is often about searching for a more meaningful existence. Well-being is linked to greater life meaning (Steger et al. 2009). In a world in which transitions are increasingly common at all stages of life (Savickas 2011), mentoring is pertinent at times of change. Significant societal and economic shifts create transitions that individuals have to deal with (Brown 2012). Often individuals find themselves steeped in uncertainty about their future. Concern over career prospects can spark questions about values and meaning in life. Significant decisions increase awareness of isolation, meaning, responsibility and freedom (Yalom 1980).

Mentees often request mentoring to help cope with the pressures and stresses of decisions based on a perceived need for change. Anxiety, to some extent, often accompanies such decision-making. Increasingly this is the experience of people at the point of life's main transitions: leaving school, changing careers, leaving work to care for a family, retiring and so on. From a personal perspective, they often require rapid decision-making so as not to lose opportunities as they materialise, and others fade. Mentoring assists in dampening anxiety and gaining a sense of control; noting that these processes may be different when people experience or respond to unexpected change compared to those that are planned.

A mentor can assist mentees in assessing their current circumstances in the hope of planning more confidently for the future. People initiate a decision-making process often basing it on their previously learned experiences (Krumboltz 2009; Bandura 1989). Specifically, mentors help mentees to (a) leverage learning from prior experiences and how they have or may respond to these; (b) perceive contributing factors to unexpected events; (c) convert an ostensible crisis into a prospect (d) minimise self-doubt and (e) actively identify and make choices (Krumboltz 2009; Krumboltz et al. 2013). The following table, based on Betsworth and Hansen's (1996) work, outlines some of these changes.

[1]***Transfer*** refers to "the influence of prior learning (retained until the present) upon the learning of, or response to, new material …" (Butler et al. 2013, p. 291; McGeoch 1942, p. 394). Butler et al. (2013), Explanation feedback is better than correct answer feedback for promoting transfer of learning, *Journal of Educational Psychology, 105* (2), 290–298; McGeoch (1942). *The psychology of human learning: An introduction*. New York, NY: Longmans, Green and Co. doi:10.2307/2262568.

| Reasons for mentoring based on change due to | Nature of change |
|---|---|
| Relationships | Relationships with employers, teachers, advisors, colleagues or friends provided advice; informal recommendations to employers; invitations to join a particular program or position, or job offer |
| Unexpected changes | Restructure; offered of a new position and not sure they can cope; temporary situation is made permanent or vice versa |
| Familial influences | Partner's career and lifestyle, type of occupation; homemaking, and non-work activities; as well as changes in these relationships including the illness or death of a partner or child; divorce; caring for ageing parents and so on |
| Influence of previous experiences including work/volunteer experience | Develop skills, knowledge attributes; gain necessary qualifications, or acquire new/additional experience in areas of interest |
| Career obstacles | Identifying and pursuing other options |

The relative impact of each of the above is highly variable from person to person and situation to situation. Mentoring is a critical process in assisting a mentee navigate the event and engage in significant learning in the process.

## 1.2 Mindful or Mindedness?

Both mindfulness and mindedness encompass emotional alertness. Mindfulness is a heightened attention to what is going on around you now (Brown and Ryan 2003). For example, a mentee may be alert to a situation and interpreted it in a particular way. After engaging with the mentor, the mentee may gain a more enhanced understanding of the context: immediate and beyond. That is, mindfulness draws attention to the "what is" and not becoming side-tracked by the "what isn't". On the other hand, mindedness is almost the exact opposite. What isn't may be just as important as what is.

Mindfulness leads to an overreliance on tangible realities, categorising and distinguishing issues based on a person's experience. People become context-dependent and, as such, oblivious to new, unconventional or different aspects of the situation that is more often than not, required in resolving issues or innovating. On the other hand, mindedness is serendipitous and encourages people to think and act beyond their usual patterns.

The primary distinction between mindedness and mindfulness is that in the latter case, new learning may be blocked through exposure to information provided by the mentor. When information is given by a perceived expert, it may be simply accepted. There may be little apparent reason to scrutinise it and thereby appreciate the ways it is person or context-specific. As a result, the mentee decides that the information is correct and blocks further potential or deeper exploration of various situations; particularly how this advice may not serve them well.

The art of mentoring is to encourage the full participation of a mentee in reflecting, questioning and achieving awareness about specific or general issues. A further important question for the mentor to ponder is why people seek a mentor. Often success stories evolve around the person attributing their success to a wise mentor. There are two parts to this. Firstly, mentees use the relationship to relate their stories to a mentor. Through the telling of the story and with the assistance of the mentor, they create meaning around the issues significant to them for consideration (Fivush 2008; McLean et al. 2007). Meaning is achieved by the autobiographical content, replete with explanation and evaluation that weave together the story line: people, places, and events imbued with psychological states, intentions, and motivations. A mentor listens and observes the content and the dynamics of the telling and deduces from this how the mentee perceives themselves both in time and place and about others. The critical point here is to begin the reflective process so that this becomes transparent for the mentee.

The second part concerns active wisdom. Most people want to increase their knowing: know-what, know-why know-how and most of all, understanding (Zeleny 2006). Wisdom and trust go hand in hand, best achieved by the mentor withstanding the irresistible pull to teach, influence or reach a conclusion for the mentee. Mentees then realise that their 'fate' is in their hands not the mentor's. It is the mentee that has to decide about whether or not to act; if so when, how and so on (Maxwell 2007). Suffice to say, the mentor needs to appreciate what is not being said as much as what is. This latter point will be discussed fully in Chap. 7.

Remember the mentee's narratives are recreated within the mentoring relationship to serve a purpose (Conway and Pleydell-Pearce 2000; Rubin 2006). That does not mean that the stories are true or false, rather how the mentor treats them is critical to the effectiveness of the relationship. As the mentee shares their personal history with the mentor using language, silence and gesture that the events of their past may take on different meanings and different evaluations of them. Listening, observing and questioning by the mentor are important in achieving this outcome where applicable.

A wise mentor guides the mentee into self-directed learning by working together rather than imprinting him or herself onto the mentee. Moreover, in so doing the mentee learns wisdom; experiencing its personal benefit and knowing its social consequences, similar to learning to live ethically (Biasi 2006; Rowley 2006). It is about finding the counter-balance between self-interest and the greater good.

Mentoring includes a full spectrum of actions including listening, reflecting, clarifying, questioning, challenging and resolving. It is a process of integration that facilitates for the mentee, an enhanced and meaningful understanding of self and context leading to the establishment of personal and professional goals, strategies and commitments for future action. Positively, the influence of a mentoring relationship is one in which mentees learn the ingredients of choice-making, how to action them and in so doing form new ways of thinking and relating to others.

However, any one definition of mentoring does not address what it means for mentors and mentees in every situation. What counts for mentoring varies as it takes many forms and serves diverse functions in different settings and different professions. Mentoring is neither an absolute nor a constant. It is considered a dynamic concept, which will change over time (from year to year/decade to decade). Participating in mentoring is satisfying a search for meaning and a process for learning about what is going on within given contexts, professional, personal or both. The mentor is significant in this process and needs to be highly experienced (and often highly qualified) in an area, relevant to the needs of the mentee in seeking a mentor.

The reason for this is that mentoring is primarily two minds coming together. It is not about inserting a supplementary "mind" of the mentor with that of the mentee rather it is about integrating their perspectives—the socio-cognitive aspects of their "worldview". Being mentoring-minded is about gaining:

(a) an informed understanding about and insight into a 360° perspective (i.e., the triad of the mentee-significant others-mentor and mentoring professional interface (adapted from Filho et al. 2007)); and the
(b) a capacity to apply that understanding and insight to inform not only the mentoring relationship but also potentially inspiring the learning of the mentee. A primary tenant of self-directed learning is reflected in mentoring where people take the initiative for planning, carrying out and evaluating their development.

Mentoring engages both the mentee and mentor in hopefully a stirring deep engagement to activate the mentee's thinking during their conversations. This mental engagement involves creative thinking processes such as retrieving information, linking ideas through association, synthesising, transforming ideas and thinking, analogical transfer and categorisation to name a few. This process is the basis of mentoring mindedness. Psychological mindedness is "a person's ability to see relationships among thoughts, feelings and actions, with the goal of learning the meanings and causes of his experience and behaviour" (Applebaum 1973, p. 36). This capacity enables reflection on motives, psychological processes, and inner experiences of the self as well as on relationships with others (Hall 1992). Mindedness is linked with self-consciousness and mindfulness (Beitel et al. 2005). However, it is a broader concept than mindfulness. Two aspects of mindedness have been identified namely an interest in and the ability for reflecting on one's psychological states and processes (Hall 1992). Mentoring is aimed at being in touch and to reflect in a nonanalytic way—is considered more fundamental than the intellectual, analytic aspect of reflection, although also significant. Focused on the rational processes of understanding actions is often "at the expense of learning about behaviour on a more affective level" (Hall 1992, p. 137). For a further example of this, Dreyfus (2007 p. 273) recounts a grandmaster, saying that under extreme time pressure he "sometimes finds his arm going out and making a move before he can take in the board position". These actions, according to Dreyfus are "non-minded" and occur without conscious thought.

In mentoring, the mentee engages knowingly at least initially as they deal with their insights as these reveal the personal relevance of their perceptions, feelings and situation. It is important to understand that mindedness is a particular attribute reflecting both an attitude (interest) and skill (ability for insight). It is something that can be learned by the mentee through active mentoring.

### *1.2.1 The Emic and Etic of Mentoring*

Another way of framing mentoring mindedness is through the mentee's account of what is going on in their world. This approach is what cultural anthropologists term an 'emic' explanation or what a sociologist or linguist would term a 'narrative'. A distinct culture is a complex whole of overlapping domains and processes that influences all thinking and actions for participants (Csikszentmihalyi 1991). Cultures provide a shared understanding of what life looks like, the types of experiences expected and the stages at which they are most likely to happen including a career. This point is discussed more fully in 1.2.2 below.

Mentoring mindedness is primarily a form of learning whereby the mentee is not only learning from the mentor but also is learning things about themselves through self-discovery. It is potentially a medium for the transmission of these learnings to others (Tomasello 2014). This transformation is the essence of mentoring mindedness. Like culture, it is a social process, the mentee letting themselves become involved rather than a rational one. Culture often feels tangible. It represents the "storehouse" of interconnected and confirmed patterns of learned behaviour typifying members of social, professional, work groups, for example, including the symbolic representation of experiences and the distinct ways in which groups of people classify and represent their collective experience (van de Walle 2008).

A critical part of mentoring mindedness is preparing mentees for cultural experiences, whatever and how diverse these may be. Mentoring due to its informal nature is often in effect developed and delivered to people with a parallel cultural orientation to those being mentored. Mentoring can easily overlook the needs of diverse workforces. Mentoring mindedness assumes that both mentors and mentees have been prepared to offer a supportive relationship with people from all backgrounds. The mentee holds assumptions and beliefs that they will have usually held for some time, based on culture-specific practices of their profession or workplace passed to them through observational learning. Any description of an event, relationship, symbols within a culture can provide an 'emic' account. This cultural matching is often a reason for its success. However, today where mentees are from many diverse backgrounds or likely to work in a less familiar work settings, this approach will be less apt and indeed, unsuccessful. In other cases, mentees will be thinking of their career from an individual perspective rather than a collective one, that is often representative of some professions, even today. In most cases, a mentee's career will have multiple orientations some cutting across the other.

Mentees will define their life and professional narratives about the cultural script that they know, intentionally or not. Mentoring helps review and refresh this cultural perception so that mentees are better prepared to deal with a broad range of situations. In constructing a sense of identity, mentees reference their achievements against their values and aspirations and also compare similarities and differences with others. A person's identity provides a link to their life story, their personal narrative (McAdams 2006). As each mentee narrates their story to a mentor, they do so using cultural expectations of what a typical life should look like for them at this stage of their development or experience.

The mentee brings this viewpoint to the mentor for 'examination' either based on their experience or as an experienced 'analyst'. Through the narrative-telling, mentors attempt to understand the "mind frame" of the mentee by asking questions as well as through deductive reasoning: positing "theories" of explanation, without feeling the need to verify them. The mentor will also draw on intuitive knowledge, hunches that they may have about what may work. This process provides an 'etic' account often referred to as 'an outsider's view' that is deductive and initiates a questioning approach within the mentee (based on Morris et al. 1999). Both the etic and emic accounts, coupled together, provide a powerful process and rich understanding of the issues for the mentoring conversation.

### *1.2.2 Developing an Identity as a Mentor*

How will mentors enact their role and assure the outcomes are for the benefit of those whom they mentor? The process of becoming a mentor and being known as a mentor is serious. Mentors need to consider how they will prepare for this role. It is a role still recognised and employed in most professions today. A mentor needs to learn something about how the process best works in the interests of the mentee.

Initially, a mentor needs to establish a presence regarding their bearing and the way they attend to the mentee. For example when a mentor meets with the mentee, they need to establish their identity as a mentor regardless of their substantive role such as a chief executive officer, a teacher, or a medical practitioner. A mentor is not a coach, a counsellor, a supervisor or a parent (in the case of young mentees). That said, it is not easy for a mentor to relinquish their professional identity or attributed status. However, it is important that there is a clear separation from their known professional identity and the one they have as a mentor. It is equally important that the mentor does not overwhelm the mentee with all the ideas that they can conjure up. If so, it is the exact opposite of mentoring. More importantly, the mentor assists the mentee to uncover their ideas and work with them to find ways that quickly convert or translate into action—a form of action learning.

What is meant by a mentor has various definitions and specifications. Becoming a mentor requires a shift in perspective that is different from functioning as a manager or teacher or professor or consultant. It involves developmental and conceptual dimensions as well as perceptual, cognitive, affective, and behavioural ones. Mentors need to think and act with consistency and accordingly within their relationship with the mentee and not overstep this role boundary. To acquire and sustain an identity as a mentor is it important to have

a. integrity, high moral and ethical standards,
b. energy, and not being "too competitive",
c. genuine interest in the welfare and accomplishment of others,
d. skill, talent, knowledge, competence,
e. respect among peers,
f. capacity for empathy, patience, enthusiasm,
g. time and availability,
h. flexible in thinking and approach especially in creating creative thinking space in conversations with mentees. Strict adherence to overt and covert rules by a mentor is likely to be insensitive to the unique needs of each mentee. Mentoring conversations need to flow naturally with a certain measure of individualisation, within ethical boundaries,
i. capable of guiding others for action and reflection. Self-reflection and self-assessment are core foundational competencies within mentoring (Kaslow et al. 2004) and consistent with the current focus on mindfulness (Shapiro and Carlson 2009),
j. being sufficiently aware of their emotional reactions to the conversation with the mentee and in each case, observing the role boundaries of a professional mentor,
k. able to sustain mentoring continuity and durability over time, and
l. affects and informs cognitive, affective, and behavioural domains of mentoring practice.

This specification serves to outline some of the crucial elements for mentoring-mindedness and action. Further, it gives substance to the depth of skill and knowledge required and distinguishes the role of a mentor from other professional positions. Mentors also are members of a range of communities and networks valued by others and depend for their endurance on this.

What is needed for mentoring is a robust parsing led by the mentor that not only indicates how complicated the dynamics of the relationship can become but also how this leads to higher order thinking such as meaning, priorities and consequences. The transference from the mentoring relationship to other professional relationships is paramount.

In mentoring, the key questions for mentors are: how are mentees best encouraged? As outlined above, ideally it would entail being: (a) nurtured by someone that promotes learning through reflective and practical experiences and (b) facilitated through being mentored by a like-minded person.

Mentorship ensures accountability of both parties and abides by the professional standards and ethics of the participants relevant to the context (school, organisation or, profession). For example, if a teacher is acting as a mentor with a younger person, then the professional and ethical standards apply as does the proper sphere of accountability.

A dynamic relationship develops gradually over time as does mutual trust and respect. This process allows the mentee to connect personally at a deeper level with a significant other, usually but not always, a more experienced person.

This *personal connection* is essential for mimicking other types of relationships (teacher, parent, supervisor, client or peer depending on the kind of mentorship it is). This representation is critical for the mentee. More importantly such relationships expedite learning in a way that may otherwise not occur or take longer if the mentorship did not exist. For example, the mentor may exclusively offer insights or opinions that may not have been imparted before to the mentee. ***Trust*** is vital in this situation as often privileged insights, knowledge and information are private, and both the mentee and mentor are relying on the other to respect sensitivities, as well as confidentiality. For example, the mentee may describe a situation where they are feeling oppressed or bullied at work and ask the mentor whether this situation is familiar to them and if so, how would they deal with it. While direct mediation is not requested and even dissuaded, the mentor may feel obliged to intercede. Their intercession depends on the vulnerability of the mentee e.g. in the case where a junior person at work is being 'bullied' by a more senior colleague, the mentor may feel obliged to act in the interests of a duty of care. This predicament could lead to a conflict of interest or moral concern for the mentor, especially if they can intervene (by dint of their influence on the relationship). However, they will feel conflicted due to the privileged nature of the communication.

Underpinning mutual trust between the mentor and mentee are *shared values and perspectives*, which are vital particularly in youth mentoring where the adult needs to work within the same "headspace" of the mentee. What aids this is mutual trust and respect leading to positive outcomes leading to a rhythm and synchronicity to the pair's cooperation?

Both parties in the mentoring relationship agree to participate, with the mentor taking responsibility for supporting the mentee. Essentially, the success of mentoring is dependent upon the meeting of two minds to carve out a shared "relaxed space" so as to progress reflection and to learn. The notion of 'mentis', the Latin word for mind, is core to this learning. Mentees need to rebuild or recreate a different ***mindset*** and even, in extreme situations, to countermand a prevailing one. The new mindset is a catalyst for fresh learning and cannot be overestimated.

Also central to mentoring is the use of ***narrative*** (Britzman and Gilbert 2004). Two people, the mentee and mentor, come together to recount events about all sorts of things, big and small, such as past achievements and failures, present and future aspirations, for the purpose of enquiry, reflection and consideration. Mentoring taps into the mentee's life story that is constructed and accounted for with a degree of subjectivity. The mentor together with the mentee reflects and interprets the issues as they arise. Mentoring revolves around the notion of "story" and cannot be taken as a mirror of the mentee's reality as it cannot take into account how accurate their account of others' perceptions and representations. However, this is not the point. What counts in mentoring are the issues that emerge in the telling of the narrative.

Further sometimes what is seemingly minor is a major learning or milestone and vice versa. It is not about the mentor giving advice as this never works. For example, most people are not very receptive to unsolicited advice. There is a high probability that gratuitous advice is ignored unless something further occurs to trigger it being enacted. In summary, skills for the mentor include:

(a) Building trust;
(b) Engaging others;
(c) Good listening and diagnostic skills;
(d) Being compassionate and understanding;
(e) Challenging assumptions made by the mentee when necessary;
(f) Raising the mentee's awareness of their actions in certain situations;
(g) Facilitating the conversation rather than directing;
(h) Being straightforward about self-limitations;
(i) Presenting feedback optimistically; and
(j) Being non-judgemental about whatever is submitted by the mentee, whether in agreement or not.

### *1.2.3 The Mentee's Story*

People at different stages in their lives, working in various occupational fields, changing roles, often seek a mentor. Some people try to find a mentor despite achieving a senior position in their profession or organisation; while others may be just starting out in their career. Others will feel "stuck" and are seeking assistance from a mentor to dislodge them from their rut.

The narratives and issues that mentees present to mentors will be multi-layered and vary depending on their demographic profiles and personal experiences (Fivush et al. 2008). Within the relationship, the mentor needs to be aware of how they perceive the mentee and how the mentee perceives them and their relationship. These perceptions shape the relationship and can facilitate or impede it. The mentoring relationship and the conversations within it acts as a "Rorschach test" (Eysenck 2004), backgrounding particular events and foregrounding others (Fivush and Haden 2003).

Individual autobiographical narratives recounted in mentoring depend on shared representations of the world and the acceptance of difference. Professional identities and characteristics e.g. perceived gender will contextualise individual stories and assume shared understandings that may not be voiced unwittingly; leading to unintentional cover up, while others will remain intentionally untold. As personal stories are repeated, the narrative becomes embedded. When some aspects of a story are retold ("recalled"), the elements become part of the mentee's repertoire (Cue et al. 2007). More importantly, aspects of the story that are not stated lead to a gap in meaning, sometimes undetected by the mentor. The mentor is inevitably biased, favouring certain aspects or evaluations of the narratives as is the mentee, while other aspects or evaluations are left undiscovered, and thus become more and more likely to remain unspoken.

Throughout mentoring, particular issues and their interpretations take hold and shape subsequent conversations, which may not always be helpful. In this way, it is sometimes beneficial for mentees to work with mentors where there are significant differences e.g. perceived gender; gender identity, age, cultural background, so that more informative content emerges throughout the conversations.

Given the diversity of mentees, there are some core issues or questions that remain central to people as they progress through their professional lives. It is these questions that require exploration in mentoring.

## *1.2.4 Creative Mentoring*

Being creative and resourceful as a mentor is about realising that for people to achieve their aspirations often relies on their engagement and commitment with a significant other. A mentor provides a sounding-board for the mentee. It is through sounding out ideas that a momentary "aha" or a dawning of understanding occurs. Both the mentee and the mentor need to be alert to this process, which often starts off with an inkling; a niggle of an idea, until it takes hold.

Being resourceful, on the other hand, requires working through frustrations, anxieties, antagonisms and withstanding the distress of being in demanding, taxing and not-so-good relationships. With a skilled mentor, people can learn how to rebalance, exit or to add to their store of resilience to work through all the significant interactions that people experience as well as becoming more constructive and optimistic about these, while remaining 'intact'.

### 1.2.4.1 Mentoring Is Expressive

Mentoring attempts to induce a response in the mentee by the mentor expressing empathy, that is building a bridge between the first- and third-person information. Other ways of achieving this are by enabling mentees to perceive other people's emotional states while distinguishing these from how they and others may be feeling (Decety and Jackson 2006). Expression theory maintains that the parties express their emotions through the act of relating and conversing; that is, it is their emotions that are being communicated. Arousal theory focuses on the emotions evoked in the mentee, mentor or both. Mentoring's expressivity is in its ability to induce emotional responses in people, critical for learning and shifting thinking. The mentor will achieve this outcome by understanding where the person "is at" by inferring their emotional responses from their vocalisations, their posture as well as what they are saying or not saying. The mentoring context can serve to simulate what the mentee experiences outside the relationship.

## 1.3 Respectful Mentoring

Mentoring opens up more possibilities for people, enhances their potential, while at the same time frames those possibilities. It is through this frame of opportunities, which develops throughout life that people "see" and review these possibilities. The opportunities are often "as yet to be experienced"; adding to the excitement and the expectation as well as potential disappointment.

Like genetics, relationships carry forward elements of our past such as emotional and intellectual ties and attitudes, as well as ways of interacting with others. These factors, in turn, influence how people experience developing subsequent relationships. This process is referred to as the "*the principle of continuity of experience*" that Dewey refers to: "every experience both takes up something from those which have gone before and modifies in some way the quality of those which come after" (Dewey 1963, p. 35).

Relationships with others provide continuity and an identity for people. Without them, people see the world as confusing and uncertain. This 'unknown' is evident when a person commences a new job in an organisation. Professional workers conduct their work across multiple boundaries within the one organisation, and more often than not this extends to inter-organisational boundaries. Teams are another example where relationships are important. Teams comprise people with different kinds of expertise contributing in dissimilar ways to resolving a problem. Often the newcomer has to come to terms with meaning-making in these contexts, trying to learn the values, understand the motives and motivations of others as they are invisible or at least ambiguous, requiring clarification. If the newcomer does not know anyone, the situation is enigmatic. If people are not able to establish relationships throughout the early phase of joining a new workplace, they can become frustrated by the incomprehensibility of it. For some, if there is not a suitable acculturation process they can despair and exit.

In this sense, creative mentoring extends beyond the personal to community-building. Mentoring can be employed within a community context. It initiates meaningful participation for newcomers, migrants and refugees and others marginalised by war, by gendered assumptions, by ethnicity, by age, by disability and so on, leading to assisting people overcome some of these challenges. These factors often become social, professional and workplace barriers. Mentors need to work hard to ensure that they do not develop mentoring barriers. Chapter 2 explores this issue further.

## 1.4 Understanding Significant Others

Understanding significant others (e.g. a relation, a friend, a colleague or a mentee) in life facilitates learning. This learning is a potent determinant of the course of people's lives and helps them to discern the intentions and desires of other people.

Relationships reveal something about us, and it is through them that people seek to realise their aspirations, make any significant choices in their lives: career, family, friendships and peace.

The value of mentoring is not the same for each participant, either the mentor or mentee. Within any relationship, people are animated by something beyond themselves even if they are not aware of this. Joining with others in a conversation is an exploratory and creative pursuit—that is, each seeks in the other something that is beyond them—unreachable and unfathomable. This process is both exciting and daunting all at the same time, especially in new encounters.

Within relationships, the arousal of something beyond ourselves is based on our past as well as our hopes for the future. For example in a letter to Blanche Jennings in 1908 D.H. Lawrence wrote: "like a positive electricity, a current of creative life runs through two persons, and they are instinct with the same life force—the same vitality—the same I know not what-when they kiss on the mouth-when they kiss as lovers do. Come to think of it and it is exceedingly rare that two people participate in entirely the same sensation and emotion …" (Lawrence 1979, p. 99). Lawrence refers to this something beyond us. He points to the fact that experience in the same friendship is not equal for each party. Emotions surrounding meeting and engaging with others are learnt and better understood through the ebb and flow of their relationships.

Research evidence indicates that people understand their potential through experiencing respectful relationships. As Alfred Lord Tennyson wrote: "*All experience is an arch where through gleams that untravelled world whose margin fades forever and forever when I move*" (Tennyson 1972, p. 40). Each relationship opens up more possibilities to the individual, enhancing their prospects while at the same time framing those possibilities; hence, the arch through which the opportunities emerge. The possibilities are "as yet unexperienced" and adding to the excitement and the expectation as well as the disappointment of relationships, hence the ebb and flow.

It is through this ebb and flow that our "*… our sympathy flows and recoils that really determines our lives*" (Lawrence 1993, p. 101). Sympathy here embraces understanding, intuiting, sensing, interpreting. Lawrence meant that a relationship "*can reveal the most secret places of life: for it is in the passional secret places of life, above all, that the tide of sensitive awareness needs to ebb and flow, cleansing and freshening*" (Lawrence 1993, p. 101).

### 1.4.1 Defining Approaches to Mentoring

Many mentors rely on a serendipitous approach to mentoring. Subsequent conversations pick up the threads and form the backbone of this process. Other mentors take an ad hoc, unstructured approach 'a talk fest' that leads to incremental improvements at best and almost always poor implementation beyond mentoring. In the latter case, the mentor does not see mentoring as developing a flow of practice for the mentee beyond mentoring.

### 1.4.2 Strategic Mentoring

Mentoring mindedness is about a structure flexible enough to suit different approaches depending on the mentee's needs. Differences between more standard approaches to mentoring and the Mentoring-Mindedness attitude are as follows:

| Conventional approaches to mentoring | A mentoring mindedness approach |
|---|---|
| Adopts a 'present to future' orientation—takes today as the starting point | Commences the conversation with "start with the future in mind"—identifies long-term aspirations and then "bridges back to present" |
| Assumes a mentor (expert) with a mentee (follower) posture | Assumes collaborative, democratic partnership between mentee and mentor |
| Accepts boundaries of the profession and organisation as given and immutable | Demonstrates a free-thinking posture, aware of the limits to practice both within the mentor and the relationship |
| Focuses on incremental, linear development | Seeks breakthrough, encourages leaps rather than step-by-step; non-linear while continuing to develop foundational thinking and skills |
| Relies on current evidence and knowledge sources | Encourages exploration of unlikely sources |
| Focuses on articulated needs of the mentee | Seeks to explore unarticulated needs |
| Seeks mentee's satisfaction | Inspired by the mentee and challenges them to experience a degree of discomfort |
| Has a one-size framework to fit all mentees | Spends time understanding the real needs of the mentee outside the conventional boundaries of the role, workplace structures, perceived gender, etc. |

Mentoring is jointly developed and agreed between mentee and mentor. It requires a generative process of insights and opportunities to break through an issue, using a creative flow process to lead to flourishing.

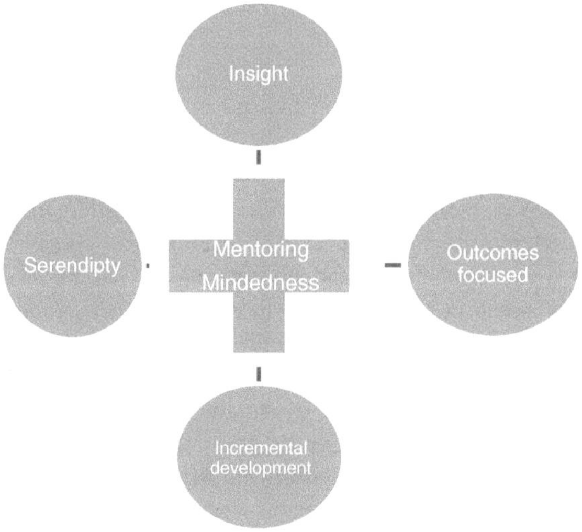

*Mentoring Mindedness* interleaves these four dimensions to produce a plan of action for mentees. The mentor facilitates the interplay between the mentee's internal capabilities, sensibilities and mental models and the externalities of their role and situation. By the mentor looking beyond the obvious, it encourages the mentee to explore a diverse array of new possibilities. It is collaborative and needs to be mentee-focused, where a deep understanding of both what is explicitly articulated and what is not, is required to understand the potential and current needs of the mentee. The mentor assists the mentee to identify tacit i.e. latent needs that sit below the surface of conscious learning. This uncovering process not only pertains to needs but also to core capabilities that are overt and dormant which could be brought to the fore and leveraged for the advantage of the mentee.

It is important to engage the mentee's readiness for mentoring. Readiness is contingent upon whether the mentee volunteers for mentoring or was volunteered by someone else. It also depends on whether the mentee was personally chosen by the mentor and the extent that empathy and overall good vibes between them are enough.

A final ingredient to mentoring mindedness is the mentee's capacity for sustained implementation of the mentoring action plan. The mentee develops or refreshes a new mindset regarding ongoing mentoring and beyond.

Most of the time what people are thinking and how they are feeling is unknown to us. However despite this, people make assumptions, infer states of mind and emotions of others by interpreting and evaluating their actions. This process is reciprocated. What one person thinks or feels is no more or less valuable than someone else's.

The focus of this book is on the composite relationship and conversations that arise within it. What constitutes mentoring is far from simple. It is a way of seeing things achieved through being as well as reflecting on issues together. For both the mentor and mentee, it needs to be a rich experience flowing out of a unique connection between the mentor and mentee, hence the notion of positivity.

### 1.4.3 Facilitators and Barriers

What is important is to find the best fit for the participants in the relationship minimising where possible any barriers to the mentor relationship e.g. age, gender and cultural. Mentoring is especially useful for people who remain under-represented in many fields and all sectors and strata of professions and occupations. This situation relates mostly to roles fixed by gender, age and background, especially in some cultures, as well as biases that become intrinsic and extrinsic constraints in a way that does not prevent, and even facilitates, the promotion of some over others. A lack of suitable information often places some people in making untenable career choices or complicating their decision-making, with little knowledge of available possibilities. Many people struggle to find suitable mentors who have access to the organisation's power structure. For example a woman manager who resists mentoring other women due to lack of time, or not wanting to share 'learnings' based on her experience, especially if they had not received help themselves. Another example is where women and men of diverse cultural backgrounds may be reluctant to initiate mentoring with each other, given the traditional norms around female—male relationships in some cultures.

Despite the challenges involved, professional mentoring remains an important strategic tool for organisations to attract and retain a diverse workforce and distribute women leadership to match men. A mentor can act as a viable source of information, guidance and foreshadow the reality for women in the workplace context so that the shocks of this are lessened. How a mentee responds to mentoring depends on the *quality of the relationship* with the mentor (Feng and MacGeorge 2006) and whether it leads to positive outcomes.

## 1.5 Beyond Positivity

Since the publication of Martin Seligman's and Mihály Csikszentmihalyi's special issue on positive psychology in the American Psychologist in 2000, there has been a burgeoning interest in positivity that has given way to mindfulness. Both Seligman and Csikszentmihalyi focused on the principles of "being positive", that is, being engaged and finding meaning, both attributes are essential for mentoring. According to their work all three elements, optimism, mutual engagement and searching for meaning are necessary ingredients of a positive outlook and withstanding negativity.

Positivity is about a subjective state of feeling optimistic rather than about having access to life's basic amenities and opportunities. Even with a high-quality standard of living, what most people can strive for is what Myers calls 'a high ratio of positive to negative feelings' (Myers 2004, p. 522). Feeling positive may be partly determined by a person's genetic predispositions, although mediated by personal and political choices that either enhance or impede positivity.

Linking positivity with mentoring may be familiar ground. For example, mentoring relationships are not always positive. Mentoring relationships can lead to negative effects on attitudes and performance (Eby and McManus 2004). Mentoring can also reproduce all the negative aspects of a power relationship (e.g. status, assumptions about gender, age) (Hansman 2002).

In this section, my aim is not about focusing on whether mentoring is positive or negative, rather how it influences the positive or negative thinking of mentees. How do people maintain a sense of optimism, harmony with others and continue to find meaning in their lives, given local and global challenges, limited opportunities and constrained choices. Being active is essential and mentoring can assist in activating the mentee's thinking, positively and negatively.

The positivity literature shines the light on the importance of relationships for becoming resilient when faced with challenges. Most people think that connecting with others is a positive experience, and for most of us, one's early relationships are fortunately so. For example, most parents are overjoyed with the birth or adoption of a new child; most people recall the delight of their first meaningful friendship or connection with a teacher. However, as life goes on, people learn that friendships change, and relationships do not always go as expected nor do we always respond according to others' expectations and vice versa. Relationships are complicated and often fraught. However, relationships are a great teacher as most people learn from and grow within them. This theme resonates throughout the following chapters.

The research findings on mentoring and its potential impact on *friendship* is important to appreciate (Algoe et al. 2008; Katzir et al. 2010). For example, this literature shows that expressing gratitude is more important in building resilience than seeking happiness. Individuals who encourage feelings of gratitude towards each other experience more closeness, more affection and tend to have positive thoughts and feelings about the other person. Building resistance is at the core of building successful relationships.

More importantly, being positive is about sustaining self-confidence (see Sect. 2.3.1).

### *1.5.1 What Does Positivity and Negativity Mean?*

Positive mentoring focuses on gaining a rich understanding of what is going on for the mentee. It epitomises open and present-minded, awareness. It enables the mentee to realise practical insights for establishing and understanding what is going on. Several questions need to be addressed: What do we understand by mentoring? What is it about a mentoring relationship that allows a person's potential to emerge, rethink and flourish? What types of mentoring are suitable? How is mentoring qualitatively different from other kinds of relationships? What are the benefits for mentors and the various ways of mentoring which are more efficient than others? Does it make a difference to the way this relationship begins? What training is available for mentors?

## 1.6 Theories of Mentoring and Its Underlying Traditions

One of the criticisms of mentoring is its lack of conceptual soundness. A broad range of activities is applied to mentoring, from speaking with a colleague through to assisting them with skill development. Mentoring outcomes are not measured. A lack of evidence is the main reason mentoring is derided. Another purported weakness is its lack of consistency. Mentoring, even if delivered by the same mentor is highly variable from one situation to the next as they are not trained in providing a standard approach. The main expectation of the mentee is for consistency. However, a similar critique is also directed towards coaching and counselling; although neither equates to mentoring. All of these processes draw from a rich tradition including Freud's psychoanalytical work (see Fisher and Greenberg

1996); behaviourism (Watson 1930; Bandura and Walters 1963) and counselling amongst many others. As indicated earlier, in the mid-20th century, humanistic psychology became influential across a range of disciplines from which mentoring emanates. Rogers (1961) developed an approach known as client-centred therapy, whereby the therapist shows unreserved favourable regard to the client. Today, this approach remains one of the most widely used models in counselling, coaching and mentoring too. However, mentoring can draw on any one or more of these traditions as follows:

Psychoanalytical theory: focuses on a person's thoughts and past experiences to understand how these might influence and explain current attitude.
Behavioural: centres on encouraging people to modify attitudes and actions to assist them to reposition their sense of self and how they present to others.
Cognitive: aims at understanding how a person's thinking patterns influences feelings and actions.
Humanistic: reflects on a person's strengths to assist them in maximising these; often referred to as strength-based coaching or mentoring.
Philosophical: concentrates on a person's assumptions to clarify, think about, question and understand these; and how a particular world-view may be self-limiting. It challenges a person to consider a wider view.
Gestalt: aimed at understanding both the personal and professional contexts and the interplay between the two.
Personal construct: shows people how they experience the world differently due to their capacity to understand the world around them, anticipate what will happen next, and create their theories to explain events (Kelley 1955).
The Narrative: personal "story-telling" depicts a person's history and their desired future (Savickas et al. 2009). The narrative allows the mentor to deepen their understanding not only of theirs and other's actions but also attitudes and motivations (Young et al. 2011). This process is useful in the construction of the meaning over a longer period of the mentee's life or career span. The narrative is core to mentoring as both the mentee and mentor tell and trade stories about their strengths and frailties. Facts are constructed, expanded, revised, developed and deconstructed. The mentor contributes to this storytelling by asking questions, challenging the "facts", the motivations, and the outcomes. Each story lends itself to the totality of understanding. The narrative provides the mentor with a point of focus and reference; it incorporates behaviour, beliefs and feelings to provide meaning. In this sense, it is a form of theory-in-action. The mentor can use to discuss how related events and activities contribute to medium term and longer term goals (Reid and West 2011).
Career counselling: the purpose of assisting a person to identify and cope with challenges related to work from occupational and role choice, managing change and other transitions such as redundancy, retrenchment, dismissal and preparing for retirement (Young and Valach 2008).

Each one of the approaches outlined above draws on and incorporates another. They are not distinct. The differences and similarities made between them concern their informative, educational or facilitative nature. However, further detailed comparison offers small value to determine the value of mentoring.

The mentoring relationship exists "outside" the roles that the mentor and mentee each holds independently of their association. The relationship develops based on the mentee revealing their cognitions and emotions, as they see fit. Nothing here is to be proved or disproved as this is irrelevant. The 'facts' are constructed by the mentee and open to questioning by the mentor. The mentee becomes the "expert" witness and the mentor assumes that these facts are how the mentee experiences them, although is entitled to question them. The mentor may Mentoring requires a suitable environment for development and growth.

## 1.7 Mentoring with a Career Focus

Since work and career are part of human development and experience, mentoring requires the mentor to see things through diverse perspectives. The psychosocial, cultural, and economic features of the local context also have the potential to shape careers (Sue and Sue 2013). Thinking about career occurs in two ways based on context: social, cultural, and economic settings. In some instances, professional cultures are less individually focused where factors other than personal desires influence the individual's engagement with work—a need to make a difference, to be part of a community of scholars, or a research team. In others, globalisation has meant that personal or portfolio careers have become a reality although there may be greater interconnections required for transactional purposes (see Arulmani 2011).

A significant consideration in mentoring is social equity, vital for professional acculturation. Social equity has its foundations in social and distributive justice regarding the way rewards and opportunities are offered and distributed. Many mentees will seek out mentoring due to inequality although this may not be something about which they are wholly conscious. It follows that mentors need to be aware of their cultural assumptions and to be competent acquire not only information but also develop and implement culturally sensitive intervention skills (Sue and Sue 2013).

While mentoring, the partialities of the mentor are transferred: the cultural nuances and semiotics of the profession or the organisation, either one of which they are a member. The mentor also assists the mentee, especially in the case of a novice, to understand what is acceptable, doable or not. In that sense, mentoring reproduces professional acculturation, mindful it could inhibit or curtail 'new blood' ideas.

Engaging in professional and vocational conversations often relies on knowing how language and humour works, for example, notions of power-distance and the like. Through this generative process, a mentor can circumvent a mentee's inexperience, highlight their strengths, and assist them in developing self-confidence. Mentors not only represent a "healthy relationship" for learning but also challenge and empower mentees with the means to accomplish more, providing they commit to doing so. In other words the highly subjective nature of mentoring amounts to questioning the background beliefs and assumptions that underpin it. In summary, understanding mentoring requires an inter-disciplinary approach.

## 1.8 The Focus of This Book

*Beyond Mentoring* also includes a wider scope and diversity of the mentoring that people can experience in their lifetime. The book shows the impact and value of mentoring not only for the participants themselves but also on the situations in which mentoring occurs and the reverberations, positive and negative, on others outside this relationship. Learning through others shapes the past and future. Mentoring is a vehicle for reflection and analysis to assist mentees to build resilience through positive relationships; reconstructing them as they go.

Everyday people demonstrate human courage and endurance as they go about their daily business, unnoticed by most and certainly uncelebrated. The ten chapters of this book show the importance of relationships with people, individually and collectively and how relationships are the DNA for an inspiring and indeed, a creative personal and professional life for people and the communities in which they engage. A distinctive feature of mentoring is revealed in each chapter.

Mentoring provides a profound sense of hope and control. People, supported in their everyday life have an opportunity to see through the randomness of life; steer it on a course, contribute and give back in some more significant way to their community, family, school or at work and that is the pathway to their achievements. It is this aggregation that contributes to positive relationships. Yielding to the unpredictability of life and believing that surrender leads us to freedom, is self-destructive. Submission leads people to become marooned on their "own island", unable to get off, stuck until someone finds them, or they succumb.

### *1.8.1 Insights*

A rich understanding of the mentoring relationship is the focus of Chap. 2. Being insightful is an important part of this, acquiring knowledge and understanding derived from developing a capacity to observe even that not immediately apparent. Being insightful is developed over time through experience and consciously taking the time to find things beneath the surface. Insight needs to be purposeful, a conscious process. The next step for both the mentor and mentee is to shape the 'lens' they are going to use to achieve insight. The lens or lenses will influence how each perceives the issues, working out the what, when, where, why and how of attitudes, actions and events without initially evaluating them. The more open to insight, the more expansive the observation, the more information gleaned and the more robust will be the analysis. Knowledge and understanding are gained and used for further insights and strategies for the mentee. Chapter 2 offers practical insights for establishing, understanding and improving mentoring relationships. Several issues are addressed ranging from self-confidence, using influence through to different approaches to mentoring as well as their outcomes.

### 1.8.2 The Mentoring Conversation

Chapter 3 assists the reader to work through a framework as a mentor to initiate and respond effectively in difficult conversations with the mentee. Some of the questions addressed include:

(a) What is the purpose of the discussion in this meeting today?
(b) How does it relate to the last conversation?
(c) What will be the issues covered? In what order?
(d) What approach is taken?
(e) What does the mentee hope to accomplish?
(f) What does the mentor hope to accomplish?
(g) What would be the best outcome for the mentee from this conversation?

### 1.8.3 The Paradox of Mentoring

Relationships are seldom what they seem. People want to develop relationships built on openness and trust. However, in truth, relationships do not always work that way. Secrecy and deceit are as much part of relationships as truth and honesty. This reality is the paradox of human nature. People are always subject to similar motivations albeit in varying ways and time: power, liking, assurance, etc. They seek to avoid the opposite of these drivers: powerlessness, disliking, fear, etc.

Mentoring relationships need to be rewarding offering integrity, learning and support to mentees. It is necessary for the mentor and mentee to know and trust each other (Cole and Teboul 2004) so as to attain the benefits that mentoring can provide. It is not possible to create beneficial outcomes in a close relationship without a great deal of shared knowledge and understanding.

A further paradox is the fact that mentoring is all about the mentee. However, selflessness is an important part of what is learned in mentoring—getting outside oneself to see how others may be seeing things and us. In so doing, there is a contradiction. As the mentee becomes the centre of attention within the mentoring relationship, this assists their internal locus of evaluation, and in so doing, becomes a catalyst for transformational learning.

Mentoring relationships work by the mentor managing a diplomatic balance of openness, critical reflection and support. How candid should the mentor be? Candor is attained through the critical guidance of the mentee so as to minimise confabulation as far as this is humanly possible. If all relationships have elements of secrecy and even deceit, though, what does this mean in a mentoring relationship? At what point does too much honesty affect the support required in mentoring? These questions will be addressed in the following chapters, see particularly, Chap. 5: *Blame*.

### *1.8.4 Blame*

The focus in Chap. 5 is working through some key dimensions of blame that will assist the mentor in working with the mentee along an agreed path. How to handle criticism from others and ways of understanding the role of blame in a person's life is important for self-regulation as well as professional and personal development and ultimately a higher satisfaction with outcomes. Mentoring can assist the mentee develop an awareness and reinforce their self-esteem in dealing with criticism, uncovering deception, dealing with the loss of credibility and so on. Engaging with a mentor is like seeking a "second opinion" for the mentee in terms of their perceptions and interpretations as well as coping strategies and feelings about this. If this is successfully worked through, mentees rebuild and gain a sense of renewed control over their social or physical environment through taking appropriate action. Is the negativity obscuring the natural flow of mutual sympathy amongst us, the simpatico that helps us restore understanding with each other and in so doing, into our life? When people take responsibility for their part in conflicts or problems or indeed forgive others and not blame them, they are released from an unhealthy quandary or relationships and find their way.

### *1.8.5 Guilt*

Guilt, the focus of Chap. 6, is closely related to blame. It is an emotional response and is experienced when a person feels they have transgressed in some way. The essence of mentoring mindedness assists mentees understand that many of their perceived constraints are cognitive and emotional impediments that have taken hold. In turn, these processes are self-limiting as they are held often as rigid assumptions and attitudes that underpin the issues at hand. Mentees through the relationship with a mentor learn they might move beyond this. The importance of reflection and feedback through mentoring is valuable in questioning these assumptions and attitudes underpinning guilt. The mentor and the mentee enhance their self-awareness as a way of encouraging them to achieve their aspirations and overcoming guilt along the way. Learning about emotions and how to deal with them through mentoring evokes, refines and develops approaches and, therefore, becomes a meaningful experience that transfers to other spheres of life: professionally, socially and psychologically.

### 1.8.6 Silence

Silence takes on different shades and tones. It can be helpful at times, less so others, and often fraught in everyday communications. Silence can be difficult within the mentoring relationship itself. It is important to understand how to use silence that builds the relationship and to minimise those "stops", which impede it. Appreciating silence in all its nuances and purposes is the aim of this chapter. Understanding the "culture of silence" is also important.

### 1.8.7 Loyalty

The focus in this chapter includes the importance of relationships for human beings, individually and collectively and how relationships are the DNA for an inspiring and indeed, creative life and community. A question that is often asked is how effective is mentoring and how do you know it is effective. What makes a difference in mentoring is the mentor's capacity to engage with the mentee: namely the mentor's position to gain rapport and engender trust? Warmth, empathy, and genuineness, as well as interpersonal activities, such as self-disclosure, intentions and response modes, are necessary (Sexton and Whiston 1994). All these elements facilitate the mentee's capacity to invest in the mentoring relationship and form a connection with the mentor. Loyalty is an enduring issue in all human relationships, from the time of a person's first friendships through to their life-forming relationships such as personal, professional and business partnerships.

### 1.8.8 Mentoring for All Seasons

This chapter contains a series of vignettes to demonstrate the positive outcomes of reciprocal feedback used across organisational settings and in workplaces. The approach is similar to that used in one-on-one mentoring albeit in a more structured way between management and staff, especially when it is embedded within other 'normal' procedures. In the same way that businesses invite feedback from customers and clients, a similar principle is relevant to staff, with value not only for staff but also for the organisation as a whole. These cases demonstrate how groups benefit by delivering mutual feedback. It is reciprocal in that it provides support for staff and creates less uncertainty. Feedback is a core part of all staff development as well as mentoring.

### *1.8.9 Mentoring for Resilience and Ensuring Its Sustainability*

The focus of this chapter is on mentoring for resilience while ensuring its sustainability. It is a worthwhile professional pursuit with value for mentees. Sustainability is always open to interpretation. Given this, how sustainable is mentoring, in the sense that it viable, workable and maintainable especially in workplaces? As stated at the outset of this book, conceptualising mentoring is not straightforward as it crosses over into coaching, sponsoring and even counselling in terms of the processes it employs and the skills that it draws upon. Elements of all of these processes are used in mentoring.

## 1.9 Conclusion

In summing up, the first point to make about mentoring is the one made by D.H. Lawrence, which is something found not only in relationships but also in creative pursuits—it is that which is beyond ourselves and provides a greater sense of meaningfulness and identity. Both mentees and mentors will find something beyond themselves in mentoring and will experience this beyond mentoring itself.

Throughout the literature, there is a continuing theme that learning through others is the best teacher. Mentoring shows how support and skills can be used to build on and rebuild resilience through positive relationships and community, reconstructing them as we go. In mentoring, people come to understand the part that each of us plays, showing courage and endurance as we go about our daily business, unnoticed by most and certainly uncelebrated. However if life is lived well by finding opportunities to contribute and give back in significant ways in communities, family, school or at work, this is the pathway to achievement. It will be noticed and matched by others even if we never know this.

Throughout their lives, what most people search for is a profound sense of hope and support when it is needed. It is the aggregation of hope and support that contributes to a positive life. Positive relationships help us restore understanding with each other and in so doing, into our life. As DH Lawrence stated: "Our civilization, with its horrible fear and funk and repression and bullying, has almost destroyed the natural flow of common sympathy between men and men, and men and women. And it is this that I want to restore into life: just the natural warm flow of common sympathy between man and man, man and woman" (Lawrence 1976, p. 101).

## References


Algoe, S. B., Haidt, J., & Gable, S. L. (2008). Beyond reciprocity: Gratitude and relationships in everyday life. *Emotion, 8*(3), 425–429.

Applebaum, S. A. (1973). Psychological-mindedness: Word, concept, and essence. *International Journal of Psychoanalysis, 54*, 35–46.

Arulmani, G. (2011). Striking the right note: The cultural preparedness approach to developing resonant career guidance programs. *International Journal for Educational and Vocational Guidance, 11*(2), 79–93.

Bandura, A. (1989). Human agency in social cognitive theory. *American Psychologist, 44*, 1175.

Bandura, A., & Walters, R. H. (1963). *Social learning and personality development*. New York: Holt, Rinehart, and Winston.

Beitel, M., Ferrer, E., & Cecero, J. J. (2005). Psychological mindedness and awareness of self and others. *Journal of Clinical Psychology, 61*, 739–750.

Betsworth, D. G., & Hansen, J. C. (1996). The categorization of serendipitous career development events. *Journal of Career Assessment, 4*, 91–98.

Biasi, P. (2006). The European University—Towards a Wisdom-based society. *Higher Education in Europe, 31*(4), 403–407.

Britzman, D., & Gilbert, J. (2004). What will have been said about gayness in teacher education. *Teacher Education, 15*(1), 81–96.

Brown, D. (2012). *Career information, career counselling and career development* (8th ed.) Needham Heights, MA: Allyn and Bacon.

Brown, K. W., & Ryan, R. M. (2003). The benefits of being present: The role of mindfulness in psychological well-being. *Journal of Personality and Social Psychology, 84*, 822–848.

Butler, A. C., Godbole, N., & Marsh, E. J. (2013). Explanation feedback is better than correct answer feedback for promoting transfer of learning, *Journal of Educational Psychology, 105* (2), 290–298.

Byram, M. (2011). A research agenda for "intercultural competence". In A. Witte & T. Harden (Eds.), *Intercultural competence: Concepts, challenges, evaluations* (pp. 19–35). Switzerland: Peter Lang.

Cole, T., & Teboul, J. C. B. (2004). Non-zero sum collaboration, reciprocity and the preference for similarity: Developing an adaptive model of close relational functioning. *Personal Relationships, 11*, 135–160.

Conway, M. A., & Pleydell-Pearce, C. W. (2000). The construction of autobiographical memories in the self-memory system. *Psychological Review, 107*, 261–288.

Csikszentmihalyi, M. (1991). Implications of a systems perspective for the study of creativity. In R. J. Sternberg (Ed.), *The handbook of creativity* (pp. 313–335). New York: Cambridge.

Cue, A., Koppel, J., & Hirst, W. (2007). Silence is not golden: A case for socially shared retrieval-induced forgetting. *Psychological Science, 18*, 727–773.

Dawis, R. V. (2002). Person-environment-correspondence theory. In D. Brown (Ed.), *Associates career choice and development* (4th ed., pp. 427–464). San Francisco, CA: Jossey-Bass.

Decety, J., & Jackson, P. L. (2006). A social-neuroscience perspective on empathy. *Current Directions in Psychological Science, 15*, 54–58.

Dewey, J. (1963). *Experience and education*. New York: Collier.

Dreyfus, H. L. (2007). Response to McDowell. *Inquiry, 50*(4), 371–377.

Eby, L. T., & McManus, S. E. (2004). The protégé's role in negative mentoring experiences. *Journal of Vocational Behaviour, 65*, 255–275.

Eysenck, Michael W. (2004). *Psychology: An international perspective*. Hove: Psychology Press.

Feng, B., & MacGeorge, E. L. (2006). Predicting receptiveness to advice: Characteristics of the problem, the advice-giver and the recipient. *Southern Communication Journal, 71*, 67–85.

Filho, G. V., Pires, A. C. J., Berlini, G. I., Hartke, R., & Lewkowicz, S. (2007). The supervisory field and projective identification. *International Journal of Psychoanalysis, 88*, 681–689.

Fisher, S., & Greenberg, R. P. (1996). *Freud scientifically reappraised: Testing the theories and therapy*. John Wiley and Sons.

Fivush, R. (2008). Remembering and reminiscing: How individual lives are constructed in family narratives. *Memory Studies, 1*, 45–54.

Fivush, R., & Haden, C. (Eds.). (2003). *Autobiographical memory and the construction of a self: Developmental and cultural perspectives* (pp. 149–168). Hillsdale, NJ: Lawrence Erlbaum Associates Inc.

Fivush, R., Bohanek, J. G., & Duke, M. (2008). The intergenerational self: Subjective perspective and family history. In F. Sani (Ed.), *Individual and collective self-continuity*. Mahwah, NJ: Lawrence Erlbaum Associates Inc.

Hall, J. A. (1992). Psychological-mindedness: A conceptual model. *American Journal of Psychotherapy, 46*, 131–140.

Hansman, C. A. (2002). Diversity and power in mentoring relationships. *Critical Perspectives on Mentoring: Trends and Issues*, 39–48.

Kaslow, N. J., Borden, K. A., Collins, F. L., Forrest, L., Illfelder-Kaye, J., Nelson, P. D., et al. (2004). Competencies conference: Future directions in education and credentialing in professional psychology. *Journal of Clinical Psychology, 80*, 699–712.

Katzir, M., Eyal, T., Meiran, N., & Kessler, Y. (2010). Imagined positive emotions and inhibitory control: The differentiated effect of pride versus happiness. *Journal of Experimental Psychology. Learning, Memory, and Cognition, 36*(5), 1314–1320.

Kelly, G. A. (1955). *The psychology of personal constructs*. New York: Norton.

Krumboltz, J. D. (2009). The happenstance learning theory. *Journal of Career Assessment, 17*, 135–154.

Krumboltz, J. D., Foley, P. F., & Cotter, E. W. (2013). Applying the happenstance learning theory to involuntary career transitions. *The Career Development Quarterly, 61*, 15–26.

Lawrence, D. H. (1976). In R. Aldington (Ed.), *Selected essays*. Harmondsworth, Middlesex: Penguin.

Lawrence, D. H. (1979). To blanche jennings, 15 December 1908. In J. T. Boulton (Ed.), *The letters of D.H. Lawrence* (Vol. 1). Cambridge, UK: Cambridge University Press.

Lawrence, D. H. (1993). In M. Squire (Ed.), Lady Chatterley's lover and apropos of 'Lady Chatterley's lover'. Cambridge, UK: Cambridge University Press.

Leck, J., & Orser, B. (2013). Fostering in mentoring relationships: An exploratory study. *Equality, Diversity and Inclusion: An International Journal, 32*(4), 410–425.

Lewis, G. (2000). *Mentoring manager: Strategies for fostering talent and spreading knowledge*. London, UK: Prentice-Hall.

Maxwell, N. (2007). From knowledge to: The need for an academic revolution. *London Review of Education, 5*(2), 97–115.

McAdams, D. P. (2006). The redemptive self: Stories Americans live by. *Research in Human Development, 3*, 81–100.

McGeoch, J. (1942). *The psychology of human learning: An introduction*. New York, NY: Longmans, Green and Co.

McLean, K., Pasupathi, M., & Pals, J. (2007). Selves creating stories creating selves: A process model of self-development. *Personality and Social Psychology Review, 11*, 262–278.

Morris, M. W., Leung, K., Ames, D., & Lickel, B. (1999). Views from inside and outside: Integrating emic and etic insights about culture and justice judgment. *Academy of Management Review, 24*(4), 781–796.

Myers, D. G. (2004). *Psychology*. New York: Worth Publishers.

Radu Lefebvre, M., & Redien-Collot, R. (2013). 'How to do things with words': The discursive dimensions of experiential learning in entrepreneurial mentoring dyads. *Journal of Small Business Management, 51*(3), 370–393.

Reid, H., & West, L. (2011). 'Telling tales': Using in career guidance. *Journal of Vocational Behaviour, 78*, 174–183.

Rogers, C. R. (1961). *On becoming a person: A therapist's view of psychotherapy*. London, England: Constable.

Rowley, J. (2006). What do we need to know about? *Management Decision, 44*(9), 1246–1257.
Rubin, D. C. (2006). The basic systems model of episodic memory. *Perspectives on Psychological Science, 1*, 277–311.
Savickas, M. L. (2011). New questions for vocational psychology: Premises, paradigms, and practices. *Journal of Career Assessment, 19*, 251–258.
Savickas, M. L., Nota, L., Rossier, J., Dauwalder, J.-P., Duarte, M. E., Guichard, J., et al. (2009). Life designing: A paradigm, for career construction in the 21st century. *Journal of Vocational Behaviour, 75*, 239–250.
Schwille, S. A. (2008). The professional practice of mentoring. *American Journal of Education, 115*, 139–167.
Sexton, T. L., & Whiston, S. C. (1994). The status of the counselling relationship: An empirical review, theoretical implications, and research directions. *The Counselling Psychologist, 22*(1), 6–78.
Shapiro, S. L., & Carlson, L. E. (2009). *The art and science of mindfulness: Integrating mindfulness into psychology and the helping professions*. Washington, DC: American Psychological Association.
Steger, M. F., Oishi, S., & Kashdan, T. B. (2009). Meaning in life across the lifespan: Levels and correlates of meaning in life from emerging adulthood to older adulthood. *Journal of Positive Psychology, 4*(1), 43–52.
Sue, D. W., & Sue, D. (2013). *Counselling the culturally diverse: Theory and practice* (6th ed.). Hoboken, NJ: John Wiley and Sons.
Tennyson, A. (1972). *A collection of poems by Alfred Tennyson*. Garden City, NY: Doubleday. (Selected and with an introduction by Christopher ricks).
Tomasello, M. (2014) A natural history of human thinking. Cambridge: Harvard University Press.
Van de Walle, G. (2008). Durkheim and socialization. *Durkheimian Studies, 14*(1), 35–58.
Watson, J. B. (1930). *Behaviorism* (revised ed.). University of Chicago Press.
Yaghjian, L. B. (2013). Hidden treasures in theological education: The writing tutor, the spiritual director, and practices of academic and spiritual mentoring. *Teaching Theology and Religion, 16*(3), 221–245.
Yalom, I. D. (1980). *Existential psychotherapy*. New York, NY: Basic Books.
Young, R. A., & Valach, L. (2008). Action theory: An integrative paradigm for research and evaluation in career. In J. Athanasou & R. van Esbroeck (Eds.), *International handbook of career guidance* (pp. 643–658). New York: Springer-Science.
Young, R. A., Marshall, S. K., Valach, L., Domene, J. F., Graham, M. D., & Zaidman-Zait, A. (2011). *Transition to adulthood: Actions, projects and counselling*. New York: Springer.
Zeleny, M. (2006). From knowledge to: On being informed and knowledgeable, becoming and ethical. *International Journal of Information Technology and Decision Making., 5*(4), 751–762.

# Chapter 2
# Positive Mentoring: Learning to Shape and Nurture Talent and Confidence

*I love to argue with people who do not disagree with me too profoundly.*
*And I like to laugh.*

James Baldwin—*Notes of a native son.*

**Abstract** This chapter will assist the reader in gaining a rich understanding of the mentoring relationship. It offers practical insights for establishing and understanding mentoring relationships.

## 2.1 Introduction

How positive mentoring is for the mentee is shaped by the quality of the relationship. Firstly, positivity in mentoring refers to the possibility of a formidable learning relationship. In today's fast-paced world, whatever one's career stage, working or studying, leading, raising a family or volunteering, learning and discovery are the mainstays of an active life. Secondly, will positive mentoring make an affirming difference for the mentee? If so, how will this be measured and understood? Thirdly, is mentoring used to counter negativity in the mentee? If in creating a positive milieu, will the mentee feel comfortable in voicing concerns; feel listened to and assisted in dealing with the issues? Fourthly, does positive mentoring mean that there is no opportunity to explore the shadows of life? Finally, is positivity achievable and more importantly, necessary for an authentic life? If the mentee is not optimistic, how does the mentor assist the mentee achieve their goals, influence others and at the same time, remain authentic and reflect the essence of their unique individuality?

Positive mentoring is about the openness of the relationship that the mentee experiences. They will feel reassured if the mentor is accepting of them and their circumstances. How does mentoring achieve this? The answer lies in two parts. The first is that it is through a mutual relationship between the mentee and mentor that



A.M. Brewer, *Mentoring from a Positive Psychology Perspective*,
DOI 10.1007/978-3-319-40983-2_2

leads to a learning experience. What is learnt are the critical dimensions of positive mentoring. Mutual learning is shared and acknowledged (based on Krauss and Fussell 1990s 'mutual knowledge' concept). It is essential for what unfolds and drives the relationship forward.

Shared learning facilitates the path of mindedness: what each knows and does not know about the issues and circumstances under discussion. Without this precondition, mentoring will not be positive as each will continue conversing on the basis of what is individually articulated rather than pooled. The reciprocal nature of pooled learning is indispensable. This learning is reinforced verbally and non-verbally (e.g. hmm-hmm, nodding, eye contact) and provides meaningful feedback especially from the mentor without dominating the conversation. The second element of positivity is being content with being you. One thing that is obligatory is the mentor creating an open space for the mentee to investigate and try out new facets of their individuality, new ways of thinking, knowledge and skill development.

Interactions between mentors and mentees are formed by how mentoring is initiated, the nature of the profession and other situational contingencies. A typical mentoring relationship involves a more experienced person, a reliable counsellor and the mentee, or the latter referred to here as a mentee. 'Mentee' is a descriptor referring to a person who has a mentor whereas a mentee conveys potential and untapped talent and, therefore, active learning. Whatever form it takes each mentoring relationship has its unique qualities. The nature of mentoring is shaped by the individuals' circumstances; the prospective outcomes; the empathy between the mentor and mentee and eventually the trust that is built; the inspiration that ignites interest and enthusiasm as well as the importance of the relationship between both parties. For the mentor how serious s/he takes on the role and for the mentee how important they regard it in a developmental sense.

The attributes of mentoring relationships include the ratio of power, mutuality of respect and support, and skills in communications and having an aptitude for conducting difficult conversations. For learning to occur, the social exchange between the mentor and mentee involves mutual influence. The last requires abilities to problem-solve, negotiate, and confront.

However, influence between the parties in this relationship is never unidirectional, with only one being shaped by the other. It is important that the mentee does not feel dominated, and this depends upon the most experienced person doing everything to neutralise the essential power imbalance between them. The best way to describe this exchange is 'mobilisation'. Moreover, while mentorship is mostly characterised as dyadic, with differential experience between the mentor and mentee, this is not always the case as will be demonstrated.

The focus of this chapter is on understanding mentoring and the reasons for its endurance over the centuries: mainly for imparting knowledge, skills and acculturation.

## 2.2 What Is Understood by the Terms: Mentoring, Mentor and Mentee?

Mentoring is the backbone of most *learning* relationships such as coaching, consulting with clients in an array of settings both corporate and institutions as well as person-centred counselling and so on. These processes should not be thought of as motley of disconnected processes as each share something in common and in practice, all of them have overlapping elements. The commonality of processes is linked to the notion of self-influence, a term first used by Manz (1992). In basic terms, self-influence is a process through which mentees, coachees and clients in counselling learn with the guidance of a mentor, a coach or a counsellor how to achieve the self-direction, self-observation and self-motivation if you like to act in ways that assist them to realise their goals.

In this section, positive mentoring is considered. To be positive is a position that is rarely questioned either in the striving or achievement of it. Positive mentoring requires a theoretical or analytical approach even though it is an applied practice. Many applications are underpinned by a theoretical framework. Mentoring is essentially initiated by a narrative, usually told by the mentee. The mentor joins into assist with framing and managing the meanings (Bolman and Deal 2008). The mentor is positive in that they display confidence in their approach. The mentee will observe the mentor's approach and may feel more optimistic as a consequence; or by the same token feel they are or never could match this approach or experience. It may lead them to feel more pessimistic if that is their predisposition prior to meeting with the mentor. Just as introversion should be more highly valued than it is, a pessimistic stance can also be positive if it leads the mentee into questioning things below the surface.

For example, the mentor facilitates this process by directing the mentor to reflect on attitudes and ways of thinking, their actions and outcomes linked to these. Mentors challenge mentees to evaluate their assumptions, beliefs and attitudes as a way of directing them towards positive self-talk. They also encourage mentees to consider how they go about doing things or not and encourage them to focus their attention on what they can do rather than what they cannot do.

Mentoring and indeed positive mentoring creates self-dialogue that generates knowledge focusing the mentor on thinking of their issues as 'mundane' as opposed to 'abnormal' so that mentees can see themselves as being within the boundaries of what society privileges as 'normal' (based on Foucault 1977).

Positive mentoring is tapping into (a) the positive orientation towards self, professional and future (Caprara et al. 2010) as well as into (b) the positive learning (Seligman et al. 2009). Mentors would orientate mentee to see the positive aspects Seligman et al. (2009) (i) as a remedy to counter dejection; (ii) a way to increasing professional satisfaction and (iii) to improve learning and generate creative thinking as a way of encouraging mentees to follow up with these new or revitalised thought patterns and actions outside of mentoring. The rationale for positive mentoring is that people need to feel inspired and optimistic in the light of inevitable disappointments that they experience. Increases in well-being are likely to produce increases in learning because positive mood produces broader attention (Fredrickson and Branigan 2005; Rowe et al. 2007), more creative thinking (Estrada et al. 1994).

Mentoring is aimed at enhancing self-awareness first and foremost which ultimately will lead the mentee to manage themselves better especially in relation to goals where they doubt their capability or politicised. Self-awareness includes self-observation that is being aware of how one's actions in response to specific triggers: people, context, etc. It also includes self-goal setting that addresses identifying areas of aspiration or need and know how to attain these as well as self-acknowledgement that is being realistic about when improvement is necessary and knowing when a good outcome has been achieved. Self-regulation is principally about managing emotions and time. In short, the mentor works with the mentee to encourage positive responses and actions that lead to effective outcomes for the mentee. Figure 2.1 is based on Manz (1992) and Bandura (1991).

Secondly the mentor works with the mentee to challenge them around why they tend to seek out certain tasks, roles and what their perceptions are for doing so. Challenging the mentee is related to the third aspect of positive mentoring which is thinking: self-analysis and questioning belief systems, creating positive mental images of self and performance outcomes in conjunction with positive self-talk.

Another important aspect to consider is self-control and its relation to being positive. Positive mentoring suggests that mentees can learn how to influence and control their thoughts and in turn actions to impact positive outcomes.

In contrast, a negative mood, the opposite of feeling encouraged (Seligman 1991) narrows the mentee's focus of attention (Bolte et al. 2003) and leads to more critical and analytical thinking (Kuhl 2000). Since mentoring is a form of problem-based learning, both forms of thinking are required. However, one form may be more motivating for people at specific times than the other, or they may need to be used in combination. A mentor will assist the mentee in achieving this balance. Positive mentoring would seek to heighten creative thinking in mentees.

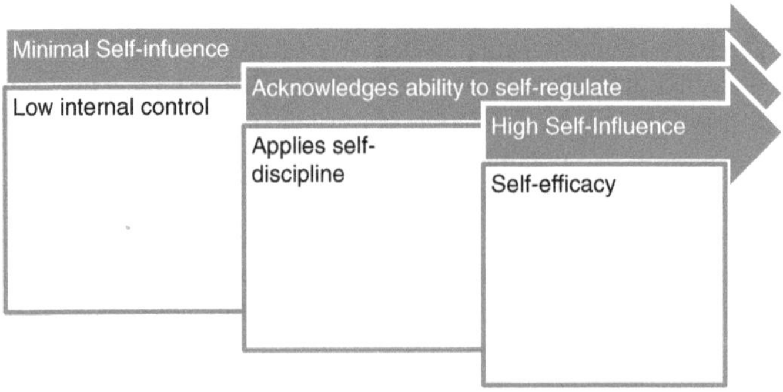


**Fig. 2.1** A continuum of self-influence

Many of the problems brought for discussion by the mentee, often take the form of solving problems, which are both revealing and enjoyable. One way to encourage a self-analytical mindset for the mentee is for the mentor to hypothesise the problem, that is create 'what if' scenarios. An example of this is when the mentor picks up on the issues and reflects them to the mentee as questions so that the mentee can consider the issues from an alternative perspective. In that way, the mentee can defamiliarise them and take a more objective view of the situation.

Mentoring is a narrative, conducted through episodic (or serialised) conversations often in a cyclical way. These accounts reported to the mentor by the mentee are a set of their experiences, constructions and reconstructions of reality. They have become codified in the mentoring conversation: firstly by the mentee in the telling and re-telling of them and then by the mentor and mentee together through their reflection and analysis. The mentee and mentor consider the various themes and threads of their conversations from one meeting to the next. They look to find the linkages between the various themes with the help of the mentor so that the mentee can see the unified meaning of what has been explored, identified and developed for action. The point is that there is some higher level of organisation of the narrative taking place in mentoring initially by the mentor, then by the mentee. Only when an issue is maintained over a number of conversations does it become a structuring force, assisting both the mentor and mentee to organise the themes and sub-themes in relation to each other so that they can start to see the threads more clearly and therefore, be enabled to address the problem more comprehensively. This organising is purposive. It is one that rarely takes place in everyday conversations. The mentee's stories combine into psychological wholes and become the artefacts of mentoring, taking on a reality of their own through the relationship between the mentee and the mentor.

Mentoring is a representation of the reality outside of mentoring for the mentee. Every story told by the mentee is essentially orientated towards a goal, the reason for the mentee telling it to the mentor in the first place. That is the mentee wishes to "... make a point, to transmit a message...often to bring about some sort of ...evaluation or implied critical judgement..." about what has happened (Polanyi 1985, p. 21). The observant mentor realises that the point of the story is the underlying goal and it requires further evaluation. It is for the mentor to uncover or unravel the goal and to reveal it for their sake and more often than not, the mentee's.

**Structuring Mentoring Conversations**

Narratives in mentoring are complex due to the porous boundary between, within and outside the mentoring relationship. This complexity could exemplify problems experienced by the mentor in managing the boundaries and limits the relationship with the mentee. In other words, the mentor attempts to take on too much in especially if the mentee is demanding or needy. Mentors need to accept positively their limitations either actual or bounded by the relationship itself. Often mentees will raise a matter that connects with the mentor as a person or their history. Mentors need to find a balance between feelings of vulnerability or being in or out of control.

While it is useful for the mentor to consider the conversations of the mentees along these lines, it is not as straightforward as that. Although the stories related by mentees follow a narrative line; they are not necessarily in the order in which a narrative might unfold. For example, a mentor will always start with an introduction or way of orientating the mentor to the story and/or viewpoint; the actions that occurred; followed by an evaluation of the actions and outcomes, for the purposes of seeking a resolution. A coda signals the finale (the aftermath following mentoring or outside of mentoring) and requires further reflection (see Labov 1972, p. 363).

Mentors need to be alert to how the conversation is initiated by the mentee. Their starting point is not necessarily the beginning of the "real story" so to speak. However regardless of this how they introduce it and what follows is highly significant to the problem in that it is stated as a way of orientating the mentor but not necessarily the initiating force of the problem itself. Even taking that into account, it is important for the mentor, and also the mentee, to understand that mentoring is not a purely formulaic process. It has natural flow and will be constructed by what the mentee and mentor each makes of it as well as what they make of it together. The element of their "togetherness" will characterise the value and outcomes of mentoring for the mentee as well as a degree of satisfaction. What is suggested here is a way for making sense and bringing some structure to the conversations. However, mentoring conversations have their own status and are and should be different to everyday conversations as there needs to be a focus on the themes and issues for their own sake.

A mentoring conversation, as stated, is not a routine conversation between two people, rather it uses particular methods by which the mentee and mentor engage together developing a fund of learning that is mutually shared during the duration of the relationship which is capable of constant development throughout it (see Bohm 2003). According to Senge (1994), dialogue helps people travel beyond the boundaries of their thinking. Through a process of mutual and reflective investigation, a deeper understanding of issues materialises with alternative constructions, bringing new insights into familiar patterns of thinking and experiences. The mentor is the 'facilitator' who 'holds the context' of the dialogue together (Senge 1994, p. 243).

The mentoring conversation is "the flow of meaning" and is catalytic in assisting people transform their current thinking by considering constraints imposed by them and others (Bell 1996). 'Dialoguing' has been discussed as a process of interactive learning together (Ballantyne 2004). The process for the mentee needs to be prompted guided by a thoughtful purpose to reach learning outcomes for the mentee. It is not an unbounded aimless conversation that a person might have with a colleague or a friend. Mentoring requires and demands 'openness', mutual engagement, genuine collaboration such that might not have been experienced by the mentee previously. It is not about conversing for the sake of it rather it will only proceed if trust, genuine self-reflection, exposure of clear and tacit ways of thinking, and willingness to grow through risk characterise the relationship (Bokeno 2007). There are three premises to this which are important and explored further in this chapter, Chaps. 4 and 10 specifically. Mentees learn how to be more creative and innovative in their thinking and problem-solving. Secondly, they acquire a greater self-awareness and acceptance and finally with reflection, how they can affect change within themselves and their situations. To achieve this requires them going beyond one's "habitual way of thinking is to make the unfamiliar as easily digestible as possible. Normally people's perceptions are "'automatic' or minimal"" (Lemon and Reis 1965, pp. 4–5).

In mentoring, it is important for the mentor to notice and steel themselves to attend to all aspects of the narrative, what is being said, what is not being said, how it is being related which refers to the non-verbal communication e.g. tone and pace of voice, facial expressions, eye contact, gestures and posture. Just as the mentor attempts to defamiliarise the mentee from their issues to provide the freedom for them to stand back, it is also important to defamiliarise themselves to become aware of their own perceptual barriers and filters for noticing, holding attention, bearing meaning and so on. The mentor needs to see the ordinary in an extraordinary light. While, in everyday conversations, parties may become aware of this either during or after the conversation, often either one or both let the issues intermingle in the narrative without foregrounding them in any way.

One of the distinctive features of mentoring mindedness is a realisation firstly by the mentor then by both mentee and mentor that the viewpoints presented by the mentee deviate from a "common sense" version of reality. A mentor may wish to employ the notion of mind style to reflect on how the mentee projects their worldview, a particular way of perceiving and making sense of the world:

> A mind style may analyse a character's mental life more or less radically; may be concerned with relatively superficial or relatively fundamental aspects of the mind; may seek to dramatise the order and structure of conscious thoughts, or just present the topics on which a character reflects, or displays preoccupations, prejudices, perspectives and values which strongly bias a character's world-view but which s/he may be unaware.
>
> (Fowler 1977, p. 103).

It may be necessary for the mentor to demonstrate the differences between the aspects of the story being presented and the prism through which the mentee is presenting them. The mentor needs to distinguish between literal and figurative accounts, both of which could be non-literal. The mentor has to employ strategies through questioning etc. to construct the mentee's intended meaning.

Language is the main vehicle used in conversation by the mentee and mentor apart from non-verbal communication. Language is social and relational (Bakhtin 1981) and is concerned with action that usually has an interpersonal purpose and outcome. The mentor is listening to the story in relation to the previous story or in relation to their own ideas and experiences which means that not only is there continual dialogue between the mentor and mentee but also within the mentor and separately within the mentee. This can create not only an internal struggle for each but an interpersonal one between the mentee and mentor especially as the conversations move to reflection, questioning and evaluation.

The outcome is that mentoring is multi-voiced not only in terms of the internal voices of the mentee and mentor, the voicing between them but also the voices which they carry inside their heads from significant others.

A mentoring framework requires a schema: "essentially, the context that someone needs to make sense of individual experiences, events, parts of situations or elements of language is stored in background memory as an associative network of knowledge. In the course of experiencing an event or making sense of a situation, a schema is dynamically produced, which can be modelled as a sort of script based on similar situations encountered previously. New experiences and new incoming information are understood by matching them to existing schematic knowledge." (Stockwell Stockwell 2002, p. 255).

The term 'mentee' rather than 'protégé' is used in this book to refer to the broad range of individuals, as previously indicated, who may be in the role of "learner" within mentoring relationships, regardless of the age or position of the mentee and mentor. Speaking of relationships, whether one is called a mentee or protégé depends on the relationship with that of the mentor. For example, the protégé-mentor relationship is used when a less experienced person shadows or is chaperoned by an "expert" in a professional and organisational learning context. However, the reverse mentoring relationship is more suitable for peer to peer situations including professionals, friends and volunteers working together on community projects.

Further, the use of the term 'protégé' signifies a more limited learning role. For example, protégé suggests the less experienced person has been selected or chosen to work with a mentor, who is more likely to supervise their professional practice or chaperon them in a specific role in a range of contexts, anywhere from business, legal, health, scientific, teaching through to creative arts and performing roles. Whatever the circumstances, mentoring needs to be encouraged rather than imposed so even if a formal program is established, participants need to be invited to participate and given reasons for doing so as well as explaining the benefits and outcomes to them. It is also important to identify and acknowledge their preferences for mentoring and a mentor before deciding upon, or indeed imposing any pairing arrangements on them.

### *2.2.1 The Context of Mentoring*

The nature of mentoring depends on whether it is (a) professional and/or workplace based or (b) community, network or relationship-based. Another consideration is that if the former, a mentee is likely to be in regular, frequent face-to-face contact with the mentor, more formal than the informality that may ensue in a mentee-mentor relationship. The latter is likely to meet less frequently say anywhere from weekly to monthly, although consistently using a variety of media and not only limited to face-to-face. However, there is another caveat: in today's world it is highly likely that Skype or similar may be used if the mentee is remotely situated e.g. any professional working in a national or international, regional setting.

In the example of (a) above, the mentee seeks a mentor for professional, training purposes as they start out or progress their early career. In this case, the mentor needs to identify the qualities together with the mentee that the latter wants to develop. Effective mentors need to demonstrate a meaningful relationship otherwise the mentee and also the mentor eventually will come to see it as a waste of time. In addition, a positive regard toward the mentee will manifest itself through the mentor's respect, encouragement, and support of them. Actions underlying effective mentoring include facilitating, guiding and sponsoring. The mentor relationship is more about teaching and sponsoring the less experienced person for a specific purpose, or so they can hone a skill or range of skills. In this case, the mentor is highly experienced and specifically trained in the mentee's field. That is not to say that a novice could not take on a mentor for non-specific purposes such as career development. If so, the relationship would be a mentee-mentor one. Sometimes the mentee is referred to as a protégé.

#### 2.2.1.1 Use of Social Media

One issue that arises in mentoring and also in coaching today is the question of whether a mentor should Google a mentee, prior to meeting with them, to ascertain information about them. This is a serious question for mentors to consider both from a process and an ethical perspective. The mentor could argue that the mentee has posted information about them online and, therefore, it is public information. No one could argue that this is not the case. However, the information about individuals online has been posted over usually a significant period, and much of it could have changed. The other issue is how relevant is it in regard to professional mentoring. While mentors do not need to be registered to guide mentees there remain ethical considerations regarding the following:

a. Informed consent to search online about the mentee
b. Failure to disclose that a search has been conducted by the mentee
c. Potential harm caused by the mentee feeling that they have been intruded on
d. Motives for wanting to conduct an online search
e. If permission is granted, when this best is done and should the mentee be present
f. What information will the mentor deem necessary or relevant, or conversely which will be dispensed with and the reasons for each

#### 2.2.1.2 Choosing Mentors

In formal mentoring programs, individuals who are deemed desirable (a teacher, a good student, a good citizen, a good manager) are usually invited to become mentors. However what is more important in selecting mentors is ensuring they can form positive relationships with the resources and capability to contribute to the learning of the mentee. Mentors do not always require the technical expertise to be successful. In many circumstances, the personal qualities of a mentor make a big difference: being a good listener is vital, capable of encouraging and creating opportunities to realise hidden talents and wanting to help people develop and succeed.

#### 2.2.1.3 Mentoring as a Bridge to Self-sufficiency

One of the most significant issues that mentees may harbour in mentoring concerns choice. The word harbour is used as mentees themselves may not recognise nor acknowledge it as an issue even though at a deeper level they will have preferences and feel frustrated if they cannot make an informed choice about mentoring and more importantly, the mentor.

The concept of making a conscious choice is essential. The choice is about more than providing a variety of options; it extends to ensuring people are fully informed and are able to make choices that take into consideration their capacity to understand the information presented to them and the implications of their actions. Ascertaining capacity can only be carried out through person-centred approaches in mentoring. It goes without saying that to apply a ‘one-size-fits-all’ approach is poor practice and fails to appreciate that each person is different and will have various views as to how they wish to receive mentoring.

The choice is so paramount that it needs to be evident in the mentoring process itself from the outset. The mentee’s right to choose can make all the difference to what some mentees will be comfortable with including the preferred setting and what information they are entitled to have remain confidential and private. Control over these factors not only will impact the mentee’s self-esteem but also contribute to expediting a trusting rapport with the mentor. It also will equalise the power between them and make them feel less inadequate should such feelings be present. The mentor may not be in a position to assess this from the outset.

Further, the range of approaches needs to be clearly explained to the mentees, so that they have a say in whether they wish to proceed, how they wish to proceed and that there are no repercussions should they decide against one or other of these.

Allowing potential mentees to state their preferred choice and selection is important. Using social media is one way of achieving this. Establishing mentoring groups, according to special interests, is another way. Facilitating people to link with a group with common needs through a website is a good way to achieve this too. Support for informal group creation, either by the mentoring program administrator or the participants themselves, including searches of mentor and mentee profiles to facilitate group formation are advisable. A SharePoint with designated areas for group discussions, Q and As, group event notices, project postings and document uploads, encouraging interaction and collaboration among group participants. Group administration and moderation are essential to assure program monitoring, evaluation and safety.

### 2.2.2 *The Mentee's Gender*

When selecting mentors for mentees, perceptions and assumptions about gender and gender identity are important considerations for a number of reasons. Being male or female is multifaceted. A woman may not feel feminine or masculine for that matter although she knows what it feels to be a woman as is the case for men. However, the gender composition of the mentoring dyad may influence

a. the ease of discussion and immediacy of engagement in the mentoring process
b. a willingness to be open and not self-protective—some mentees will be more open to others of the same gender, and this needs to be assessed. Equally, the same gender of both may facilitate the mentor being more readily able to relate to the mentee (Underwood and Moore 1982). However, a balance needs to be maintained to ensure there is a degree of partiality too (see Sect. 8.1).
c. the ownership of issues;
d. the signs of distress or embarrassment; and
e. past experiences with one or other in a parallel process such as previous mentoring, coaching, counselling and so on.

Pairing up with a mentor is about the individual preferences of the mentee and whom they feel most comfortable with regardless of gender. More importantly, gender preference is related to the issues that the mentee wishes to discuss. The mentee's perceptions of whether the mentor will understand these and be able to guide them based on their own experiences or knowledge of the context will determine the choice of mentor. What is important is how connected the mentor is with the mentee (see Sect. 2.3.5).

### 2.2.3 *Gaining Agreement About Process*

As in everyday life, difficulties arise in mentoring, and these largely relate to communication issues. What largely goes amiss is the failure to establish a shared understanding rather than agreement. Mentoring aims to establish a "shared social reality" between the mentee and mentor. It is important to keep in mind that people in a relationship do not assume that they operate on the same information, assumptions and interpretations. To achieve this requires continuous checking largely through a questioning process.

To minimise communication deficits, it is important that the mentor, in particular, is continuously observant to conflict and errors in information sharing and identifying this as a possibility with the mentee. The approach by the mentor needs to be constructive (an element of positive mentoring) by either personally attributing the error to him/herself or to a situation. In both cases, the checking needs to facilitate inquiry rather than lay blame. This approach will reinforce cooperative learning, enhance the sharing of information with both parties adjusting as they see fit. The approaches used in mentoring are discussed in further detail in Chap. 3.

In some mentoring relationships, the issue of silence is a challenge experienced differentially by both the mentee and mentor. Silence is open to misconstruction. Sometimes in conversations, silence means agreement, and it can equally mean disagreement. Sometimes both mentees and mentors are disinclined to raise personally and politically sensitive matters. From the mentee's perspective, it may be through fear of being judged. From the mentor's perspective, it may be uncertainty about the resilience of the mentee to cope with this. Silence is explored further in Chap. 7.

Although mutual expectations within a mentor-mentee relationship might not always be explicit, a commitment to the agreed objectives, a willingness to learn within the mentoring relationship, a resolve to devote the necessary time and energy to the agreed goals, and an expectation that the mentee becomes increasingly independent are essential prerequisites.

### 2.2.4 Mentoring Stages of Learning

To define mentoring in stages does not always reflect the reality of the developing relationship and the evolving conversations. The stages or phases of mentoring and the nature of conversations within this are shaped by the mentee's needs such as whether they require skill development, career guidance, transitioning from one role to another. Career advancement or relocation, repatriation, retirement, or disappointment in not getting the highly sought after promotion are all reasons for a person seeking mentoring. Each of these will have a different focus although each might contain elements of the other, albeit nuanced. For role transition, the focus might be on identification, internalisation and accommodation or the transition from peer to the teacher is a difficult one especially if the mentee's colleagues are more likely to have problems with letting go and acknowledging the new status of the formerly junior colleague. In each case, there is development from establishment through to redefinition which both the mentee and mentor need to address both interpersonally and circumstantially. One will be affected considerably if the mentoring relationship is required rather than based on the mentee's preferred mentor. Where mentoring has been imposed, the relationship may take longer to establish and for each to connect as the mentee will be warier of the mentor's motives and confidentiality. The effectiveness of mentoring depends on a resolution of each of the phases in mentoring to the satisfaction of the mentee. Table 2.1 summarises the alignment of the purpose of mentoring with the nature of the relationship.

**Table 2.1** The alignment of the purpose of mentoring with the nature of the relationship

| Purpose of seeking mentor | Type of mentoring relationship |
|---|---|
| (a) Guidance in a general or specific (e.g. professional area, identity, role clarification) | Protégé-mentor relationships |
| (b) Early career development | Protégé-mentor relationships |
| (c) Assistance in navigating professional and/or institutional structures including conflicts and contradictions | Protégé-mentor relationships |
| (d) General personal development questions or issues as a professional or employee | Mentee-mentor relationship |
| (e) Broad career development | Mentee-mentor relationship |
| (f) Ethical and moral guidance | Mentee-mentor relationship |
| (g) Moral and ethical concerns | Mentee-mentor relationship |

#### 2.2.4.1 How Do Mentees Learn?

Mentees learn through of process of gaining insight, which entails observing, noticing what is being observed and then realising and drawing from the subsequent knowledge that arises from this. This process is conducted conjointly with the mentor. The mentor and mentee need to test the observations through a questioning process e.g. How does the mentee feel about the observation? This is an important question. The first answer may be different if the mentor asks the question again later in the conversation when the mentee has had a chance to explore it further first. Another question to ask is: Is the mentee focusing on the totality of the situation or a selected component of it? Are they open to considering it from a different or new perspective?

The mentor will guide the mentee back to the point of problem initiation or where the mentee feels this issue first arose. Together the mentor and mentee will uncover the evidence through questioning, explore what is discovered and eventually hypothesise alternative ways of seeing this. At first, the mentor needs to start this process with the points of greatest foci for the mentee. Otherwise, they will lose interest and see it as irrelevant (for further questioning also see Sects. 3.3 and 10.2). Observations include the target of the observation, any one or all of the following: attitude, action, relationships or an event. In order to understand these and gain insight it is important to view them as objectively as possible without evaluating them. Mentors work the mentee to assist them to observe it as if seeing it for the first time as well.

As information is revealed, issues and concepts can be further explored. A further way to consider doing this is by choosing an appropriate set of lenses. Analysis through a 'lenses' approach is a micro process used within mentoring or a macro-process that encapsulates the mentoring relationship. An example of this is learning through three lenses: transformational, humanistic and emancipatory

(Merriam et al. 2007). The first, transformational, facilitates mentees to discover meaning within their own experiences through critical self-reflection (Mezirow and Taylor 2009; Taylor 2008). The second perspective, humanist, allows mentees to develop or hone their critical thinking skills by using existing knowledge and motivations to develop their own approaches to self-learning through their own or mentor's direction. Once the information and understanding are creatively opened up them, the mentor and mentee seek to make sense of it gaining further practical understanding and skills.

In the third, emancipatory perspective (Mezirow and Taylor 2009), mentees become positioned for action based on an analysis of role and context: (a) organisational and legal contexts; (b) cultural including political situations; (c) learning about technical systems and processes e.g. policy context; and (d) motoric techniques e.g. performance of techniques through to the overall performance of a role e.g. clinical relationship with clients. Essentially, there are very few instances when issues cannot be resolved in some way. Many issues are created, exacerbated or suffered because people do not seek to stop, observe and explore them further. On more occasions than not, the way to resolve them is embedded in the challenge that the person is experiencing, and the issue is either how the person is viewing it, a lack of observation or within the relationships. This is what is meant by mentoring mindedness.

By opening up a situation for observation, exploration, reflection and analysis, some resolution can be found. If not, then the mentee can perhaps use the insight to gain an understanding of how to accept or use it as a turning point in their life. Many creative opportunities emerge from such realisations.

Reflection can be initiated by a "big picture" view using a qualitative, unstructured, open-ended, spontaneous approach guided by the mentor. At some point, this approach needs to become more focused and organised around the issues or questions that the mentee needs and wants to address.

**Gaining Insight**

Becoming insightful is picked up from cues that people detect instinctively and deliberately through focused concentration (Bautista et al. 2011). Further, the more people know, the more they use this knowledge to gain insight into new areas or to challenge their thinking. Both increase a mentor's capacity for insightfulness.

One of the main reasons that a mentee may request a mentor is that they realise they are cannot get a handle on the situation. They sense there is something deeper although unsure about this and have no way or system for "testing" their hunch. This sensation is a form of cognitive dissonance and mentees feel blocked. The positive side of this is that the mentee through their discomfort is keen to learn how to get out of it. Mentoring is not about a quick fix to resolve the mentee's level of discomfort rather it about working with the mentee to develop an approach where they can learn to lift themselves out of the dissonance by themselves. Table 2.2 is an outline of an approach to achieve this outcome. The mentor commences the process using examples familiar to the mentee to encourage the development of insight—a form of learning.

**Table 2.2** Gaining insight in mentoring

| Mentee's approach | Mentor's approach | Learning principle |
|---|---|---|
| Discusses uncertainty about current context, role, stakeholder perceptions of them and to other | Wide—ranging experience of different organisations and workplaces | Use an analogy to draw the comparison between past situations that the mentee knows well with the current one |
| Undetected misunderstandings | Questions to drill down into misunderstandings and errors in assessment of the current situation | Queries the mentee on how they arrived at their mistaken conclusion |
| Understanding is based on superficial descriptions and structures in the situation | Questions the mentee so that they look beneath the surface | Uses examples that the mentee can identify with showing the difference between the tangible representations of the situation and people and the less perceptible |
| Thinking is chaotic rather than working through a guided approach such as the five "W" questions | Asks the five "W" questions focusing on why, what, who, when, where + how | Asking questions and not accepting things at face value nor taking observations for granted |
| Tends to rely on what they have learnt technically and through observation | Encourages mentee to distinguish how they know things: technical knowing; through observation; through reading and listening and using these forms to diagnose what they need to know in a professional or work context | Provides feedback and chooses another example for practice.<br>Insight learning is useful for problem-solving especially where people are uncertain about the outcome or disagree about this |

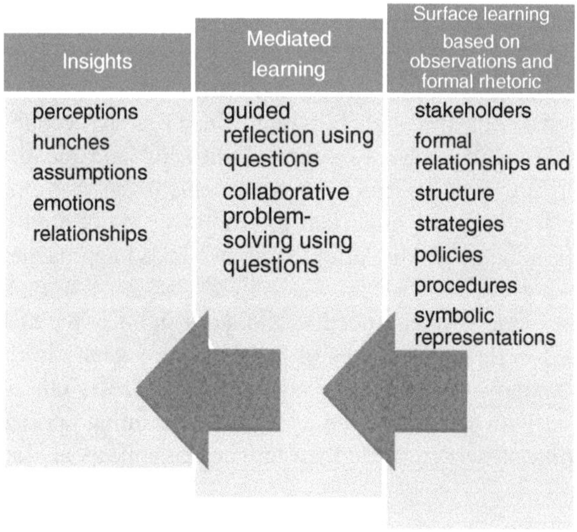

#### 2.2.4.2 Divergent Thinking

Taking these various frames as reference points, the joint focus of the mentee and mentor is not only about the purpose of the connection, either cognitive dissonance, a perceived capability gap both identified by the mentee, or about relationships with their supervisor, peer or significant other but also role and context. The deficit may be more tangible for example, having to do with the mentee taking their next career step, changing careers or widening their influence or engagement in circles other than their immediate professional or work spheres.

It is the task of the mentor to work out whether or not the perceived gap is real or merely a perception. Even if the latter the mentor needs to work with the mentee to alter the perception if it is impeding further development of the mentee in desired directions. In doing so, the mentor needs to work out with the mentee whether there is a tacit acceptance of the gap or whether there is tacit capability or other capability gaps that the mentee is oblivious to.

Mentors need to assess their own capability including potential gaps for assisting a mentee, either through self-assessment or peer-review through a colleague or friend. Mentors have a responsibility to establish a good relationship with the mentee through example and modelling, to maintain satisfactory standards in their own professional role of mentor (as well as their role outside of mentoring); to remain up to date not only in their professional knowledge of mentoring but also in maintaining an awareness of their own strengths and weaknesses. The focus of the mentor is in creating high standards of mentoring through an engaged process built on mutual learning.

It is then that the mentor can focus on the nature of the capability gap for the mentee, real or perceived. They both work together to understand and then figure out what the issues or questions that brought the mentee to the mentor. Then potential goals need to be planned and prioritised. A mentor intervenes in the learning process through listening, facilitation, challenging and providing overall support to assist the mentee in identifying and examining these aspects and seeing whether these are aligned to actions and plans. A formal mentoring conversation usually includes preparation, dialogue, commitment and closure to each meeting. It also involves agreement about goals around the process, accountability of each party to each other, and a plan of action. Following and identifying outcomes, opportunities for further development or advancement, assessing progress towards goals, and using feedback are important in producing the desired learning.

In terms of learning, mentoring draws upon two broad approaches: divergent and convergent thinking.

The divergent mode is open-ended, exploratory, inquiry-based focusing on the future and is used in the early phases of mentoring especially in the first meeting. A mentor will employ this mode throughout the process. Often some mentors become frustrated with what they see as a time-consuming approach and quickly want to get to some answers, especially if the mentee appears anxious in this regard too.

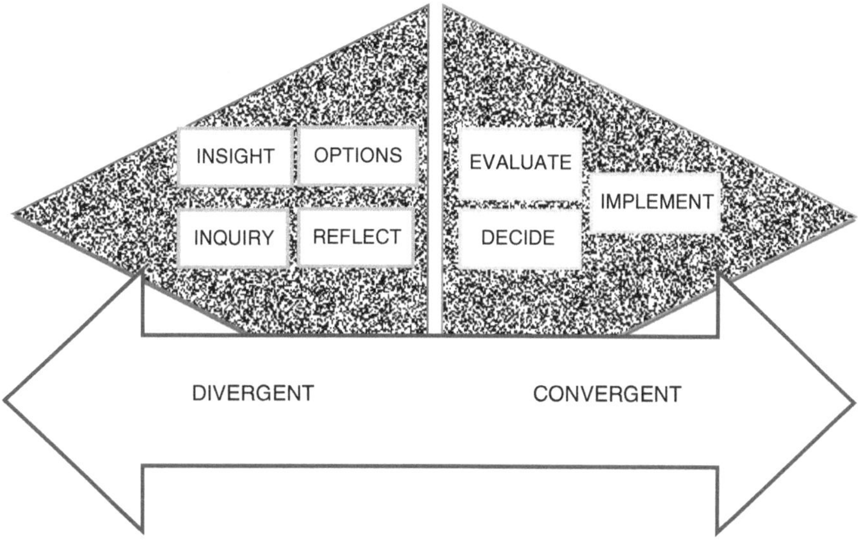


**Fig. 2.2** Divergent thinking is supplemented by convergent thinking

Divergent thinking is supplemented by convergent thinking which is more analytical, evaluating the options that emerged through the divergent process. While the elements of the learning process generally occur in a particular sequence, there is no one right linear path. Mentoring is flexible and creative, providing the linkages and the flashes of insight that form it and lead to great outcomes for the mentee (Fig. 2.2).

Throughout the divergent learning process, mentors do not try to persuade or coerce, rather *encourage and challenge* their mentees. This is the phase for inspired learning, imagining what might be, followed eventually by a phase of pragmatic planning as they both move together towards convergent thinking—the end stage of mentoring. Between the beginning and end phases of mentoring, the mentee and mentor interweave divergent and convergent thinking depending on the issues at the end.

During the divergent phase, the mentor needs to assess the mentee's readiness for the mentoring process and then in the convergent phase, their readiness for commitment to implementation action plans arising from the mentoring. The mentoring readiness is relatively straightforward as it depends on the mentee-mentor relationship and how this develops. Compared to 'implementation readiness' this is much trickier as it depends on the professional context, supporters of the mentee, resources such as time and energy, resilience to withstand push back and so on.

Once readiness in the implementation phase is confirmed, then mentoring is based on supporting the mentee in this process. This will include assisting them prepare the ground for making changes such as applying for a new role inside or outside their current employer, providing comment on a business case for a new project, communicating with key stakeholders, building a personal brand and so on. However, it may be nothing more than the mentor encouraging the mentor to remain focused, assess priorities and make decisions as appropriate.

## 2.3 What Is It About the Mentoring Relationship that Allows a Person's Potential to Emerge, Be Shaped or Flourish?

Learning is, more often than not, accidental or unintended, whether it is planned or not. Mentoring facilitates the mentee to progress from inadvertent learning towards intended learning, self-knowledge and building the personal capability to deal satisfactorily with the ups and downs of life. This type of learning is positive in that it builds self-awareness, knowledge and ultimate resilience.

An unfolding narrative facilitates an exploration between the participants to find out what is going on in the situation under focus and what does it mean for them. What can they learn from this? People get little practice or opportunity for intrapersonal reflection. Mentoring offers the opportunity to learn this skill with a person who is prepared to explore, challenge and listen and reflect together on the responses and outcomes.

Let's consider the broader question of what a mentor offers the mentee and how this influences them throughout the relationship and beyond. In many situations, public and private, people learn from each other informally through observation, modelling or shadowing, and also through conversations and conflicts. How many times does one hear the expression "if only I'd thought of that at the time" indicating that people reflect on past conversations after the event and learn from the further contemplation about the experience. Mentoring facilitates deeper contemplation, either during or post conversation. It is through this process where further self-learning occurs, not only the process but also useful outcomes.

While mentoring varies from situation to situation, at a macro level it requires the following three dimensions: issue exploration, identification of the prime issue, agreement and then analysis about where to from here. To further demonstrate the learning component of mentoring, take the example of a younger, less experienced person working with a seasoned mentor where the mentor is assisting the mentee in steering a new or career-changing direction. Part of the exploration is working out the reasons for the change, making explicit the assumptions on which the analysis is based, the purpose for doing so and the risks associated with the likely outcomes. In this brief scenario, the mentee and mentor have to trust each other's openness, to believe that any proposed new direction is emanating from the mentee principally and not being imposed as well as it being in the mentee's best interest and for the mentee to accept that the mentor is acting in good faith. Trust is crucial for "unpicking" the current action and formulating new goals. Furthermore, trust can be divided in terms of emotional and instrumental trust (based on Zhu et al. 2013). The former focuses on sentient, and interpersonal aspects of the relationship whereas instrumental trust represents the characteristics of the mentor and mentee such as their capability and consistency within the relationship. Emotional trust facilitates the relationship between the mentor and mentee which points to the magnitude of affective trust as it involves the deeper emotional state of the mentee. Affective trust allows individuals to be honest about their susceptibilities and diminishes fears and lack of confidence which may hinder learning and performance in their roles beyond mentoring. The emotionally arousing nature of trust leads to mutual exchange and rapport which eventually translate into positive work outcomes for the organisation (Zhu et al. 2013).

Building new personal capacity requires expanding our network of relationships and this also takes time. So often in mentoring, the mentee has to step back rather than forward, a process that is never easy those mentees who are keen to progress rapidly. Helping mentees to take a step back is never easy nor is supporting them to rethink and to fortify their personal capability. Both are crucial for their future development.

## 2.3.1 *The Role of Confidence*

Confidence is a cognitive skill which is equated with self-efficacy, defined as "people's judgments of their capabilities to organise and execute courses of action required to attain designated types of performances" Bandura (1986, p. 391). Simply expressed, self-efficacy is self-belief in what a person can or cannot achieve. This is very powerful. The beliefs people have about their capabilities are significant in shaping not only their own perceptions of their capability but also those of others. If a person believes they will not succeed, this is communicated to others subliminally.

Upon commencement of the mentoring relationship, some mentees may present, experiencing low confidence, which is inevitably inhibiting their overall capability in some way. This wearing down of self-confidence is often a gradual process over time so that by the time the mentee presents in mentoring, their low morale is apparent, and they have realigned their expectations accordingly. In other words, their talent resource is eroded too.

In other cases, a low self-belief may be less apparent as the mentee has now become skilled in covering it up. This is harder for the mentor to detect and if sensed, discuss. However, a similar pattern may be occurring where the mentee has downgraded their expectations about possibilities, which is also part of the "covering up" that they have achieved.

In both scenarios, people learn to become risk averse. Their personal judgments about their capability to perform can influence how they think, feel and behave, especially as work tasks increase in demand. If the demands become too great, mentees may become overly prudent in taking up challenges leading others to make negative evaluations of their capability. These external assessments are more to do with mentees in this situation being overly cautious than the capability per se.

Often self-confidence originates due to comparisons, real or false, with others e.g. peers, supervisors, and is intensified when those others are also evaluating the mentee's performance and indirectly, their capability.

The experience of low confidence may be a tacit one. In mentoring, a person's self-efficacy can be viewed through a prism of their achievements, their perceptions of situations and their comparisons with others that they bring to the mentor for discussion.

One approach is for mentors to suggest new approaches with mentees to see how willing they are to take on something novel or unfamiliar to them. Mentors who give mentees options may observe them consistently taking the less challenging option. Mentors can use such insights from these conversations to work with the mentee in getting to the source of the issue, which is whether it is low confidence, poor capability, both or some other factor.

Self-efficacy is learned and, therefore, is a skill. It is important that mentors understand the process structuring these conversations and how they can work with mentees to enhance their self-efficacy in the same way that any other skill is learnt and developed.

The mentoring relationship can falter if mentors neglect to develop the self-efficacy of their mentees, especially if this is at the heart of the matter for the mentee. If neglected, the mentee with low self-efficacy is likely to become disheartened as they had hoped that mentoring may be a chance to re-invigorate and boost their confidence. If the mentor does not engage on this level with the mentee targeting the nub of the issue, mentees will become easily disheartened, and either gives up on mentoring or if in a formal program, go along with it until they can be released from it without losing face. They certainly will not call upon their mentor to assist them further.

On the other hand, the mentor may find that they invest an inordinate amount of time trying to re-invigorate mentees or to reassure them over and over again. For example, Karen, a hardworking team member volunteered for formal mentoring to assist her take the next step in her career, a team leadership role. After some weeks of getting nowhere with her mentor, Karen was offered another mentor to replace her current one who was leaving the organisation. With much persuading, Karen admitted she had lost confidence in her desire to move forward as she felt her mentor had not assisted her in keeping her embryonic aspirations of becoming a leader alive. This led to a useful discussion of realistic expectations for herself with her new mentor. Eventually over a few more meetings, Karen re-engaged and set out a career plan with actions for this future prospect.

When a mentor does not boost, or worse, deflate the self-efficacy of the mentee by not dealing with it directly, the relationship will stall and become ineffective. From thereon in, mentoring is a waste of time. Whenever the real issues are not discussed, this is the outcome. See Chap. 3 on how to structure the mentoring conversation.

As self-efficacy of the mentee decreases and the longer this occurs, there is increasing probability that they will not achieve the required competence to prepare them for the next step, which is a double jeopardy for them leading to increased anxiety and opportunities for them to opt out. Dealing with this predicament is a must.

Past performance accomplishments are the most dependable source of information that influences self-efficacy judgments because they rest on actual mastery experiences (Bandura 1977). The relationship expectations of self-efficacy and outcomes are reciprocal. When a person feels in control, they align their expectations accordingly, and this influences their performance including what opportunities they will engage in, being less cautious about this, re-attempting after a failed first attempt, the amount of effort expended and the duration of effort and preparation for what lies ahead. The cumulative effects of this process increase a person's perceived control of a task, especially if this is accompanied by trusted feedback from a mentor. When mentees better understand their past performances and why and how they achieved the outcomes they did, they are more likely to feel efficacious. A sense of efficacy motivates their determination to success. Consequently, they are more inclined to try again and apply what their learning in specific situations to broader ones; and take similar risks in a new one. In addition, mentees may persist if at first they do not succeed, learning more about how to improve their performance and outcomes in diverse contexts, and in this way increase their sense of control, which feeds into their self-confidence.

There are several ways to do this: confidence is developed more sustainably where mentees achieve tasks which are relatively straightforward but have not been attempted previously with negligible external assistance and also on more difficult tasks (Bandura 1986). Once mentees have tried it for themselves, this is enormously powerful and confidence-building for them.

To summarise the approach and to experiment it within the mentoring context first as follows:

(a) A mentee reflects on past situations. The mentor works through these with open questions.
(b) A mentee reflects on comparisons with others. The mentor works through these with open questions. In conversation, it is more than likely that (a) and (b) will be integrated.
(c) For both (a) and (b) above, the mentor explores the situations by asking

    I. Why aren't you good enough? Waits for a response.
    II. In response I am not good enough to take on that role or perform the task, the mentor can ask, "who says?"; "compared with whom?" It is useful to work with the mentee to uncover and deal with their faulty logic especially if they are basing it on an idealised version of self.

(d) The mentor provides and elicits feedback and observes the mentee's emotional expressions including commenting on if there is a detectable change in conversational climate.
(e) The mentor elicits key thoughts from the mentee about their observations.

(f) Together they plan a new cognitive approach using a specific situation—start with a successful one then work to one which is more challenging.
(g) The mentor guides discovery through planned risk-taking by the mentee in a given situation fully supported.
(h) A time is set aside to reflect and work out what worked and what didn't.
(i) The mentor assists the mentee to apply fresh understanding and new actions.
(j) Then the mentee practises, practises and practises with the mentor.
(k) Then applies it in a real situation without the mentor.
(l) The process of reflection with the mentor is recommenced working through what happened in (i) above.

### 2.3.2 *Self-sufficiency*

Whereas, in Aristotelean times, autonomy was predominantly used to describe city states, now autonomy is interpreted as self-sufficiency and applies to individuals. Relational accounts of autonomy have proposed to widen the perspective to the social context of choice (Berofsky 1995). Philosophically, personal independence (self-sufficiency) and the capacity for decision-making (or competence) is related. All things considered, self-sufficiency is the capacity for people to make choices and act on them based on their own reasons, desires, values, commitments and emotions at any given point in time. Decision making occurs following a period of deliberation—short or long—by the person.

### 2.3.3 *The Value of Self-sufficiency*

Fostering autonomy is one of the main purposes in mentoring to assure a strong mentee and mentor relationship. A mentoring relationship needs to be open, reassuring and accepting. Self-sufficiency or sense of personal autonomy (albeit semi-autonomy) is valued in most societies albeit in varying degrees both historically and situationally. The issue for the mentor and mentee is to become self-sufficient by questioning for: why, in what circumstances and how? For instance, self-sufficiency is considered to be a public good in society on the grounds that the moral and legal rights of individuals are respected and protected. It also guards people in both states and institutions against total authority and exploitation and indeed, over-protectiveness (e.g. the Nanny-State). Moreover, most societies pay lip service at least to ensuring that children are reared to be self-sufficient as this is associated with upstanding, moral purpose and values. However in most societies there are children growing up "on-the-street" and who survive on "their wits" by being self-sufficient and resilient although not necessarily acting morally or legally, either out of the necessity of subsistence or otherwise. The same could be said for individuals participating in many different settings including institutions, work situations and community locales. Regardless of the circumstances self-sufficiency is important. Otherwise, individuals experience low self-efficacy and resilience, low accountability and responsibility and feel less authenticated which leads to a sense of uncertainty, low self-esteem and eventually anxiety.

In these settings moral purpose and rationality are taken-for-granted but this varies depending on a person's understandings, capacity to control or influence the situational contingencies such as formal/procedural processes as well as substantive ones.

Reflective understanding is paramount in considering the struggle for self-sufficiency for the mentee regardless of which stage they are in their professional life cycle. In an age of entitlement, many people are now struggling with wanting something and wanting it immediately, even though it is may never be attainable.

There is also the issue of lack of self-sufficiency by default—automatic response without reflection. In short, the person is not reflective enough to realise that they have some control over the situation and if the action that is expected does not fit in with their preferences, they do not need to follow.

The second issue is the moral purpose and rationality underlying the action and to the extent that the mentee supports it or not or indeed is obliged to support it legally or by virtue of the profession that they have signed up to perform.

Teasing out legal and professional reasons from personal preferences and emotions allows the mentee to prioritise preferences and choices as a way of sifting through the parameters of significant decisions to act in one way as opposed to another. It also means that the person's sense of self and their right to act on their needs is taken into account as well as the value pluralism of the contexts in which they participate.

The mentor needs to be able to assist the mentee to question their world view, their perception of the contextual factors and participants as well as their beliefs, desires and preferences. It is through this process that self-sufficiency further develops which is associated with self-efficacy and resilience.

The notion of world-view is a very important concept for the mentor to use as a tool. By examining the mentee's world view, the mentee is able to view different perspectives and how and why they took them in particular situations. From this both the mentor and mentee can engage in making inferences and test out how the mentee's actions may be being evaluated by others (Ruby and Decety 2004). This tool is a salient one for the mentor in considering issues such as blame, guilt, silence and loyalty in the latter half of this book.

However, the mentee needs to be within the bounds of the morally permissible to count as (genuinely) autonomous (Meyers 1989). Self-sufficiency means that individuals self-legislate according to their interpretation of the moral dictates of the situation as far as they realise it (O'Neill 2003).

Self-sufficiency has its limits due to the evident pluralism of values and assumptions of rationality within modern societies. Mentors and mentees face the challenge of being sufficiently broad to be compatible with this pluralism, but also pragmatically attuned to how this is applied in relevant settings for mentees. It is a challenge because people assume that at least once they reach early adulthood they have the right to self-determine and in doing so often do not meet standards of substantive rationality. In fact, respect for individual autonomy within liberal states includes the legal protection of irrational, 'unwise' choices.

Collective efficacy is the relationship between the mentor and the mentee that is required for effective mentoring. Collective efficacy could also be used beyond this relationship as the mentee learns to build a network with others for support.

### 2.3.4 The Role of Influence in Mentoring

Throughout such processes, the success of mentoring is about the mentor influencing rather than "telling" the mentee. The main process for this is 'listening' to the mentee, which sounds simple enough. However, the failure to listen well is a frequent barrier. It leads to a faulty exploration between the mentor and mentee, conversations that go nowhere, overly prolonged mentoring or an eventual breakdown in the mentoring relationship. Mentors need to understand that they do not need to come up with answers for everything.

Influence relies on this important listening skill. If a mentor listens well, a mentee will follow suit eventually. Each is subjected to the other's energy, control and resistance. The mentor influences the mentee, although as stated previously, this is never a one-way exchange. Influencing each other flows from the deepest source of human understanding. The challenge for each is to accept or counter the other's influence depending on the nature of the persuasion and to what purpose it is being addressed. The mentee should never be dominated by the mentor, who may be revered for their achievement or status (seniority) as this would defeat the purpose of mentoring. However, the mentee needs to be open and also listen to consider alternative questions if they are to explore well and learn. Indeed, one of the outcomes of mentoring is to improve one's capability to influence others and not to be dominated by them, particularly where one's own ideas are being subjugated.

Mentoring reveals the role that power and influence play in every relationship and how to act vigorously to participate in this process and not stand on the sidelines. Selecting an appropriate mentor is important in learning to find and balance power in this relationship so as to experience and learn from it. Further, mentors need to be well connected so they can call upon these resources, although ideally they should not be the mentees' supervisor as the capacity to be open may be thwarted due to their potential power to reward and sanction. That is not to say that supervisors cannot use mentoring as a device for developing skills in their staff teams as it can work in general terms.

An unsuccessful mentoring relationship is like an accident that makes people reluctant to participate in again. "A negative relationship can affect morale, stress levels and even turnover rates. Those who have a bad experience with mentoring are often reluctant to take part in another relationship." (Cranwell-ward et al. 2004, p. 209). Empowering participants rather than incapacitating them is the key to exerting positive influence with mentees.

### 2.3.5 *What Makes a Successful Mentoring Relationship?*

Firstly, as already suggested, mentees are required to commit to acting on their new learning and make decisions about how to modify their actions, their thinking and their approach to others. This is as much about refreshing mindsets, self-reflections, re-evaluating and a commitment to change. It is a form of learning where the mentee has to 'be' in the present and not 'absent', unlike in other learning situations, such as the classroom or in a clinical therapeutic situation where the "learner" can "switch off" does not necessarily "buy into" the process. If mentees become disinterested or preoccupied, the mentor needs to be attuned to this and bring them back into the moment.

Secondly, mentoring takes time. The amount of time devoted to mentoring will vary depending on its nature and the roles and experience of the people involved. Some pairs will meet regularly and frequently while others will agree to get together as needed. The former is suited where young and less experienced mentees are involved and the latter where it involves professional equivalents or differently experienced people of similar status. Whatever the circumstance, successful mentorship requires frequent meetings at the beginning of the relationship so as to establish a good foundation for moving forward. Meetings do not always require personal contact and could be achieved through Skype, email or phone. Peer mentoring can be done in a similar way and through electronic discussion fora too.

Thirdly, for mentoring to be effective, sponsorship needs to be a significant feature of the mentoring relationship whereby the mentor can draw upon their influence and networks to gain some advantage for the mentee e.g. additional resources, career opportunities, and the like. For example in Australia and other western countries, women aspiring to become board members of listed companies are seeking out formal mentors with the expectation that this will give them a real opportunity to gain a seat on boards (Korporaal 2010). It will not if they have not built up a track record of effective board participation, and this usually starts with an introduction by a mentor to a board or committee that is within their early experience.

## 2.4 The Outcomes of Mentoring

A core benefit of mentoring for both parties is multi-dimensional learning. Learning through feedback, how to make decisions, impact others as well as understanding how to align individual goals with actions, resources and plans are often dealt with simultaneously. Learning is two-way: mentors offer valuable knowledge and skill development based on their experience to provide a pathway out of life's cul-de-sacs. Equally, mentees can offer valuable resources to the mentor to reciprocate their support (Mezias and Scandura 2005). Moreover, mentoring provides for both, individually and together, feedback about their assumptions and roles (Hall 1996) and is an effective way for both to broaden their vision on career development (Liu et al. 2009).

Other benefits from a positive mentoring relationship are feeling more self-aware and self-confident; more closely connected to the organisation and finding work more satisfying and meaningful. Mentoring maximises knowledge and can be passed onto others outside the relationship. "It helps people build new relationships and strengthen existing ones; people become more collaborative in their performance and learning, and individuals feel more prepared to offer themselves as mentors to others" (Zachary 2005, p. 9).

## 2.5 How Is the Mentoring Relationship Qualitatively Different from Other Types of Relationships?

Mentoring is a primary *conversation* whereby the mentees need to feel "*protected*" by the mentors and that the mentor is "there" for them. This is particularly important for Generation Y workers who respond well when they are provided prompt feedback and credit for results achieved (Martin 2005; Southard and Lewis 2004).

It revolves around a personal, intimate conversation transmitting shared meaning; it is responsive, deeply satisfying, trusting and influential (Nezlek 2001). All of these characteristics make life more fulfilling and *positive*. Intimacy inherent in mentoring is impossible in situations where there are more than two people present, such as group training sessions, apprenticeships or on-the-job training. Consequently, a one-on-one mentoring relationship becomes extremely significant and worthwhile if it works. So while mentoring does *occur within, overlap* and *parallel* other forms of collaborative, learning relationships, these rarely contain the particular ingredients and benefits that mentoring affords its participants, both for the mentor and the mentee (Tenner 2004).

Mentoring covers the full gamut of learning relationships from the novice (who is highly educated and wanting to learn more in a specific field) to the highly experienced (someone who has wide-ranging experience and is able to know a situation based on their past experience). Elements of counselling, coaching and team building comprise mentoring. Although the learning outcomes are critical for the mentees, the value of mentoring as distinct from other learning relationships is that the process itself is as important source of modelling, transforming and self-development. A focus on process entails unpacking the thinking and feelings of the mentee, reflecting on the degree of coherence between emotions and reasoning, intentions and aspirations, implementation and follow-up. What contributes to the effectiveness of mentoring is the degree of self-engagement and the nature of the interpersonal communication between the mentor and mentee and how this affords them a store of information including sensitivity to contextual meanings, perceptions, interpretations as well as being able to tease out the distinctions between these. In other words, the communication is primary.

### *2.5.1 Types of Mentoring*

Mentoring Relationships are established in various ways. Some of the major ones are considered here used exclusively or in conjunction with one or more of the others.

*Traditional One-on-One Mentoring*

Traditional one-on-one mentoring is a type of apprenticeship whereby the most junior mentee learns from a more experienced mentor. As the label suggests, its aim is to groom the mentee for their next step, focusing on the values, decisions and performance. This is often formalised, although rarely compulsory, and the mentor or mentee are often selected and matched. It is used in schools and all types of organisations for supporting people to develop or learn new skills. However, mentoring can be informal where one or other party is sought out by the other. Whether it is formal or not, traditional mentoring may vary in its philosophy in regard to whether the mentor's viewpoint is that the mentee's thinking needs to be 'aligned' to that of say an organisation (dubbed 'alignment mentoring') or allows the mentee to come to their own position through reflection and reflective practice, more akin to professional mentoring.

*Professional Mentoring for Practitioners*

This is similar to traditional One-on-One Mentoring and primarily focuses on reflective inquiry into how the junior professional is improving the quality of their decisions and actions as a practitioner, for example, a medical practitioner, lawyer, teacher, social/youth worker, counsellor or nurse. Professional mentoring is often mandatory such as peer supervision for psychologists, coaches and the like. It provides a standards and an ethical base that enable the practitioner to evaluate their own approach, analyse their dilemmas and work through problems to resolution.

*Mentoring versus Sponsoring*

Sponsoring is a form of mentoring with one difference: "Sponsors go beyond giving feedback and advice; they advocate for their mentees and help them gain visibility in the company" (Ibarra et al. 2010, p. 83).

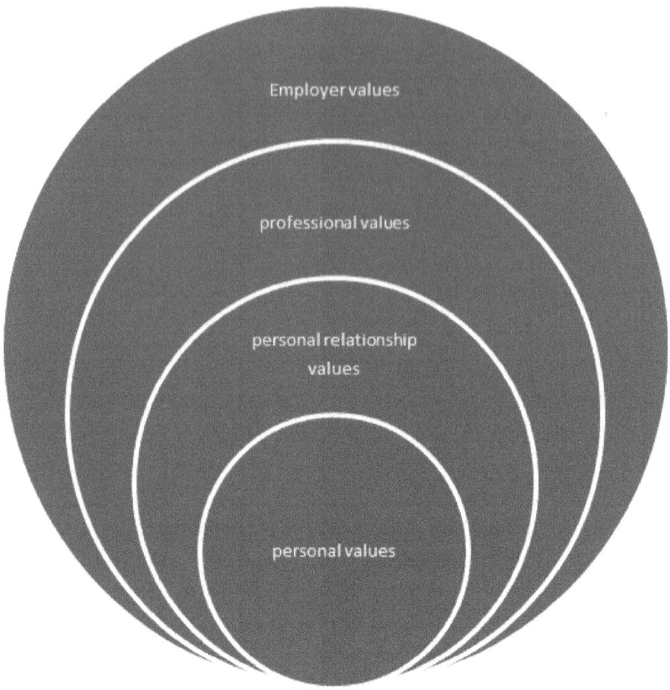


**Fig. 2.3** The spheres of cultural influence

*Cross-Cultural Mentoring*

Culture is an integral part of person's identity and, therefore, cross-cultural considerations need to be taken into account. Cultural values are realised from a person's family of origin, family of procreation, friends, profession, religious institutions and the surrounding society. Figure 2.3 exhibits the spheres of cultural influence.

The mentee's values can equivocate between different sets of values depending on the strength of relationships with each, incentives, conflict or dissonance at relational interfaces and other situational dependencies. If a mentee is from a collectivistic culture, its dominant values are group orientation, coexistent with a religious ideal, with nature/land as is the case with indigenous peoples in particular and/or focus on the past. A person's cultural orientation will influence the choice of a mentor and mentoring as well as its impact. Both may need to be adapted accordingly. Suffice to say that mentorship has the potential to offer opportunities for genuine acculturation and cultural competence.

Culture not only influences how mentees and mentors think and feel but also their identity and their perceptions of how they think the other sees them. Identity is significant in all facets of a person's life and changes albeit slowly throughout life's course from a small child, student to a fully-fledged employee or professional.

In mentoring it is important for mentors to appreciate both the interfaces and intersections of the mentee's cultural values and belief systems. In professional relationships, people can maintain a certain distance (i.e., objectivity, neutrality) from the other whereas in mentoring it can be highly personalised and emotionally charged to all involved (Buckley and Foldy 2010).

Identity, on the other hand, is another multifaceted aspect of social and personal functioning that identifies the individual and gives them credibility and some self-esteem. Cultural identity highlights a person's uniqueness and could include, for example, gender, ethnicity and occupation.

Cultural identity combined with personal attributes influences the way a mentee presents initially and how they approach mentoring and realise its benefits. For example, a mentor needs to take into account a person's ethno-social position e.g. consider a Muslim woman working in a male-dominated western institution and the potential stressors for her in relation to her colleagues especially male; her home life that she leaves and returns to each day; her personal attributes and capacity to integrate with this organisational culture; any culture-bound beliefs; practices; codes of conduct and expressions of distress. It is inevitable that cultural identity will be fluid and may well change in response to a number of factors especially during mentoring. It is essential that mentors take this into account.

All mentoring should be conducted from a cross-cultural perspective. Cross-cultural mentoring not only refers to ethno and religious spheres but also the different value systems imposed on the mentee by virtue of their professional orientation and employment. Understanding mentoring from a cross-cultural perspective encourages and assists the mentee to probe into their underlying assumptions, values that impact on their perceptions and actions in the host culture. It is mentoring between people of different cultures such as in "ex-pat" situations. It works through an approach whereby the mentee is required to walk along two paths. A good example of this would be integrating an indigenous approach within the mainstream culture, especially where the mentee has to relate to people from their cultural background. Napier has explored the cross-cultural exchanges between foreign 'experts' who work as mentors in developing countries and local 'learners' who possess a great deal of locally-relevant knowledge that the foreigner needs and lacks (Napier 2006). The dialogue, learning, teaching and support across cultural differences are a vital component of cross-cultural mentoring relationship. The interaction between the two parties happens within the institutional context, and the decision to engage in those actions is influenced not only by the individual, but also by the institution's culture, faculty expectations, mission, and history.

*Peer Mentoring*

Mentoring between peers of similar status such as school or University students is also beneficial in sharing information, problem-solving and support for each other. It overlaps with informal mentoring and is probably the most common and therefore, invisible form of mentoring. The key factor here is that peer mentoring includes personal approaches that are not always dealt with in formal programs.

*Reverse Mentoring*

The mentee stereotype is typically conceived as a young or "junior" status person is paired with a more experienced, older person assisting their advancement (knowledge and skill development, work or career opportunities, job promotion) (Wanberg et al. 2003). Effective mentors could just as easily have less experience and provide a basis for new learning for others regardless of individual characteristics or experience. Similarly, the notion of Generation Y approaching work with different expectations compared to previous generations may also be over simplified. Over the ages, humans want, more or less, the same things from their working life regardless of whether it is a short or long career, continuous or not, that is, they desire security, satisfaction, belongingness, acknowledgement and growth. Many motivational theorists and research attest to this. Consequently, the stereotypes applied to Gen Y could just as easily be applied to the over 50s group. If one thinks of the baby boomer generation, the amount of change and innovation that has occurred in their lifetime has far outstripped that of Gen X or Gen Y. They were the first teenagers, the first hippies and transmogrified into "yuppies" and more recently, "sea and tree changers".

While structured mentoring schemes are well-established for senior mentors and junior protégées, reverse mentoring schemes are relatively new (Greengard 2002) whereby the over 50s generation are paired with a Gen Y, for example, with a specific purpose in mind. However, there is widespread recognition that reverse mentoring, broadly defined as a one-on-one relationship in which the senior person learns from a younger/junior one, is more common than is acknowledged, if only because it happens informally and goes unnoticed. Reverse mentoring originates in the trend away from concepts of knowledge and power that parallel traditional mentoring to an equal relationship, whereby all participants, regardless of age, have something of value to contribute (Darwin 2000; Tempest 2003).

Trust is also essential in reverse mentoring especially where one member acts as a sounding board or takes on the role of the questioning partner: "why are you doing that? What are you trying to achieve? Wouldn't you be better doing it this way?" and so on. (Welch and Welch 2006). This approach benefits younger people, giving them a voice in the leading to feeling more confident and valued by others (Cotugna and Vickery 1998; Leh 2005; Morgan and Streb 2001). This approach may be of particular value to Generation Y, whom some authors claim to be more interested than earlier generations in the moral, civic and social value that their work provides (Allen 2004; Cone 2006; Crampton and Hodge 2009; Glass 2007; Pekala 2001). The benefits of reverse mentoring open up networking and other benefits for young people (Leh 2005; Wong et al. 2008; Zanni 2009).

*Group or Situational Mentoring*

While learning is often best served through a traditional one-on-one mentoring experience, sometimes it works better when people interact with multiple learners (group mentoring) or with multiple experts (situational mentoring). Different learning situations are important (Emelo 2010) and various approaches may need to be trialled and used. Peer coaching and mentoring circles are alternatives to encourage relational learning beyond the one on one. For example, some employers have experimented with forms of peer coaching for cultural change and personal transformation. Others have established mentoring circles for the purpose of facilitating development. An example of this is where a senior leader, trained in managing group dynamics, meets with a small circle of people regularly to discuss particular issues that may be shared among them and uses the group's skills and knowledge to learn.

### 2.5.2 General Approaches to Mentoring

There are many approaches to mentoring including person-directed learning (Hezlett and Gibson 2005; Jones 2012; Lankau and Scandura 2007) and is often ignored (Allen et al. 2006; Baugh and Fagenson-Eland 2007; Eby and Lockwood 2005; Parise and Forret 2008). The approach selected is often determined by the mentor or the human resource management department if conducted in an organisational setting. The range of approaches is primarily dictated by the focus which is often determined by the mentee including:

(a) Attaining specific goals e.g. career,
(b) Exploring future opportunities e.g. change of career or life focus, developing a new specialisation; or changing organisations or locations,
(c) Gaining higher levels of understanding,
(d) Assuming greater responsibility for developing capability in a specific or range of areas,
(e) Dealing with specific conflicts professionally, in the workplace or in personal life,
(f) Re-energising their thinking for professional purposes, and
(g) Dealing with diversity e.g. self in relation to others.

Each approach may require the mentor working in different ways: focusing on some issues and not others that emerge in the conversation, working with the mentee in contrast to guiding them; setting goals with or for them or not; questioning openly or challenging; giving examples; interpreting; permitting the mentee to control the rhythm and pace of the relationship or just being an "ear" and listening.

The important thing is that the approach is discussed and actively selected by the mentee with the mentor's guidance; adjusting the approach to the needs of the mentee as it flows. The nature of the conversation, the questions, amount of listening, pause and silence are each aligned with the general approach. This is discussed in more detail in the following chapters.

Within the selected approach, there is an important foundation for mentees and mentors to consider, which becomes evident as the dialogue between them continues. The conversations will manifest mutually consistent interpretations between the mentee and mentor about issues under discussion, inconsistent interpretations as well as some that do not make any sense immediately. All three standpoints are useful for discovery and reflection, and so this warrants further questioning as follows:

a. What are the commonalities of interpretation?
b. What are the differences in interpretation?
c. What are the ambiguities and complexities that neither mentee nor mentee appreciate and that need to be teased out further? and
d. What purpose does each of (a), (b) and (c) above serve, especially in the mentee's world beyond mentoring?

One of the learning points for mentees is that learning uncovers resistance both within themselves and within their relationships. A mentee might want to discuss that they are dealing with a cohesive team, that is riddled with tension. Moreover, a cohesive group may disagree with the leader. However, their dissent has not been broached openly for various reasons. The mentee confronts the conundrum and brings it to mentoring for discussion (See Chap. 7).

### 2.5.3 *Diversity*

Since diversity is a critical fact in professional and work life, this approach will be discussed first as many of the other methods listed above are co-related. While most people experience their world as diverse, most have a limited exposure to the complex nature of diversity. Globalisation and commoditisation of products, services, travel and social media have made our experiences of diversity more varied than probably any previous decade or time in history. Most institutions whether they are government, business, education, health, defense or religion respond to diversity through political measures, laws and legal norms surrounding minority rights as well as framing a new language and syntax in an attempt to inclusive of social groups. Some people would regard the latter as banal and purely cosmetic rather than a truly felt value. Despite this, diversity means different things to different people with many being indifferent to its social and political significance. As developing countries take their place in the supply chain of globalisation as they supply labour and resources, diversity is further nuanced through "the emergence on the political stage of local communities, indigenous peoples, deprived or vulnerable groups and those excluded on grounds of ethnic origin, social affiliation, age or gender, has led to the discovery, within societies, of new forms of diversity. The political establishment has in this way found itself challenged" (Unesco 2009, p. 4).

Diversity is often distinguished between dimensions of difference that are considered either "given" or "assumed" (e.g. age, ethnicity, gender identity, race, physical abilities, sexual orientation) or "adaptable" through education, belief, social status and so on. Both are visible in the sense that Alcoff (2006) describes although some are more permanent and less variable for obvious reasons e.g. race, age, gender—although this too is changing.

How tangible diversity is in most people's everyday lives is an interesting question. Part of the answer lies in whether a person or not is largely representative of mainstream society or not. This question is relevant for mentoring that is, how people define and perceive diversity. The significance attributed to diversity will depend on the degree of palpability of the felt identity by individuals and how this creates differences between themselves and others; whether this is personally or socially attributed or both. Perceptions of group composition especially of the "in" group and the "outgroups" are related to how accepted people feel, how the institution values diversity and lives up to its policies and language. Diversity points what is valued and in relation to career and career prospects, this is vital.

### *2.5.4 Gender and Social Inclusion Focus in Mentoring*

Diversity is a value that most institutions publically claim; how it is experienced by staff and other stakeholders is an open question. Whether public or private, most organisations protect the 'goodwill' of their business and do everything they can do to preserve it. Goodwill is an asset, something to be quantified and valued like reputation and brand, especially at the time of either selling the business, takeover or merger. It is also used in calculating the performance of the Board and the CEO. Goodwill has both a qualitative and quantitative aspect in terms of an organisation's standing as a 'good employer' or a 'good service provider'. The "good employer brand" is powerful in trying to attract the best and brightest talent.

And yet diversity and efforts in striving to become socially inclusive does not always form a significant part of goodwill or the organisation's "good employer" brand. To be fair, an increasingly number of employers today perceive themselves as such, at least philosophically even if they cannot always directly apply their policies to the fullest extent or attain the desired targets. Most large organisations have a charter of equality on their official website accompanied by images depicting the diversity of their staff, customers, and clients as well as marketing collateral to that effect. In the banking industry, for example, it goes without saying that banks play a significant institutional role in most economies, given their huge workforces and dominance on the listed market. There are a number of other similar non-listed institutions in the financial, education, health and commercial sectors of most economies. Universities are another important example given the value of the education to export markets. It is safe to conclude that such institutions are important in leading diversity even if they are not always making significant progress in real terms.

Just as gender and ethnocultural inclusion are important aspects of institutional branding, these organisational attributes are critical to the employment relationship and its associated aspects (e.g. appointment to positions of power, remuneration, role and managerial transitions) as is a disability. Gender, for example, plays different roles in people's professional development as well as their cultural identities. The existence of a glass ceiling has been well documented (Cotter et al. 2001; Maume 2004; Elliott and Smith 2004). The reverse for men working in female-dominated professions is not founded by research; in fact men experience a certain amount of favouritism in recruitment, selection and promotions to higher-paying, more prestigious positions in these fields (Budig 2002; Snyder and Green 2008). However, the research also shows that men from mainstream backgrounds are more likely than minority men to benefit from working in female-dominated jobs (Wingfield 2009). This reality affects mentees and is an issue that frequently precipitates the search for a mentor. What is going on here?

Figure 2.4 outlines the situation in any given workplace and attempts to explain the interaction between a number of key factors used in the professional milieu, industry and workplaces. Specifically, employment is guided by merit, variously

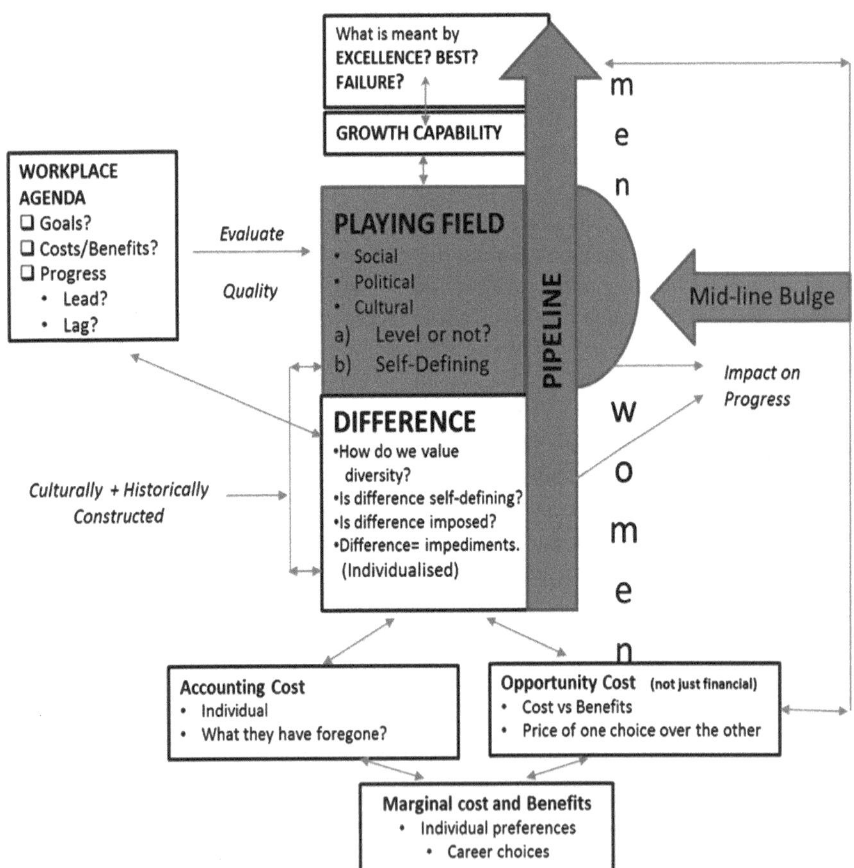


**Fig. 2.4** Workplace culture, goals and the pipeline

referred to as seeking to employ the "best" talent. Many decisions that are taken based on this, however, have an adverse impact on building the talent pool which depends on growing capability especially for the pipeline of talent, diversity, equality and individual performance and progress. This point will be demonstrated below. Each factor applied to any given workplace seems fine at face value. However within the state of affairs depicted in Fig. 2.4, there are opportunity costs for all, especially women, and those from diverse cultural backgrounds and with disabilities.

In this context, an opportunity cost is a depleted value to the business of some people not being employed or promoted at the expense of others. In selecting staff, it is rare for this to occur that is, to quantify and qualify the value of two individual's capability, current or prospective experience is evaluated against the benchmark of merit. Noting that merit is often not explicitly defined other than being thought of as the "best" person for the job or in some cases, indicators such as revenue growth, cost savings, new services, etc. It is important to analyse what is meant by opportunity cost. In the case of talent decisions it includes both

a. quantitative factors (e.g. budget capacity to hire, skill acquisition and development, training costs, familiarisation costs, capacity to work non-flexibly, level of experience (often narrowly conceived and assumed), salary costs) as well as
b. qualitative ones (e.g. unrealised performance and outcomes, learning capacity, new ideas, considering lateral experience, motivation, fitting in with a team, working collaboratively, leading culturally) and the
c. trade-offs within selection decisions.

In hiring and promoting staff, selectors are evaluating the costs (usually only quantitatively) between appointing one person over another. In the variables [(a)–(c) above], subjective assessments are made on each rather than any objective evaluation. No harm in that on the face it. However, decisions based on merit are assumed to be purely objective and when merit is discussed this issue is rarely raised. It is what happens in how selectors deliberate on these factors that render them highly subjective and this fact is never really made evident.

Consequently opportunity costs are often unstated and therefore, overlooked in selection decisions making. Factors such as the value of (1) social diversity to an existing team, (2) any differences that women, staff from culturally diverse backgrounds or those with disabilities may bring due to their experiences, and (3) their work being at least equal or greater to the person being selected. These opportunity costs are feasible and may have significant value longer term, not only on productivity for example but also in regard to cultural transformation, even though they may not have an immediate efficiency or monetary value. Because opportunity costs remain tacit, selectors are blind to their effect on decision-making.

The question to ponder is what is the opportunity cost to organisations, when employers continue to select and appoint people from a narrow subset of the talent pool, usually male and from mainstream backgrounds as the statistics attest, to midline and higher order positions within industry, professions and organisations?

The opportunity cost also includes the value of extending the talent pool as well as demonstrating tangible commitment to the organisation's policies on social inclusion, flexible work, family friendly and the like. This is one of the great challenges in thinking and applying diversity, that is addressing and overcoming conscious and unconscious bias at critical points in decision-making in regard to decisions about selection, promotion and performance and so on. One way to address this is to ensure that people who participate in selecting talent, mentoring, coaching or sponsoring staff are aware of bias, and this is best achieved through training and development.

The following example shows that overlooking the opportunity cost of appointing women for example in flexible roles does have an effect on the bottom line of the organisation. This example is based on the *Ernst and Young Productivity Pulse Wave 3* study, where researchers found that women in flexible roles waste only 11.1 % of work time, compared to an average of 14.5 % for the rest of the working population. Given that in this study's sample, 43.2 % of women in the workforce worked part-time, compared to 13.5 % of men, this translates into an important quantitative indicator that few selectors measure or consider in their trade-off decision-making when selecting staff. More importantly, the researchers found that women working flexibly contribute an extra week and a half of productive work per annum, simply by using their time more wisely. The E and Y researchers conclude that for every 71 women employed in flexible roles, an organisation gains a productivity bonus of one additional full-time equivalent staff member.

Mentors in particular but also mentees need to appreciate how to evaluate opportunity costs if they are to influence the culture of their professions and workplaces and turn around the inequality (both explicit and implicit) present. In decisions about staffing, the value of the seemingly "next-best" person may in fact not be the best outcome overall, especially in the longer term e.g. productivity, pipeline effect and a positive cultural outcome showing tangible support for policies.

While, in the past, opportunity costs have been considered for things like environmental issues, it is time to consider them in regard to the talent pool. For example, the *Ernst and Young Productivity Pulse Wave 3* determined the extent of Australia's female productivity potential. It also quantified how much low female workforce participation is costing Australia for example, which is relevant to other OECD economies. The Ernst and Young (E&Y) report demonstrated that after 2002 in Australia some gains in female workforce participation have been attained, with the rate rising by just over 4 %, largely due to older women re-entering the workforce, post child-rearing. Australian research attests to this too. For example as shown in Fig. 2.5, Australia's major banks remain well short of their own gender diversity targets, despite continuing efforts to achieve greater balance on their boards and in senior management ranks.

The Australian Newspaper (March 12, 2015) reported that the percentage of women on the Boards of Australia's major four banks remains has barely altered over the last five years, although female membership at executive committee level as increased—4 more since 2010. Like many institutions referred to in the first

**Women on major bank boards and executive committees**

| | Board | | Executive committee | |
|---|---|---|---|---|
| | 2015 | 2010 | 2015 | 2010 |
| Westpac | 2 (8) | 3 (10) | 2 (11) | 1 (13) |
| ANZ | 2 (8) | 1 (8) | 2 (12) | 3 (10) |
| NAB | 2 (11) | 2 (13) | 3 (10) | 3 (12) |
| CBA | 3 (11) | 2 (9) | 5 (13) | 1 (11) |
| **TOTAL** | **9 (38)** | **8 (40)** | **12 (46)** | **8 (46)** |

**Fig. 2.5** Female representation in banking. *Source* The Australian Thursday, March 12, p. 23. *Note* Number in brackets is the sample size; for example, two of Westpac's eight directors are women

paragraph of this section, banks have growing numbers of women in the pipeline but there is a bulge at the midline.

By the financial year (2012), the Australian Bureau of Statistics (ABS) recorded male labour force participation at 79, 14 % higher than the female rate of 65 %. The labour force participation rate was higher for males than females across all age groups. The E&Y report also explored opportunities about how to increase representation of women across all industries and at all levels.

Based on the evidence provided by this E&Y report, it can be seen that most selectors of talent operate within a narrow set of decision parameters, and many easily pass over opportunities for talent growth not only within their immediate and broader pipelines but also in the case of individuals. Most selection decisions are made without thinking more broadly about how this interfaces or interacts with other policy decisions. As a result, selectors avoid pursuing value-maximising opportunities, assuming that the best is defined quantitatively. Instead, workers slave to achieve target production goals and avoid any changes that might hurt their short-term performance, for which they may be continually evaluated.

When selecting people for positions and roles it is time to consider that:

1. Most people will overlook opportunity costs.
2. Opportunity costs are tangible and affect the triple bottom line. By choosing from a narrow subset of the talent pool, the cost of the decision made assumes the cost of the option not taken (Edgeman et al. 2015).
3. Opportunity costs are often not realised until later; every attempt needs to be made to make them explicit and attempt to quantify and qualify them within every workplace and professional setting.

How do we address these issues? Using a logistics pipeline analogy; there are a number of factors pulling women up the line e.g. properly implemented policies and a number of push factors which suggest that women have a talent impediment (e.g.

lack of experience or skill mainly as this is evaluated differently to that of men or that women sabotage their own chances by psychologically impeding their own progress).

Needless to say, that both sets of factors are resisted. In regard to the pull factors such as organisational policies and targets, these are often resisted by those concerned, that they are being overlooked for promotion and claim that merit is being thwarted. In pushing or encouraging women to hang in there or "lean in" there is push back from women who opt out of being considered or exit the organisation completely, due to the burden of having to work beyond expectations so as to avoid the implication that merit is being breached. Sponsoring women, which is in such short supply is required urgently to overcome these push factors. The real impediment is the specific culture of the organisation and the assumptions, values and norms it reinforces to support both the push and pull factors. As indicated in Fig. 2.5, diversity like 'risk' should be placed on the agenda of every meeting of a division, unit, subunit as well as other committees that may transverse these. For example, if safety rather than diversity was being discussed, then much stronger attention would be placed on it. A diversity culture like a safety culture is synonymous with climate. The question would be asked: what are the essential characteristics of a 'good' safety culture and how might they be best measured, what are the reliability, validity and utility of existing measures of safety culture, and how does the concept contribute if at all, to good safety systems and performance. This framework needs to be applied to diversity.

And if an employer was trying to improve their safety they would target both best practices as well as quantifying outcomes in terms of a number of incidents and so forth. A suggestion for improving the diversity culture is to develop 'targets' into 'quotas' making explicit the guidelines for merit decision-making within these. One reason why the introduction of quotas is resisted so strongly is that the resistors know that merit is a policy that often lacks substance or real application in decision making. It is imperative that there is much to be gained from a rigorous and controlled focus on both merit and the diversity culture. Another suggestion is to ensure that at least 50 % of candidates on interview shortlists are female, that all interview panels have more than one female member and that the 50 % rule applies to all talent development and workforce planning. Other initiatives include invited women leaders to address fora on a regular basis in organisations for both men and women. In other words, all programs addressing diversity should contain 50 % men.

Dismissing opportunity costs, knowingly or unknowingly, goes to the heart of the professional and workplace culture. Employees decide whether to trust their organisation or professional body based not only on the policies that are developed but also the commitment to those policies through the decisions made and actions taken. A further test is whether or not these met the employees' expectations about not only what is in their best interest but what is right in any given context (Barbalet 2009; Hetherington 2005; Giddens 1990; Rousseau et al. 1998).

Professional and organisation trust is based on goodwill as to whether a system is operating in the best collective interest and competent in dealing with issues or problems (Das and Teng 2001; Malhotra and Lumineau 2011).

As indicated at the outset of this section and in the context of this discussion, goodwill needs to be understood apart from its usual accounting concept which even there can be a bit of a black box. It is one thing to understand goodwill it is another to experience it in action. Like opportunity costs, it has quantitative and qualitative aspects (Dahmash et al. 2009; Dorata 2009). Drawing on the work of Johnson and Petrone (1998), two main perspectives on goodwill can be observed, i.e. a top-down perspective and a bottom-up perspective. From the top-down perspective, goodwill may be little more than expedient for an organisation to proclaim its values, reputation and brand (Cooper 2007). In addition, goodwill could include the value of non identifiable intangible assets such as important stakeholder relationships and synergies e.g. government, business, professional associations, educational institutions. From a bottom-up perspective, goodwill is perceived by those working within the profession and organisation. The values employees observe may be somewhat at odds with the official line. What they observe and experience needs to make sense to them and also be aligned with the organisation's brand and reputation. These cultural artefacts are a crucial link between institutional trust (Schyns and Koop 2010; Tan and Tambyah 2011). Diversity is an important aspect of this. As the talent pool widens and opens its narrow neck at the centre to more diverse employees, it becomes the vehicle to introduce new ideas and concepts into the organisation, enables concurrence of cultural artefacts, reorders thinking around the status quo and taken-for-granted aspects such as "best" and "excellence" and challenges thinking that resolves incongruities (Leung et al. 2008). Making sense of the world is key and making social comparisons plays a significant part in shaping choices, decisions and outcomes all leading to enhancing or diminishing trust (Dunn et al. 2012).

Returning to the notion of triple bottom line (TBL), mentioned briefly above is an important way to view the "bottom line" of organisations because the social and people aspect is brought into the picture and takes account of opportunity costing. Using TBL ensures sustainability of diversity and the pipeline effect. Sustainability reporting is the practice of measuring, disclosing and being accountable to internal and external stakeholders for organisational performance toward the goal of sustainable development of its diverse talent pipeline.

### *2.5.5 Gender and Social Exclusion—Barriers to Effective Mentoring*

Gender and social exclusion are frequent barriers to effective mentoring. Why? Firstly, mentors tend to choose mentees who mirror themselves. Even if the mentor and mentee differ by culture, ethnicity, religion or gender, both the mentee and mentor may need to work harder to gain mutual understanding, gain *simpatico* with each other and resolve misunderstandings. It also increases the risk of incompatibility and mentoring ultimately being less effective. Secondly, mentors are likely to have greater personal or positional power in relation to the mentee and may use this to assuage the differences between them. This may become a barrier. Where the mentee is able to have a shared history or understanding, it stands to reason that they may be able to maintain better well-being than those who are unable to do so.

Can similar barriers in the workplace be addressed through mentoring or will they just mimic each other?

Women are not minorities. While the participation of women in the workforce and in education has reached unprecedented high levels, representation of women and other diversity groups has not kept pace with this. For example, diversity groups are rarely represented or integrated within in senior leadership teams, or even in some industry sectors. Populations are diverse. Australia, which is geographically distant from most other continents, has one-third of its population born overseas.

Women's careers are dampened by their unequal access to powerful mentors, and conversely having potent mentors would improve their prospects for advancement. Mentoring or rather mentoring by a sponsor is essential for most women, as Having a sponsor-mentor influences the outcome of career success. In academia for example and equivalent roles, women with mentors have more publications, more time spent on research activities, and higher overall career satisfaction (Poteat et al. 2009). Similarly, individuals experiencing extensive mentoring relationships reported receiving more promotions, had higher income, and were more satisfied with their pay and benefits than individuals experiencing less-extensive mentoring relationships (Dreher and Ash 1990).

Barriers to the advancement of women and others from diverse groups include discrimination, lack of appropriate mentors and sponsors, and lack of or poor policies for career development and advancement or ineffective implementation of these. Women, as discussed above, may find it difficult to secure a senior female mentor or sponsor. Even if they do, this may not prove to be beneficial, if the female mentor does not give peer support and open up opportunities for networking for the mentee.

Issues in mentoring relationships exclusive to women and especially female minorities include family obligations, gender protocols, patriarchal family structure, performance pressures, isolation, and limiting role expectations. It may be that a member of a female minority is not permitted a male mentor, even if one is available and willing. Female professionals from minority groups lack the availability of role models, mentors, and sponsors.

Women's career development and prospects substantively influence them in real ways and emotionally. Women are concerned about how to present "self" at work and in particular roles, and struggle with this in terms of their own perceptions and those of others. Women are more concerned than men about expressing emotions at work as well as initiating and maintaining personal relationships and usually these are with men. So women may self-exclude in terms of social functions by virtue of avoiding developing personal attachments or lack of time due to family commitments. Attachments and relationships play a central role for women in both identity-formations professionally and lead women to disempower themselves at work. The phases of a woman's career life cycle may incur limits too. Early adult transition years (ages 17–29) may find women concerned over educational attainment or early partnerships; ages 30–40, in addition to requirements of career development, may require women to focus on their "biological clock," and middle adulthood in rearing children and then, increasingly in later adulthood having to care for elderly parents or relatives. They are also disadvantaged by age as they near retirement with less financial resources than men due to lower remuneration and career gaps.

Issues for diversity groups in mentor-mentee relationships are even more complex, especially for women from specific cultural groups. A Muslim woman working in the Finance industry in Australia seeking a female Muslim mentor would be an example of this. Despite expanding Muslim communities in some parts of the country. Although minority women are reportedly more likely to mentor others from similar backgrounds or disadvantage, the number of mentor-ready women available to serve is limited.

Racial, ethnic, or gender identities are 'visible identities' a term coined by Alcoff (2006), i.e., where she argues "what" people are as well as "where" they are socially located has implications at work, organisationally and so on. She goes on to argue that such identities lead to separation, reification, and reasoning problems as each has its own assumptions about the nature of what they represent and the nature of their difference to each other. Firstly "strongly felt" ethnic, racial, or cultural identity separates people from each other. The second problem claims that when strongly felt or represented these identities reify the abstractness of such identities. Furthermore, since these categories come with scripts, determined by social expectations and stereotypes, they serve to undermine individual autonomy. The third issue assumes that strongly felt social identities interfere with the status quo, especially concerning political, ethical, and cultural matters. Strongly felt identities, and the expectation of loyalty and authenticity that comes with them, interfere with the so-called natural order of things which is largely Western, male and white.

Simply put, critics charge that identity politics compels individuals to value the good of their group over that of the common good.

It may be that diversity programs have the opposite effect than that intended on benefits for women and members of diversity groups. While no one doubts the intentions, there may be time to rethink the approach. Mentoring alone will not work nor will mentoring and sponsorship in all situations. Targeting women and members of diverse groups for preferential treatment or to meet targets or quotas is having the opposite effect including those who are the potential beneficiaries. No amount of positive mentoring will alter this. Mentoring can address the consequences of the discrimination that women and minorities experience and how to deal with it but mentors alone cannot address the structural inequities existing in most organisations (Ibarra et al. 2010). In a few Australian organisations, especially in the banking and financial sector where women are increasingly powerful customers, groups are being set up to deal with this. However most have a narrow remit and need to be encouraged to commission research so that they can institute remedies for structural barriers that their members identify.

Effective formal mentoring programs "are attentive to differences across gender, race, ethnicity, culture and generational lines" (Cariaga-lo et al. 2010, p. 21). The challenges here are that usually women experience more mentoring than men while men are more likely to be the direct beneficiaries of sponsorship (Ibarra et al. 2010). Men mainly introduce other men into their networks and are usually promoted through the ranks more quickly than women.

In a 2008 Catalyst survey of more than 4000 full-time professional men and women, 83 % of women and 76 % of men say they had one or even more mentors at a certain time in their career. However, more mentoring does not necessarily lead to career advancement. A 2010 follow-up survey showed that men received 15 % more promotions than women. One of the main reasons that are mentoring failed women in terms of promotion is the difference between having a mentor and a sponsor (Ibarra et al. 2010). Compared with men who are more ready and willing to both offer and seek a mentor, women mentors need to be encouraged and sought out (Laff 2009). And they will provide more psychosocial functions since they are more relationship-oriented (Okurame 2007).

Further, women's mentors usually possess less hierarchical power due to their position in the organisation. In the 2008 Survey, 78 % of men and 69 % of women were actively mentored by a CEO or other senior executive. A mentor's position in organisations is closely related to mentee's career advancement.

One way to address this challenge is to reduce mentoring from a top-down, one-to-one relationship to cohort associations based on flexible networks of support Sorcinelli and Yun (2007, p. 58), with men and women engaged in parallel as mentees. Women would be able to observe directly the strategies that men employ. The diverse characteristics of the participants in the mentoring relationship can affect how individuals participate and benefit from the mentoring experience. At the conclusion of formal mentoring programs, mentoring relationships will inevitably lead to deeper relationships and spawn new mentoring arrangements. This creates an ideal setting for wider learning communities.

Mentors for women and members of diversity groups need to be selected with due consideration. The issues that mentoring deals with are sensitive both personally and culturally. Given the unique challenges involved in cross-gender mentoring especially, it is important to assess the overall goals and the receptivity of available mentors. Further, addressing the dynamics of mentoring and how to prevent issues both at an interpersonal and legal perspective is important for successful mentoring to take root in any organisational setting.

## 2.6 What Are the Benefits for Mentors and the Different Ways of Mentoring Which Are More Effective Than Others?

Mentorship is not a situation where one party acquires all the benefit and the other very little, as is often assumed. Sometimes a mentor is viewed as the one giving all or even making sacrifices for the other. However this is rarely the case. The benefits to each participant will vary according to the quality of the relationship that is generated between them. Mentors learn a lot about mentoring and themselves from their mentees which can heighten their performance and acknowledgement, especially where outcomes are substantiated (Ragins and Scandura 1994; Russell and Adams 1997). This in turn can afford them enhanced career satisfaction, renewed effort and interest from collaborating with others (Johnson 2002, p. 87).

The mentoring relationship is a microcosm of the mentee's behaviour. As a result, mentors not only assist mentees and provide them with feedback on their interpersonal dynamics but also find that they learn to communicate more effectively themselves regardless of whether it is a traditional or reverse mentoring relationship. Being a mentor inevitably fosters one's understanding of how other people think, feel and act and their interrelationships. Seeing life through the eyes of others is an important learning source for mentors (Eby and Lockwood 2005; Wanberg et al. 2006) and one that is often overlooked. Different perspectives such as these broaden the mentors' understanding and allow them to address some of the challenges they face in their own lives. Through self-reflection activated during the mentoring process, mentors learn by appreciating how they (or their roles) impact others and how this leads them to modify their approach as well as enhance their communication with people who have different values and backgrounds.

Mentoring makes a difference when it is voluntary even if participating in a formal program and both respect each other and believe each is achieving some value from it. Voluntary mentoring relationships have a better chance to succeed because of the self-motivation to engage. Take the Lawyers Encouraging and Assisting Promising Students (LEAPS) project for example. This is a workplace learning program for students working with a lawyer mentor currently employed and provides them with the opportunity to learn about the profession as well as assist them with their studies and career planning (Australian Youth Mentoring Network 2010). No doubt this is followed by lawyers sponsoring students into jobs once graduated. The benefit of the profession is they get to select from an elite group of high-performing students and the socialisation into the profession has already commenced with less teething problems upon the commencement of employment.

## 2.7 Does It Make a Difference the Way the Mentoring Relationship Comes About?

The manner in which mentoring programs are established leads to differential outcomes. Men and women usually find their mentors by themselves instead of relying on formal programs.

Formal and informal mentorships vary in the ways they are established and acknowledged. Often informal mentorships are established by selection of participants based on mutual appeal and convenience, which may not be officially endorsed by management. On the other hand, the institutional orchestration of formal mentorship means that formal mentors may not view the mentee as worthy of special attention and support; mentees may be seen as undeserving of the benefits of mentorship or the special attention it affords them. Such "assigned" relationships may lack compatibility, interpersonal ease, as well as the longevity required to develop trust and the provision of psychosocial dynamics so critical to achieving the best outcomes (Chao et al. 1992).

Further, mentors in formal programs may be more visible and, therefore, less able to sponsor and promote their mentees because these actions may be construed as favouritism by co-workers (Ragins and Cotton 1999). DeLong et al. (2008) see a disadvantage. They claim mentoring often relies on the selection of 'A-grade performers', that is, the top 10 % of the internal workforce, and do not include the 'B-or C-grade performers', that is, the bulk of the internal workforce who are good, albeit invisible, workers who get more than the lion's share of the work done, especially the burdensome work and often remain loyal to the organisation for longer periods. However, much of the value of those exclusive, one-on-one, power-dependent mentoring relationships depends on context-specific knowledge, which is less and less relevant to sustaining career learning especially as career mobility increases (Darwin 2000).

A formal mentoring program is likely to match the aims and attributes of the parties more effectively than informal ones with a more beneficial outcome. In a 2010 follow-up survey, women receiving formal mentorship were more likely to be promoted than those who found mentors by themselves (by a ratio of nearly three to two) (Ibarra et al. 2010). Leaders need to be responsible for seeking out "ways to help people foster their own developmental networks that include relationships providing various types and amounts of support" (Chandler et al. 2010, p. 49).

Mentoring helps ascertain information about, for example, what is it like to join this organisation as a newcomer, student, staff or client, customer or manager? What does it feel like to be promoted or not promoted here? How are people treated when faced with leaving? What do we learn when we take on a new management or leadership role? What is it like to change career focus? Answers to these questions are vital for designing mentoring programs.

## 2.8 What About Training for Mentors?

Potential mentors and mentees need to be identified in all institutions, whether staff, students or leaders. This allows a development path to be planned for each depending on how their knowledge and experience is to be developed and utilised. This way the new recruit, student or staff is assigned a mentor and tracked. Similarly, a training pathway for the mentor can be designed and planned. This approach can suit one-on-one mentoring or a circle of peer mentors. Performance feedback training for mentors will be of value in terms of their effectiveness as a mentor as well as their retention in the organisation.

### 2.8.1 Handling Conflict in the Mentoring Relationship

As conflict and change are inevitable in relationships, conflict handling is a vital skill for effective mentoring. Influence, conflict and negotiation are important parts of mentoring especially for the mentee to learn and test their skills and reactions to conflict. No matter how productive conflict is between two people, it is still challenging. Mentorships will sometimes produce disagreement, strain relationships and consequently be distressful for individuals (Johnson et al. 2000; Johnson and Nelson 1999; Levinson et al. 1978; O'Neil and Wrightsman 2001). Learning to cope with conflict and examining both sides of an argument, while suspending judgment is a critical outcome.

### 2.8.2 Communication

Communication training boosts confidence and credibility with the mentee and strengthens the mentor relationship. In particular, people are less likely to listen today for a range of reasons: less time and are likely to interrupt, they think they should have the answers and, therefore, do not ask questions or worse still, they think they know the answers. Consequently, people often do not hear what is said or certainly do not remember it.

Mentors need to listen well so as to give those frequently not heard, a voice in what sometimes can be described as "silent culture" in the organisation, where difficult issues are not voiced and avoided. In learning how to voice issues, mentees gain a sense of being a more powerful unique self.

A good question for a mentor to ask is: "what do you need to know right now?"

Listening lessens the likelihood of conflict as each has more understanding of the situation and less likely to be across purposes.

### 2.8.3 Team Building

Training in team development is critical to mentoring. It permits diverse perspectives to be shared so as to facilitate a common outlook on issues, which in turn is more likely to engender trust and transparency amongst team members and leaders (Jones et al. 2007; Reilly and Lojeski 2009). In spite of best efforts and attention, some people will be poorly suited to mentoring.

### 2.8.4 *Boundary-Setting in Mentoring*

All human relationships have boundaries or "rules" about what is or isn't allowed in the relationship. Boundaries are expectations of what can be achieved and are essential for framing a mentoring relationship and distinguishing it from other relationships. Boundaries set in mentoring assist the mentee establish boundaries in other aspects of their life. The following typology is a way to consider boundaries:

(a) Physical boundaries include access to a person's body and possessions e.g. whether or not a person shakes hands with another; lends their personal possessions, such as your money, car, clothes, books, food, or toothbrush.
(b) Space boundaries pertain to an individual's personal and cultural space and their rights to privacy.
(c) Mental boundaries apply to thoughts, values, and opinions. Questions here include: Are you easily influenced? Have they formulated their own ideas, values and philosophies? How flexible are they in their thinking?
(d) Emotional boundaries: how easy is it to distinguish responsibility of role or profession from felt emotions?

Boundaries are significant in the mentoring relationship and in the mentee's life. It allows them to understand where to "draw the line" with regard to taking responsibility for themselves, or for another. It also assists in dealing with guilt (see Chap. 6). Further if people find it difficult to control their emotional highs and lows it may lead them to consider re-setting their boundaries so they can gauge their responses to situations.

For this reason, mentors need to think in advance about setting appropriate boundaries, expectations, accountability of each with their mentees and discuss these to reach an agreement about them from the outset. For example, respect is an important boundary in any relationship and is relevant in informal mentoring and peer mentoring.

Confidentiality is an essential element here too. Mentors need to establish rules of confidentiality in the relationship and discuss it with the mentee at the outset. Regardless of the type of mentoring, personal issues are likely to be explored in mentoring situations to some degree especially when interfere with the mentee's positive feeling about themselves in the school, workplace or organisation.

## 2.9 Mentoring Is More Than a Fleeting Connection

Before anything else, the mentoring process needs to be strengths-based and gender-sensitive. Mentorship, if effective, can become the mainstay of a significant learning relationship for both mentors and mentees and even a friendship that extends beyond the initial need. Durable mentoring is vital for young people in particular. In order to maximise the benefits, design and plan a mentoring program according to the principles outlined in this chapter, assuring quality and consistency and preparing potential mentors and mentees in advance even from the time they enter their organisation. Mentoring requires strong support from within institutions and the community to encourage as many people as possible to volunteer and participate. Mentors should not be paid.

This chapter has shown how mentoring occurs and how it contributes to learning, improved critical thinking, analysis and understanding values as well as outcomes. Economic and social changes have somewhat transformed us and the communities in which we reside and the institutions in which we study and work. Mentoring connects both mentor and mentee to these changes. Increasingly people are engaged in small to medium sized organisations with flatter hierarchies, with people working alongside their "bosses" or collaborating with their teachers or lecturers. Although there is increasing ageism, it is not the inter-generational issues that are the points of difference between different experience levels in mentoring. People today are concerned about the environment, education, the economy, refugees, and their futures. There is a greater expectation for social justice, "fair play" in all aspects of their lives with a belief that our leaders have an obligation to deliver this through procedural fairness. People want better lives and given that work and study is a fair chunk of this, they want leaders and followers to work together on common challenges and endeavours. Mentorship is an important micro-relationship to assure that this happens at the macro-level.

The challenges are to integrate the view of all layers of society into a defining vision and reflect this in laws, regulations, opportunities and educational programs. By reconciling the financial imperative with social justice and innovation, mentoring harnesses the power of relationships to develop a resolution to numerous social and economic issues.

## References

ABS 4125.0—Gender Indicators, Australia. (2012 January). Australian Bureau of Statistics.

Alcoff, L. (2006). *Visible identities: Race, gender and the self.* Oxford: Oxford University Press.

Allen, P. (2004). Welcoming Y. *Benefits Canada, 28*(9), 53.

Allen, T. D., Eby, L. T., & Lentz, E. (2006). Mentorship behaviours and mentorship quality associated with formal mentoring programs: Closing the gap between research and practice. *Journal of Applied Psychology, 91*, 567–578.

Australian Youth Mentoring Network. (2010). *LEAPS.* http://www.youthmentoring.org.au/program_details.php?id=220

Bakhtin, M. (1981). *The dialogic imagination* (C. Emerson & M. Holquist, Trans.). Austin: University of Texas Press.

Ballantyne, D. (2004). Dialogue and its role in the development of relationship-specific knowledge. *Journal of Business and Industrial Marketing, 19*(2), 114–123.

Bandura, A. (1977). *Social learning theory.* Englewood Cliffs, NJ: Prentice Hall Inc.

Bandura, A. (1986). *Social foundations of thought and action: A social cognitive theory.* Englewood Cliffs, NJ: Prentice Hall Inc.

Bandura, A. (1991). Social cognitive theory of self-regulation. *Organisational Behaviour and Human Decision Processes, 50*, 248–287.
Barbalet, J. (2009). A characterisation of trust, and its consequences. *Theory and Society, 38*, 367–382.
Baugh, S. G., & Fagenson-Eland, E. A. (2007). Formal mentoring programs. In B. R. Ragins & K. Kram (Eds.), *The handbook of mentoring at work: Theory, research and practice* (pp. 249–271). London, UK: Sage.
Bautista, A., Roth, W., & Thom, J. (2011). Knowing, insight learning, and the integrity of kinetic movement. *Interchange, 42*(4), 363–388.
Bell, M. (1996). Dialogue in the public sector. *Management Development Review, 9*(3), 20–21.
Berofsky, B. (1995). Liberation from self: A theory of personal autonomy Cambridge: Cambridge University Press.
Bohm, D. (2003). *On dialogue*. New York: Routledge.
Bokeno, R. M. (2007). Dialogue at work? What it is and isn't. *Development and Learning in Organisations, 21*(1), 9–11.
Bolman, L. G., & Deal, T. E. (2008). *Reframing organizations: Artistry, choice, and leadership* (4th ed.) San Francisco, CA: Jossey-Bass.
Bolte, A., Goschke, T., & Kuhl, J. (2003). Emotion and intuition: Effects of positive and negative mood on implicit judgments of semantic coherence. *Psychological Science, 14*, 416–421.
Buckley, T. R., & Foldy, E. G. (2010). A pedagogical model for increasing race-related, multicultural counseling competency. *The Counseling Psychologist, 38*, 691–713.
Budig, M. J. (2002). Male advantage and the gender composition of jobs: Who rides the glass escalator? *Social Problems, 49*(2), 258–277.
Caprara, G. V., Steca, P., Alessandri, G., & Barbaranelli, C. (2010). Optimal functioning: Contribution of self-efficacy beliefs to positive orientation. *Psychotherapy and Psychosomatics, 79*, 328–330.
Cariaga-lo, L., Dawkings, P. W., Enger, R., Schotter, A., & Spence, C. (2010). Supporting the development of the professoriate. *Peer Review* Summer, 19–22.
Chandler, D. E., Hall, D. T., & Kram, K. E. (2010). A developmental network and relational savvy approach to talent development: A low-cost alternative. *Organisational Dynamics, 39*(1), 48–53.
Chao, G. T., Walz, P. M., & Gardner, P. D. (1992). Formal and information mentorships: A comparison on mentoring functions and contrast with non-mentored counterparts. *Personnel Psychology, 45*, 619–636.
Cone, Inc. (2006). *The 2006 Cone Millennial cause study*. Boston: Cone Inc.
Cooper, J. (2007). Debating accounting principles and policies: The case of goodwill, 1880–1921. *Accounting, Business and Financial History, 17*(2), 241–264.
Cotter, D., Hermsen, J., Ovadia, S., & Vanneman, R. (2001). The glass ceiling effect. *Social Forces, 80*, 655–682.
Cotugna, N., & Vickery, C. E. (1998). Reverse mentoring: A twist to teaching technology. *Journal of the American Dietetic Association, 98*(10), 1166–1168.
Crampton, S. M., & Hodge, J. W. (2009). Generation Y: Unchartered territory. *Journal of Business and Economics Research, 7*(4), 3.
Cranwell-Ward, J., Bossons, P., & Gover, S. (2004). *Mentoring: A Henley review of best practice*. New York: Palgrave Macmillan.
Dahmash, F. N., Durand, R. B., & Watson, J. (2009). The value relevance and reliability of reported goodwill and identifiable intangible assets. *British Accounting Review, 41*, 120–137.
Darwin, A. (2000). Critical reflections on mentoring in work settings. *Adult Education Quarterly, 50*(3), 197–211.
Das, T. K., & Teng, B. S. (2001). Trust, control, and risk in strategic alliances: An integrated framework. *Organization Studies, 22*, 251–283.
DeLong, T. J., Gabarro, J. J., & Lees, R. J. (2008). Why mentoring matters in a hyper competitive world. *Harvard Business Review, 86*(1), 115–121.

Dorata, N. T. (2009). History repeats itself: The acquisition method and nonrecurring charges. *Accounting Forum, 33*, 11–26.

Dreher, G. F., & Ash, R. A. (1990). A comparative study of mentoring among men and women in managerial, professional, and technical positions. *Journal of Applied Psychology, 75*, 539–546.

Dunn, J., Ruedy, N. E., & Schweitzer, M. E. (2012). It hurts both ways: How social comparisons harm affective and cognitive trust. *Organizational Behaviour and Human Decision Processes, 117*, 2–14.

Eby, L. T., & Lockwood, A. (2005). Protégés and mentors' reactions to participating in formal mentoring programs: A qualitative investigation. *Journal of Vocational Behaviour, 67*, 441–458.

Edgeman, R., Eskildsen, J., & Neely, A. (2015). Translating triple top line strategy into triple bottom line performance. *Measuring Business Excellence, 19*(1)

Elliott, J. R., & Smith, R. A. (2004). Race, gender and workplace power. *American Sociological Review, 69*(3), 365–386.

Emelo, R. (2010). Increasing productivity with social learning. *Industrial and Commercial Training, 42*(4), 208.

Ernst & Young. (2012). *Australian Productivity Pulse™ Wave 3*, November cited in Ernst and Young *untapped opportunity the role of women in unlocking Australia's productivity potential*. July 2013.

Estrada, C. A., Isen, A. M., & Young, M. J. (1994). Positive affect improves creative problem solving and influences reported source of practice satisfaction in physicians. *Motivation and Emotion, 18*, 285–299.

Foucault, M. (1977). *Discipline and punish*. London: Peregrine.

Fowler, R. (1977). *Linguistics and the novel*. London: Methuen.

Fredrickson, B. L., & Branigan, C. (2005). Positive emotions broaden the scope of attention and thought-action repertoires. *Cognition and Emotion, 19*, 313–332.

Giddens, A. (1990). *The consequences of modernity*. Stanford, CA: Stanford University Press.

Glass, A. (2007). Understanding generational differences for competitive success. *Industrial and Commercial Training, 39*(2), 102.

Greengard, S. (2002). Moving forward with reverse mentoring. *Workforce, 81*(3), 15.

Hall, D. T. (1996). Long live the career—A relational approach. In D. T. Hall & Associates (Eds.), *The career is dead—long live the career: A relational approach to careers* (pp. 1–12). San Francisco: Jossey-Bass.

Hetherington, M. J. (2005). *Why trust matters: Declining political trust and the demise of American Liberalism*. Princeton, NJ: Princeton University Press.

Hezlett, S. A., & Gibson, S. K. (2005). Mentoring and human resource development: Where we are and where we need to go. *Advances in Developing Human Resources, 7*, 446–469.

Ibarra, H., Carter, N. M., & Silva, C. (2010). Why men still get more promotions than women. *Harvard Business Review, 88*(9), 80–85.

Johnson, W. B. (2002). The intentional mentor: Strategies and guidelines for the practice of mentoring. *Professional Psychology: Research and Practice, 33*(1), 87.

Johnson, W. B., Huwe, J. M., & Lucas, J. L. (2000). Rational mentoring. *Journal of Rational-Emotive and Cognitive-Behaviour Therapy, 18*, 39–54.

Johnson, W. B., & Nelson, N. (1999). Mentoring relationships in graduate education: Some ethical concerns. *Ethics and Behaviour, 9*, 189–210.

Johnson, L. T., & Petrone, K. R. (1998). Is goodwill an asset? *Accounting Horizons, 12*(3), 293–303.

Jones, J. (2012). An analysis of learning outcomes within formal mentoring relationships. *International Journal of Evidence Based Coaching and Mentoring, 10*, 57–72.

Jones, K. W., Hardcastle, V., & Agnich, L. (2007). *A guide to mentoring*. Lexington, KY: University of Kentucky.

Korporaal, G. (2010, August 11). Women make mark on boards. *The Australian*.

Krauss, R. P., & Fussell, S. (1990). Mutual knowledge and communicative effectiveness. In J. Galeghar, R. Kraut, & C. Egido (Eds.), *Intellectual teamwork: Social and technological foundations of cooperative work* (pp. 111–146). Hillsdale NJ: Lawrence Erlbaum.
Kuhl, J. (2000). A functional design approach to motivation and self-regulation: The dynamics of personality systems and interactions. In M. Boekaerts, P. R. Pintrich & M. Zeidner (Eds.), *Handbook of self-regulation* (pp. 111–169). San Diego, CA: Academic Press.
Labov, W. (1972). *Language in the inner city: Studies in the Black English Vernacular*. London: Basil Blackwell.
Laff, M. (2009). The guiding hand: Mentoring women. *T+D, 63*(9), 32–35.
Lankau, M. J., & Scandura, T. A. (2007). Mentoring as a forum for personal learning in organizations. In B. R. Ragins & K. E. Kram (Eds.), *The handbook of mentoring at work: Theory, research and practice* (pp. 95–122). London, UK: Sage.
Leh, A. S. C. (2005). Lessons learned from service learning and reverse mentoring in faculty development: A case study in technology training. *Journal of Technology and Teacher Education, 13*(1), 25–41.
Lemon, L. T., & Reis, M. J. (Eds.). (1965). *Russian formalist criticism: Four essays*. Lincoln, Nebraska: The University of Nebraska Press.
Leung, A. K., Maddux, W. W., Galinsky, A. D., & Chiu, C. Y. (2008). Multicultural experience enhances creativity: The when and how. *American Psychologist, 63*, 169–181.
Levinson, D. J., Darrow, C. N., Klein, E. B., Levinson, M. H., & McKee, B. (1978). *The seasons of a man's life*. New York: Ballentine.
Liu, D., Liu, J., Kwan, H. K., & Mao, Y. (2009). What can I gain as a mentor? The effect of mentoring on the job performance and social status of mentors in China. *Journal of Occupational and Organisational Psychology, 82*(4), 874–876.
Malhotra, D., & Lumineau, F. (2011). Trust and collaboration in the aftermath of conflict: The effects of contract structure. *Academy of Management Journal, 54*, 981–998.
Manz, C. C. (1992). *Mastering self-leadership: Empowering yourself for personal excellence. Englewood Cliffs*. NJ: Prentice Hall Inc.
Martin, C. A. (2005). From high maintenance to high productivity: What managers need to know about Generation Y. *Industrial and Commercial Training, 37*(1), 39–44.
Matt, H., & Cohen, P. (2004). Occupational segregation and the gender gap in workplace authority: National versus local labour markets. *Sociological Forum, 19*(1), 121–147.
Maume, David J. (2004). Is the glass ceiling a unique form of inequality? Evidence from a random-effects model of managerial attainment. *Work and Occupations, 31*(2), 250–274.
Merriam, S., Caffarella, R., & Baumgartner, L. (2007). *Learning in adulthood: A comprehensive guide* (3rd ed.) San Francisco: Jossey-Bass.
Meyers D. T. (1989). *Self, society, and personal choice*. New York: Columbia University Press
Mezias, J. M., & Scandura, T. A. (2005). A needs-driven approach to expatriate adjustment and career development: A multiple mentoring perspective. *Journal of International Business Studies, 36*, 519–538.
Mezirow, J., & Taylor, E. (Eds.). (2009). *Transformative learning in action*. San Francisco: Jossey-Bass.
Morgan, W., & Streb, M. (2001). Building citizenship: How student voice in service learning develops civic values. *Social Science Quarterly, 82*(1), 156–169.
Napier, N. K. (2006). Cross-cultural learning and the role of reverse knowledge flows in Vietnam. *International Journal of Cross Cultural Management, 6*(1), 57–74.
Nezlek, J. B. (2001). Causal relationships between perceived social skills and day-to-day social interaction: Extending the socio-meter hypothesis. *Journal of Social and Personal Relationships, 18*, 386–403.
O'Neill, O. (2003). Autonomy: The emperor's new clothes. *Proceedings of the Aristotelian Society, 77*, 1–21.
O'Neil, J. M., & Wrightsman, L. S. (2001). The mentoring relationship in psychology training programs. In S. Walfish & A. Hess (Eds.), *Succeeding in graduate school: The complete career guide for the psychology student* (pp. 113–129). Hillsdale, NJ: Erlbaum.

Okurame, D. E. (2007). Perceived mentoring functions: Does mentor's gender matter? *Women in Management Review, 22*(5), 418–427.
Parise, M. R., & Forret, M. L. (2008). Formal mentoring programs: The relationship of program design and support to mentors' perceptions of benefits and costs. *Journal of Vocational Behaviour, 72*, 225–240.
Pekala, N. (2001). Conquering the generational divide. *Journal of Property Management, 66*(6), 30–38.
Polanyi, L. (1985). *Telling the American story: A structural and cultural analysis of conversational storytelling*. Norwood: Ablex Publishers Co-operation.
Poteat, L. F., Shockley, K. M., & Allen, T. D. (2009). Mentor-protégé commitment fit and relationship satisfaction in academic mentoring. *Journal of Vocational Behaviour, 74*, 332–337.
Ragins, B. R., & Cotton, J. L. (1999). Mentor functions and outcomes: A comparison of men and women in formal and informal mentoring relationships. *Journal of Applied Psychology, 84*(4), 529–550.
Ragins, B. R., & Scandura, T. A. (1994). Gender differences in expected outcomes of mentoring relationships. *Academy of Management Journal, 37*, 957–971.
Reilly, R., & Lojeski, K. S. (2009). Leading the dispersed workforce. *Mechanical Engineering, 131*(11), 30–34.
Rousseau, D. M., Sitkin, S. B., Burt, R. S., & Camerer, C. (1998). Not so different after all: A cross-discipline view of trust. *Academy of Management Review, 23*, 393–404.
Rowe, G., Hirsch, J. B., & Anderson, A. K. (2007). Positive affect increases the breadth of attentional selection. *Proceedings of the National Academy of Sciences of the USA, 104*, 383–388.
Ruby, P., & Decety, J. (2004). How would you feel vs. how do you think she would feel? A neuroimaging study of perspective-taking with social emotions. *J Cognitive Neuroscience, 16*, 988–999.
Russell, J. E. A., & Adams, D. M. (1997). The changing nature of mentoring in organisations: An introduction to the special issues on mentoring and organisations. *Journal of Vocational Behaviour, 51*, 1–14.
Schyns, P., & Koop, C. (2010). Political distrust and social capital in Europe and the USA. *Social Indicators Research, 96*, 145–167.
Seligman, M. E. P. (1991). *Learned optimism*. New York: Alfred Knopf.
Seligman, M. E. P., Ernst, R. M., Gillham, J., Reivich, K., & Linkins, M. (2009). Positive education: Positive psychology and classroom interventions. *Oxford Review of Education, 35*, 293–311.
Senge, P. M. (1994). *The fifth discipline: The art and practice of the learning organisation*. New York: Doubleday/Currency.
Snyder, K. A., & Green, A. I. (2008). Revisiting the glass escalator in a female dominated occupation. *Social Problems, 55*(2), 271–299.
Sorcinelli, M. D., & Yun, J. (2007). From mentor to mentoring networks: Mentoring in the new academy. *Change* November/December. 58–61.
Southard, G., & Lewis, J. (2004). Building a workplace that recognises generational diversity. *Public Management, 86*(3), 8–12.
Stockwell, P. (2002). Schema poetics and speculative cosmology. *Language and Literature, 12*(3), 252–271.
Tan, S. J., & Tambyah, S. K. (2011). Generalized trust and trust in institutions in Confucian Asia. *Social Indicators Research, 103*, 357–377.
Taylor, E. W. (2008). Transformative learning theory. In S. B. Merriam (Ed.), *Third update on adult learning theory. New directions for adult and continuing education* (No. 119, pp. 5–15). San Francisco: Jossey-Bass.
The Australian. (2015, March 12). Female representation in banking (p. 23).
Tempest, S. (2003). Intergenerational learning: A reciprocal knowledge development process that challenges the language of learning. *Management Learning, 34*(2), 181–200.

Tenner, E. (2004). The pitfalls of academic mentorships. *Chronicle of Higher Education, 50*(49), B7–B10.
Underwood, B., & Moore, B. (1982). Perspective-taking and altruism. *Psychological Bulletin, 91*, 143–173.
UNESCO. (2009). *UNESCO World report: Investing in cultural diversity and intercultural dialogue Paris*. Scientific and Cultural Organisation: United Nations Education.
Wanberg, C. R., Kammeyer-Mueller, J., & Marchese, M. (2006). Mentor and mentee predictors and outcomes of mentoring in a formal mentoring program. *Journal of Vocational Behaviour, 69*, 410–423.
Wanberg, C. R., Welsh, E. T., & Hezlett, S. A. (2003). Mentoring research: A review and dynamic process model. In J. J. Martocchio & G. R. Ferris (Eds.), *Research in personnel and human resources management 22* (pp. 39–124). Oxford, UK: JAI Press/Elsevier Science.
Welch, J., & Welch, S. (2006). *Winning, the answers: Confronting 74 of the toughest questions in business today* (pp. 96–98, 187–189). London: HarperCollins.
Wingfield, A. H. (2009). Racializing the glass escalator: Reconsidering men's experiences with women's work. *Gender and Society, 23*(1), 5–26.
Wong, M., Gardiner, E., Lang, W., & Coulon, L. (2008). Generational differences in personality and motivation. *Journal of Managerial Psychology, 23*(8), 884–885.
Zachary, L. (2005). *Creating a mentoring culture: The organisation's guide*. San Francisco: Jossey-Bass.
Zanni, G. (2009). Reverse mentoring: An effective strategy for career growth. *The Consultant Pharmacist, 24*(6), 465–467.
Zhu, W., Newman, A., Miao, Q., & Hooke, A. (2013). Revisiting the mediating role of trust in transformational leadership effects: Do different types of trust make a difference? *The Leadership Quarterly, 24*(1), 94–105.

# Chapter 3
# The Mentoring Conversation

*The meeting of two persons is like the contact of two chemical substances. If there is any reaction, both are transformed*
(Jung 1933, p. 49).

**Abstract** Working through this chapter assists you to understand a mentoring framework to initiate and respond effectively in conversations with the mentee. Some of the questions addressed include: a) What is the purpose of the discussion in this meeting today? b) How does it relate to the last conversation? c) What will be the issues covered? In what order? d) What approach is taken? e) What does the mentee hope to accomplish? f) What does the mentor hope to accomplish? g) What would be the best outcome for the mentee from this conversation?

Human interaction remains the keystone of learning. Mentoring is no different given its learning value through guidance, socialisation, facilitating and sponsoring. The mentoring relationship is remarkably complex and extremely important developmentally for the mentee. The mentee has to be the major focus of the relationship, a person who is also remarkably complex and multi-faceted. First and foremost each mentee is the embodiment of their experiences; secondly they are a social being who has to relate to others professionally and beyond and finally they are self-interested which renders them political. Problems that mentees bring to mentoring are not isolated incidents. These situations need to be reflected only for the obvious issues but also for the more deep-seated cultural and social issues, including the contradictions, resistance, struggles and conflicts. All of these are inter-related and provide opportunities for creative learning.

## 3.1 The Formal Mentoring Relationship

The mentoring relationship prescribed or not, is established in a range of contexts including professional, organisational and personal. In the previous chapter, mentoring was viewed as a relationship built on trust, with two people conversing

 
A.M. Brewer, *Mentoring from a Positive Psychology Perspective*,
DOI 10.1007/978-3-319-40983-2_3

together with the mentor listening and observing for much of the time and assisting the mentee through guided reflection as well as providing feedback in the form of guidance, support and encouragement (Hartley 2004).

A mentoring relationship involves typically a more experienced person, usually one who acts as the critical guide for the other, less experienced person or newcomer. However, reverse mentoring may engage a less experienced person mentoring a more experienced one; for example, an older worker with a younger mentor who wishes to re-enter the workforce and requires new understanding about current work practices, service processes and technologies.

A mentoring relationship is not always limited to two people and may involve a group. Whatever the nature of the mentoring relationship, all parties have the capacity to benefit from it, although not necessarily in equal measure. So while there is usually a deemed recipient, and in most cases more accurately described as a mentee, the focus is to unleash their potential, their untapped talent while at the same time developing the opportunity for active learning from within the mentoring relationship (Brewer 2011). Mentoring is about problem-solving and deep learning.

No matter what type of mentoring, mentors and mentees engage with each other so they can reveal what is in each of their own "black box" which they carry around with them. The opening of the mentee's black box for the mentee is to share with the mentor an explicit understanding of what participation means for them in their working life for example. In opening the mentor's "black box", they are sharing the learning processes that the mentor has used successfully or not and how these might differ from that of the mentee. The difference between the mentee and mentor concerns the distinction between practice and analysis which is only disentangled for the purposes of the mentoring conversations.

## 3.2 Multiple Streams of Conversations

In mentoring, there are multiple streams of conversations which are often interwoven with each other. Some of these will be addressed in this chapter which is directed towards understanding better the mentoring conversational framework embracing the series of conversations over time between the mentee and the mentor. The *main conversational stream* originates from the first meeting between the mentor and mentee and concludes usually at their last meeting. The duration between the first and last meetings varies from case to case. In normal circumstances, it is recommended that the mentoring conversation is sustained initially for ten regular meetings with one—three weeks approximately between each meeting.

The *second stream conversation* is a series of conversations held at each meeting. The second stream has its own conversational logic, viewed as a separate conversation, although part of a series where the mentor picks up the threads of the previous meeting in each subsequent one. This process builds the spine of the mentoring relationship and is the strategy used for sustained learning. However the mentee brings to this main conversation, other multiple conversations and narratives often presented as snippets from other conversations external to the mentoring relationship. The mentor needs to keep on track and not be diverted; only harvesting information necessary for the main learning goal. The method guides the mentee towards reflection and further learning. This is done through the conversational method outlined below in this chapter.

Finally, there is a *third stream,* and this includes self-dialogue, which the mentee and mentor each has apart from the mentoring conversations. These are ideally reflective conversations where each mull over "what was said" between them. These reflections would then be brought into each of the above conversational streams initiated by the mentor or the mentee.

Conversations are enjoyable and difficult—sometimes in the one conversation. They should never be boring or too easy. Having said that many people avoid having difficult conversations with people especially at work: with our supervisors, our staff and our peers. Almost all of us do not wish to be on the receiving end of a difficult conversation. Most of us avoid it because we are fearful of the consequences regardless of our role or who initiated it. The more anxious people become about the conversation; the more likely they are to avoid it until finally they are forced to initiate or participate in it, and the more problematic the outcome is. A difficult conversation should be seen as a learning opportunity regardless of context.

The aim of this chapter is to employ a framework to enable the mentor to initiate and respond effectively in difficult conversations primarily with the mentee, although much of what is focused on here applies in areas of life beyond mentoring. Some of the questions addressed include:

1. What is the purpose of the conversation in this meeting today?
2. How does it relate to the last conversation?
3. What will be the issues covered? In what order?
4. What approach should be taken?
5. What does the mentor expect to accomplish today?
6. What does the mentee hope to accomplish today?
7. What would be the best outcome for the mentee from this conversation?

## 3.3 The Conversational Method

The method used will focus on a step-by-step negotiated understanding of the main conversational framework.

### *3.3.1 Preparation*

An important part of the work in mentoring is the work that mentors do in preparing themselves to be effective as they can. Becoming empathetically focused is an important first step. Empathy is an overused expression to the point where it has lost its significance. "It means temporarily living [in the mentee's] life, moving about in it delicately without making judgments" (Rogers and Sanford cited in Kaplan and Sadock 1984, p. 1378). There are several aspects of developing empathy for the mentor including:

a. Connecting with the mentee using appropriate non-verbal behaviour (discussed below);
b. Demonstrating an appropriate amount of emotional interest in the mentee's issues;
c. Giving the mentee plenty of time to respond to questions, and reflections;
d. Ensuring that the reflecting questioning is done using a sensitive vocal tone so that the mentee picks up on the mentor's intended aim. (Watson 2002), and
e. Not rushing to a conclusion on behalf of the mentee.

Being overly empathetic may mean that the mentor is less partial than is helpful in the mentoring relationship. This point needs to be considered when matching mentors and mentees. Sometimes choosing a mentor with an opposite "profile" may facilitate a more objective stance for both.

A mentor needs to maintain oversight of the purpose and their emotions in comparison to those of the mentee, ensuring high levels of mental acuity for engagement throughout the relationship.

To relate well to mentees means that the mentor needs to become a critically-conscious person. Prior to the first conversation with the mentee, the mentor needs to identify any faulty logic in their thinking or the way they plan to engage with the mentee. In order to achieve this, mentors need to be able to reflect on their own values and needs accordingly: What are the needs and fears of the mentor? Are there any particular concerns that they have personally or professionally? Have they skewed their perceptions in some way? How? What buttons of theirs are being pushed by the mentee intentionally or unintentionally? Consequently, it is important for the mentor to work out:

1. Why have they accepted the role and the responsibility of being a mentor?
2. Why has the mentor accepted this particular mentee? Was the mentee simply assigned without the mentor selecting them?

Exploring the responses and reasons to these two questions is important for an effective mentoring outcome. It allows the mentor to sharpen purpose and intention which inevitably assists the mentee in achieving the outcomes they need.

Most mentors have had opportunities to initiate complex and layered conversations on a frequent basis. These conversations may not have always felt like "opportunities" especially if they proved to be challenging. If that is the case, mentors need to reflect back on some of these conversations and work out how they handled each one and asked: what worked well? What did not? What were the peculiarities of each? Did they have any concerns about them at the time and if so what were they? Did they take appropriate steps to ameliorate the concerns? If not, why not?

It is important to remember before embarking on a mentoring journey, whether as a mentor or mentee, that neither one can anticipate what is going to happen. This is true in everyday conversations too. Sometimes these conversations and relationships do not progress as people expect or want.

From the outset, the mentor needs to explore with the mentee, the types of issues or situations have they found to lead to difficulties in the workplace or in a professional setting of their choice. This assists both to consider the factors that can exacerbate these situations or prevent the mentee from going in the desired direction with participants following through with preferred actions.

The conversation might start with the mentee describing a situation either one that has taken place or construct a scenario which they would like to see happen. The following questions could be posed to the mentee for a given scenario, either within a mentoring session or for "homework" so that they can address them from their perspective:

1. How would/should they like to have acted?
2. What would/should others have done in this situation?
3. Did they act wisely?
4. Did they act well?
5. What were their motivations?
6. Were their feelings? Are these morally justified?
7. What could they have improved?
8. What do they need to do to make the situation better in future?
9. Have they learnt anything from the mentoring conversation?

During the conversation where the mentor works with the mentee or when the mentee returns from reflecting on them alone, the mentor follows up by asking: *When you address these nine questions, do they help or not? How? Why?* Why not? Through this process, the mentor becomes aware of the mentee's own context, content and what they would like to see achieved through mentoring.

Often during mentoring, a situation or question is raised by the mentee in which they demonstrate discomfort and either find it difficult to respond or avoid a tricky question. One way to tackle this is for the mentor to make a note of it and return to it later. Whenever it is tackled, the mentor can explore it further by asking the mentee: "*Have they had related experiences*?" If so, the mentor can then explore the differences and similarities between that situation and the one under discussion. In exploring this, the mentor observes the mentee's non-verbal behaviour which is so crucial in detecting discomfort or concern that they might have about an issue:

(a) Word choice
(b) Tone of voice
(c) Eye gaze
(d) Facial expression
(e) Placement of hands, legs, etc.
(f) Posture

This attentiveness to non-verbal cues is important in all interactions with the mentee including the following barriers which are also having an influence.

a. **Personal barriers**:

- Expectations (prior or current)
- Educational background presupposes assumptions and values
- Emotional baggage due to the nature of the working relationship
- Being self-focused
- Overburdened by tasks, expectations: personal and others

b. **Communication barriers**:

- Poor communication skills especially listening
- Misperceptions
- Poor evidence

c. **Cultural barriers**:

- Differences in backgrounds: values, beliefs, rituals
- Preferences: cultural and personal

d. **Environmental barriers**:

- Contextual factors and distortions

A further finding requires the mentor to analyse the differences between the mentor's and the mentee's view of events. The mentor needs to be mindful of becoming too eager to get to the solution. If this sense starts to take hold or occur and especially if they are unaware of their haste, it can lead to the mentor talking too much and blocking the mentee, with a deleterious effect on the outcome. Accordingly, the mentee may be less forthcoming and withhold information. Another risk here is that the mentor becomes energised because s/he both identifies too closely with the mentee's situation and starts offering advice based on their own personal experience. This type of response can undermine the mentor's relationship with the mentee. More troubling is that such a response from the mentor may reflect some of the things the mentee may be experiencing with others in positions of authority such as feeling incapable, belittled and so on. Consequently, in conversation with the mentee, mentors need to be aware of their:

(a) Own intentions
(b) Impact the mentee in mentoring
(c) Their contributions to any difficulties they have had in conversing with the mentee
(d) Their impact on the perceptions of the mentee as well as themselves in the role of mentor, for example, unintentionally and unduly influencing the mentee in taking on their perceptions.

At some stage early in the relationship the mentor and mentee need to discuss their respective values. The timing is important as it needs to be discussed when a good rapport has been struck between them. The conversation could be initiated by the following questions:

1. What are the values of your organisation? How different are these to your profession? Your own?
2. How do you practise and represent these values?
3. What is challenging about these values? How do you overcome these?
4. What do you do to deliver core values to your team (if relevant)?
5. What support would be helpful to you in practising these values? Who from?

### *3.3.2 Exploring and Gaining Agreement for Purpose*

The mentor and the mentee explore what they want from mentoring overall. In order to achieve this, a mentor-mentee agreement is developed and signed once both parties have been selected and agreed to proceed after an initial introduction.

During the introduction, each provides a summary of their backgrounds, interests, and what they seek in the relationship. This step will reveal the potential elements for a workable partnership, and if both can satisfactorily commit to working toward the goals that they develop in the agreement (attached). If contented, they can begin to work together to establish aims, specific and achievable, using the agreement form. If they agree to enter into a mentoring relationship, the agreement underpins the mentee-mentor relationship for the time period specified within it.

## 3.4 The Mentor–Mentee Agreement

The following agreement is made on a voluntarily basis, entering into this mentoring relationship indicates that both the mentor and mentee agree to work to ensure it is a constructive and valuable experience. It is important that both the Mentee and Mentor agree to the following terms:

Confidentiality: All information between the Mentee and the Mentor shall be confidential and only shared with other parties if both agree.

Expectations: Mentors will work to the best of their ability and knowledge, and both parties will work together to identify the Mentee's professional goals and develop a plan for achieving those goals.

Meeting: The Mentee and Mentor will seek to agree about the frequency of meetings, format, i.e., in person as well as where and when. The frequency, timing and venue for these meetings are agreed and can vary with agreement from both the Mentee and Mentor.

Duration: The Mentee and Mentor agree that the professional relationship will be evaluated at a date to be specified and agreed. The duration may be 10 meetings over 2–3 months, and this is a good time to check into appraise the benefit of continuing mentoring. Either party should have the option of discontinuing the relationship for any reason provided there is formal notification of this. In the case of the mentor terminating the relationship, a reason needs to be stated.

This following agreement reflects the terms of the relationship that both the Mentee and Mentor enter into at this point in time. The terms of this agreement may be changed at any time provided that both parties agree and document such changes in writing. Both Mentee and Mentor should keep a copy of the co-signed agreement.

**The Meeting Plan Template**

At the end of each meeting, a meeting plan is completed and reviewed as follows.

| Mentor/Mentee Agreement | | | |
|---|---|---|---|
| Mentee Name: | | | |
| Contact Information: | | | |
| Mentor Name: | | | |
| Contact Information: | | | |
| Duration of Agreement and Frequency of Meetings | | | |
| Agreed Start Date: | Agreed Finish Date: | | |
| Frequency of Meetings: | Duration of Meetings: | | |
| Objective(s)/Strategies | | | |
| No. | Target Achievement Date | Overarching Goal: *Example of broad goal—work out next step in my career path*<br>Strategies/Activities: *Example of how—Discuss ways to increase my visibility professionally*<br>Outcome: *Example of achievement indicators—resume updated, sponsors identified, positions earmarked, short-listed for a number of positions* | |
| 1. | Specific objective: | Strategies/Activities: | • |
| | Outcome: | | |
| 2. | Specific objective: | Strategies/Activities: | • |
| | Outcome: | | |
| 3. | Specific objective: | Strategies/Activities: | • |
| | Outcome: | | |
| 4. | Specific objective: | Strategies/Activities: | • |
| | Outcome: | | |
| 5. | Specific objective: | Strategies/Activities: | • |
| | Outcome: | | |

(continued)

(continued)

| Mentor/Mentee Agreement | | | |
|---|---|---|---|
| 6. | Specific objective: | Strategies/Activities: | • |
| | Outcome: | | |
| 7. | Specific objective: | Strategies/Activities: | • |
| | Outcome: | | |
| 8. | Specific objective: | Strategies/Activities: | • |
| | Outcome: | | |
| 9. | Specific objective: | Strategies/Activities: | • |
| | Outcome: | | |
| 10. | Specific objective: | Strategies/Activities: | • |
| | Outcome: | | |
| 11. | Specific objective: | Strategies/Activities: | • |
| | Outcome: | | |
| 12. | Specific objective: | Strategies/Activities: | • |
| | Outcome: | | |
| Agreement/Signatures | | | |
| We agree that mentoring conversations will be conducted within the following guidelines:<br>• Conversations will focus on the professional and career issues and outcomes.<br>• All communications will be confidential.<br>• Mentors/mentees agree to maintain confidentiality and respect of each other.<br>• Mentors/mentees can mutually modify the agreement, or can opt out without ill-will. | | | |
| Mentee(Name): | (Signatures) | | |
| Mentor(Name): | (Signatures) | | |

And then what they want to have happen as the conversations unfold. *What are their expectations at the end of each conversation? Do they know what they want or what they are ambivalent about?* Intentions are often invisible. The mentor is seeking to get beyond the stated purpose to ascertain whether there are any underlying concerns for the mentee especially in conversing with the mentor. However, this may take time and should not be rushed. It may take more than one meeting to reveal their real goals and motives.

The next step is to decide with the mentee what it is they want to accomplish and whether this can be achieved through the mentoring conversation. It may be that the mentee requires additional support from others outside the mentoring relationship.

## 3.5 Key Questions for the Mentor

(a) What is the mentee's purpose for having the conversation?
(b) What do they hope to accomplish?
(c) What would be an ideal outcome?

Once this is discussed and agreed, the real conversation unfolds.

### *3.5.1 Conversation Opening and Initial Assumptions*

The mentor initiates the conversation knowing there will be differences in each of their perspectives. From the outset, the mentor is modelling a framework that the mentee may learn from and emulate to some extent with others outside of the mentoring relationship. During the initial phase of the first conversation and over the next few subsequent meetings, gaining the trust of the mentee is utmost. The mentor needs to be perceived as responsible and effective. One way of achieving trust is by the mentor listening carefully to each of the mentee's aims and reasons for seeking a mentor as well as descriptions and responses to the questions they pose.

Eventually and usually not in the initial meeting, the mentor begins to focus on assisting the mentee question their assumptions about some issues or observations aimed at helping the mentee make a difference. Initially, this approach rarely produces a major breakthrough and needs to be recycled sensitively through multiple conversations. In fact, it may simply open another avenue to explore, exacerbating the complexity of the situation for the mentee. If this is the case, then it is all the more reason for the mentor to permit the mentee to choose the lines of inquiry as well as the pace of the exploration.

The mentor, picking up from the pace of the mentee, guides the mentee using their experience and knowledge base, and this is likely to lead to more moments of insight for the mentee than rejecting their theories-in-practice as it were. The mentor only accelerates the process, if the mentee is dragging it for reasons of not wanting to engage in the process. At this point, a diversion might need to be taken to investigate the perceived blockage. Mentees may be finding it difficult to consider breaking with the current patterns of working, relating to others, or seeing things differently. It may be that they are weighed down by the assumptions and positions of others, and this is imposing on their aspirations and capacity to think differently or develop new ways of doing things.

### *3.5.2 The Continuing Conversation*

The conversation between the mentor and mentee is about sharing information with the aim of mutual learning. Almost never should it be about getting the "facts right" per se as this is fruitless and largely irrelevant. Facts cannot be proved one way or the other (see Losch 2009). It is not about what is true or not, rather what is important for the mentee. People's perspectives and explanations (theories-in-practice) shape how they see and experience the world. Many of these have been programmed by their socialisation since early childhood and from there positively reinforced throughout their further schooling, education and professional development. This does not mean that these explanations are not real or factual. They are for those who see and experience it that way. If there is a close correspondence of the two, then it is deemed "true" or real for the mentee. The role of the mentor is to assist in exploring and discovering a better understanding of the mentee's context towards observing the proximity of the association between perceptions and actions.

The mentee's explanations need to be understood in the context of the relationships amongst the significant players in a specific context, for example, the supervisor, the supervisor's boss, peers, subordinates and so on. In other words to appreciate how the social structure that overrides the context provides value, meaning and shapes interests of each of the players including the mentee. It is also important to understand the signs that the mentee is selecting to understand their significance in context.

The mentor as a listener has a significant role to play which cannot be understated and is conspicuous in the interpretation of what they hear. For example, insights occur when both the mentee and mentor interweave their understanding. If the mentor uses the mentee's assumptions and ideas rather than their own, the insights will occur on familiar ground and therefore, can be more readily internalised and called upon in action (see Koestler 1964).

There are a number of ways of achieving this. For example, insights can take the form of elaboration with the mentor adding new information to that brought up by the mentee. Alternatively the mentor could facilitate the mentee into re-coding the way they have represented the issue, colouring it differently while building on the original concept. Another way for developing familiar insights for the mentee is for the mentor to ask what if that "rule" or that "assumption" did not apply in this situation, what would you do then? This leads to a relaxing of perceived constraints for the mentee. Another approach might be for the mentor to consider re-sequencing the order of events or steps in the problem to be "solved" or asking the mentee to seek a different form of information or further evidence (based on Cunningham et al. 2009).

In the main most problems proffered by the mentee probably do not require a major discontinuity in their thinking rather an evolution of thinking building on what they know or do not know they know. This is particularly the case in the early part of mentoring. It may progress to more radical form. However, this should only occur once a rapport and trust has been established.

Further, mentors need to be aware that a context can be analysed according to how it is constructed and related by the mentee. The following parameters could be utilised to achieve this:

1. Cognitive context: constructed by the mentee's own perceptions or that of other's which they are "owning" intentionally or otherwise, as their own; how perceptions cohere with what else is known.
2. Cultural context: values, language.
3. Socio-political context: relationships, interests.

The mentoring conversation is focused on how the mentee considers conflicting perceptions, interpretations and values. This process is orchestrated by the mentor.

However, mentors ought not to assume they know the intentions/emotions of the mentee. A consideration of the difficulties that a mentee may be having with others is useful here:

a. Experienced/assumed disagreement: conflicting views translating into a win-lose situation
b. thinks they are right
c. thinks they're wrong on most things, and their supervisor is always right
d. feeling aggrieved
e. believes that their behaviour (even if inappropriate) is justified
f. overly sensitive to criticism
g. feels shame
h. shifts blame to someone or something else
i. thinks their position should not be questioned if the role they have one of authority
j. believes they always have the best interests of their organisation or someone else
k. doesn't want to make the same mistake again

It is important for the mentor to check with the mentee to see whether they understand what others may want from the situation they are describing. *Are their similar needs or ones different to their own?* The mentor needs to work with the mentee on the real aspects of the problem and to work on ameliorating them.

## 3.6 Step 1: Inquiry by the Mentor

The mentor needs to "enter" into the mentee's experience of the situation. How do they achieve this? The first step is by cultivating an attitude of discovery and curiosity. The mentor's attitude is conveyed by their personal approach: asking questions not making statements; using an inquiring tone, withholding judgement and relaxed posture.

Secondly through questioning: the mentor needs to learn as much as possible about the mentee and their point of view by asking:

1. **Why would you like to gain from having this conversation with me?**
   The mentor is aiming to derive the following from the mentee's responses:
   (a) Purpose
   (b) Assumptions
   (c) Interests
   (d) Values
2. **Who is significant to them in the context that they describe?**
   (a) Are they relevant?
   (b) Are they credible?

3. **What's the issue?**
   (a) Where's the evidence?
   (b) Is it relevant?
4. **What outcomes are being sought?**
   (a) Are they relevant?
   (b) Are they credible?
5. **What actions are required?**
   (a) What will be the impact?

One useful device employed by mentors is to imagine that they are entertaining a visitor who is new to the current context (without conveying this to the mentee of course). In other words, avoid proffering their conventional and presumed knowledge of the situation. It is necessary that the mentor does not assume that they know this situation well, that is, "they've seen it before" which can block firstly the mentor listening to new information and secondly and more seriously, the mentee being forthcoming in describing and revealing their observations, assumptions and concerns about it. A mentor needs to find out how things look to them from their perspective; how certain events affect the mentee, and what the values and priorities they have in regard to this context.

If the mentee was really from another planet, the mentor would be hyper-vigilant, watching for signs including their body language and listening for the unspoken meaning and energy as well. The mentor needs questions themselves at this point: *What does the mentee really want? What are they not saying?*

The mentor lets the mentee talk spontaneously until they are finished. It is important that the mentor does not replace any restrictions on them nor interrupt them except to acknowledge what is being said. Whatever the mentor hears, they do not jump in too quickly and make assumptions, evaluate the statements or extend advice, yet. The mentor's task at this point is to learn as much as they can in this phase of the conversation. There is plenty of time for diagnosis and structuring the analysis in due course.

*Opening the Inquiry*

How does a mentor enter the conversation? Usually by speaking calmly and audibly—never equalling the mentee's pitch or pace, especially if they raise their voice, converse in an excitable or aggressive way. However, the mentor is mindful of the varying tones and pitches of the conversation of the mentee as this is useful information as well as being observant of their own presence. If the mentee is not readily forthcoming initially, one suggestion for *opening the* inquiry phase is to state:

"*I have something I'd like to raise with you.*"

"*I'd like to talk about ____________ with you, but first I'd like to get your point of view.*"
"*I need you to explain something to me.*"

*Or if you have had a misunderstanding or as disagreement with the mentee you can ask:*

*"I need you to help me understand what just happened. Can we just reflect on that for a moment?"*

*"I think we differ on ____________________. What do you think?"*

*"I'd like to discuss ____________________. I think we may think differently about this? ____________________."*

*"I'd like to see if we might reach a better understanding about __________. I really want to hear your feelings initially about this, and then I will share my perspective as well."*

*The mentor needs to focus on the mentee's emotions: Talk about the mentee's feelings by first; asking them about these, without patronising them. For example, never state:*

*"I see you are upset about this." Instead ask: "is this upsetting for you?"*

The mentor glides above the context and hovers, helicopter-like, taking the time to judge possible points of entry into the conversation. In the initial phase, the mentor is building an overview, sizing up the situation, and figuring out what the mentee wants to accomplish overall in this first meeting. Later, the mentor's overview may change as well as their goals. The mentor then begins to ask questions, focusing on the specific situation. Context matters here.

At this stage, questioning needs to be accurate based on what the mentee has expressed. Questions asked include those most relevant to their current situation based on the mentee's evidence provided to date. The mentor avoids posing non-specific questions.

Two principles that are important in guiding questioning at this stage are situational relevance and professional or personal significance for the mentee. The mentor chooses to explore some issues more deeply by interspersing gently, probing questions, and all the while ignoring the less relevant or tricky issues. The mentor maintains a circumstantial focus rather than a problem-solving one at this early stage.

Mentors could keep in the mind the following guidance for their questioning. Some of these questions are more appropriate for later conversations, rather than the opening phase, in the mentoring relationship.

1. **Relevance**: Do we need to talk about ______________ now or later, if at all?
2. **Clarification**: What do you mean by ________________________________?
3. **Assumptions**: What are you assuming ______________________________?
4. **Values**: What's important to you in this ____________________________?
5. **Evidence**: How do you know ______________________________ is true?
6. **Contributing factors**: What's affecting ________________________ _____?
7. **Action**: What are you planning to do next?___________________ And then?
8. **Outcomes**: What would you like to see happen? _______________________

**Outcomes of Step 1: Inquiry**
By the end of Step 1, the mentor has learnt something about and from the mentee, their context and some of their reasons for seeking mentoring. These need to be noted if not during the conversation, as soon as the mentee leaves the room.

## 3.7 Step 2: Acknowledgment of the Mentee

Acknowledging the mentee and what they are expressing to the mentor is influential for building rapport and strengthening the mentoring relationship from the outset and needs to be maintained all through the relationship.

By listening to what the mentee is saying and not rejecting or deflecting it. Mentors need to show that they are hearing, understanding and not evaluating or agreeing with the mentee. *How does the mentor best acknowledge the mentee?* This is achieved by:

- Listening calmly; nodding gently and being mindful of facial expression and posture.
- Giving feedback to the mentee and avoid over-explaining as it deflects from them and the mentor is likely to lose credibility.
- Try to understand them so well that they can experience this.

An example of a worthwhile interchange here between the mentee and mentor might be as follows. Before you read on you may wish to refer to the beginning of Chap. 1 and the discussion around how the mentee presents with an "inner voice" that is accessible only to them and not to others.

The mentor can utilise the difference in the inner and outer worlds through externalising the issue at hand otherwise it is tricky if the mentee perceives the "self" as the blockage. They may express things which lead the mentor to think that the mentee as a poor self-conception. The mentor can utilise the distinction between inner and outer self by employing "linguistic distance" between so-called character traits and the self and then contextualises and researches (Bird 2004, p. 9). For example, if a mentee describes her/him as aggressive, the mentor may ask as follows:

'Has aggression blocked your goals in any way do you think?' Or
'This aggression, has it increased over time?'

Creating linguistic distance in this way opens a way for the mentee to reflect and provide both with further insight. The mentor is intent on using the mentee's own self-descriptions and using linguistic distance so that the mentee can begin to separate them from his or her inner self.

Where the mentor might acknowledge what the mentee is saying, it is important that this acknowledgment does not mean that the mentor imposes the self-concept nor replaces it, nor does it equal agreement. A mentor needs to distinguish one from the other. A reflective question is one of the best ways to achieve this by asking for example:

"Do I understand that this means that …?" (This does not mean agreement).

The mentee will probably respond positively. If so, conserve this information for later. It is best not to augment their response at this point by offering suggestions. In other words, the less additional information from the mentor, the better it is for the mentee. The mentor continues to ask questions (even the same ones) if they need to know more. It is important to avoid sounding condescending by making statements such as: "this sounds really important…,". A simple nod of the head will suffice.

**Outcomes of Step 2**

Acknowledgement is best shown by the mentor's engagement and interest and empathic understanding. The processes described in Step 2 guard against the mentor imposing their views on the mentee and in so doing, equalise the partnership in the mentoring relationship.

Further, the mentor shuns being positioned as an all-knowing, wise observer—a frequent perspective of mentees especially if they form a good rapport with the mentor. A mentor needs to present as a collaborator or a facilitator in the process of investigating what is and what the future might hold for the mentee in terms of professional or capability development. There is a move from observing mentees to understanding them with a view to investigating their experience and future aspirations for development alongside their relationships with others and self-descriptions, often while exposing their strengths and weaknesses about their impact.

The mentee is at the centre of the process and needs to become influential in it. The mentor is influential in their critique and guidance of the process through questions and reflections that make it possible for mentees to (a) informatively explain alternatives for their work, roles and career, (b) investigate some of the neglected territories of their work lives and selves, and (c) become significantly acquainted with those skills of their lives and selves that are relevant to addressing their current work concerns. The mentor is not influential in the sense of offering solutions. The mentee needs to discover and test these in action themselves—a form of action learning.

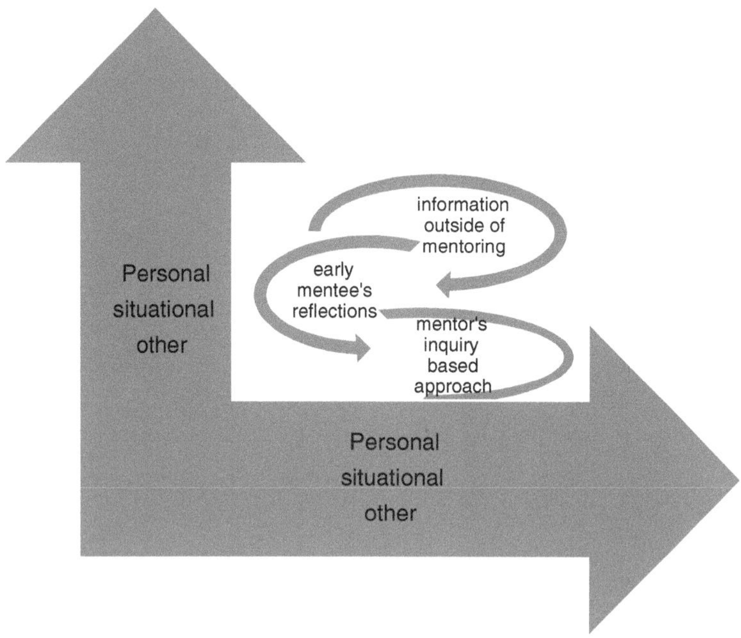


## 3.8 Step 3: Reflection

This is a process of inductive reasoning used by the mentor in conjunction with the mentee. Inductive reasoning works by moving from specific observations made by the mentee in the situation to broader generalisations and explanations expressed with the mentor. It is a "bottom-up" approach. Using this approach the mentor begins to detect patterns of thinking, actions and uses questions to formulate some tentative suggestions that can be explored with the mentee, and finally ending up with something that the mentee can "take away" and work on in the situation under focus or another one. Reflection is not about the mentor telling or giving the mentee their explanation of what is going on. The offering of advice too early is the opposite of reflection which is learning through explanation and discovering of meaning for the mentee. It is a skill that people use professionally and can be practised for life (Fig. 3.1).

Reflection is an opportunity for the mentor to re-orient the mentee to focus on how they process their thoughts both in terms of beliefs, moral and social, as well as their feelings about this and the situations that they describe. For reflection to be successful and involve in deep learning it requires genuine self-awareness and self-reflection. If these skills are developed during mentoring, it will hold the

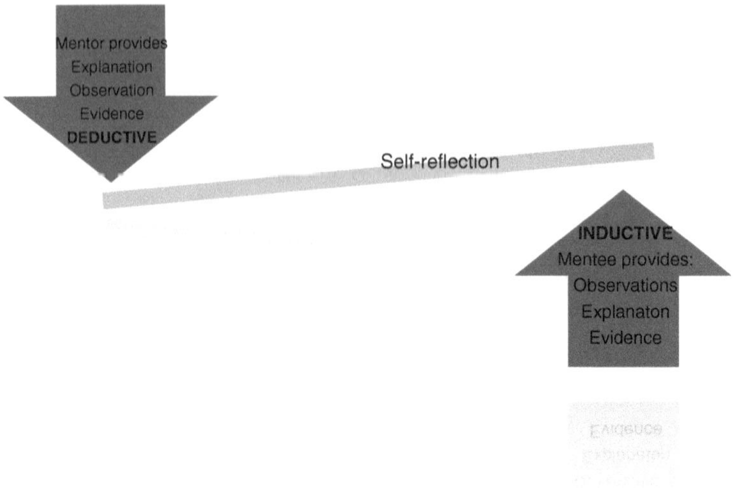


**Fig. 3.1** Guided reflection

mentee in good stead for dealing with future choices, decisions and subsequent actions. It is also important for the mentor to guide the mentee to separate and distinguish their 'self' from what is happening and to reflect on their own cognitive and affective states as opposed to those of another person (Salovey and Rodin 1984).

Through reflection, the mentor guides the mentee to drill down beneath the surface situation so as to observe situation's attributes other than its obvious effects and impact and the influences underlying the main actions and impacts. This process assists the mentee to see and develop a view on the second and third-order issues other than the obvious first order ones (see Argyris and Schön 1996). According to Argyris (2000) learning occurs when inconsistencies or misjudgements are noticed, and an attempt is made to ameliorate these. Single-loop learning occurs when mistakes are amended without altering the overarching governing values held by the players in the situation such as assumptions about power and control and who has the right to it; compete with each other, suppress what one is really thinking/feeling and rationality prevails (e.g. the facts are given and the same for all concerned). In this case the players have different understandings of what is going on, compete to win and defend their positions (Argyris and Schön 1996). Mistrust ensues. If the mentee is experiencing this at work, they are less likely to question, be open to questioning and the opportunities for new learning are stymied. The results for the players in the situation are what Argyris (1985) referred to as a skilled lack of awareness and skilled incompetence. A mentee brings skilled unawareness into the mentoring conversation, and the mentor needs to understand the possibility of this and is amenable to dealing with it. For example, when a supervisor needs to conduct a difficult conversation about performance with a team member they are deeply concerned about misdirecting their energy and focus. Panic and confusion characterises their feeling state, and this is transferred to the team member. Consequently they do not prepare, lack evidence to support their performance evaluation and so focus on simplifying the conversation for fear of getting it wrong. The difficult conversation is characterised by non-directive questioning and face-saving devices. This leads to a cover up and subsequent concealing that they are covering up. The status quo prevails, and they feel like they are hitting their head against a brick wall. One way out of this is for the mentor to guide the mentee by guided reflection to double-loop learning.

Double-loop learning occurs when errors are corrected by changing the governing values in Box A in Fig. 3.2 and then the actions as outlined in Box B.

Eventually, the mentor offers the mentee a guided assessment of the situation based on Single-Loop Learning Model 1 and then Double-Loop Learning Model II so the mentor may further reflect on what is/might be happening using as many of the mentee's phrases as possible. The mentor tests to see what the mentee's hopes might be by asking open questions and continuing to acknowledge their position. Mentees will find it difficult to budge from their views unless they are persuaded to see the fault lines in their logic, the gaps or differences. The reason for this is most people's assumptions about why things happen the way they do are reinforced continuously over many decades. It will take time for people to appreciate the Double-Loop Learning Model II unless they have been previously exposed to that way of not only thinking but also acting. It takes skill and confidence not only to see this but also to act upon it. Until then, a mentee will be less inclined to modify their thinking and should not be forced to do so. There are no guarantees about this and reflection should never be rushed so as to get to a resolution.

One way to release the mentee's thinking is for the mentor to respond judiciously on whatever they can to the mentee, including confessing at times to their own issues and associated defensiveness, if it comes up. For example, in an argument with a colleague that they are describing to you, the mentee may notice that the mentor has become defensive, or the mentee has become defensive with the mentor. The mentor may acknowledge this and explain that they have experienced

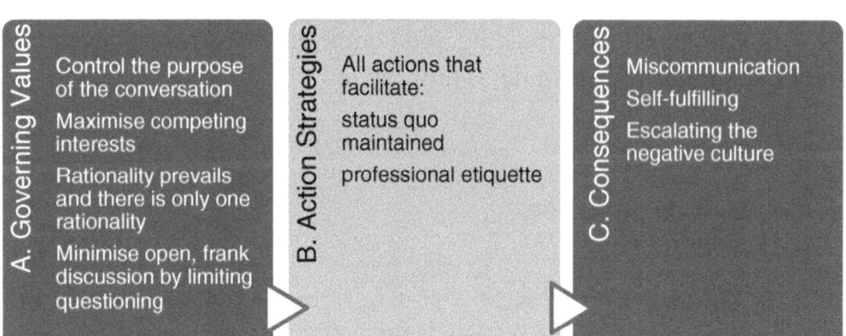


**Fig. 3.2** Single-loop learning

similar situations. This is an example of empathic understanding and learning. The mentor should then re-centre and continue the reflective process with the mentee using their own situation to unpack Models I and II as outlined above.

### *3.8.1 How to Engage the Mentee in Reflection*

The mentor asks the mentee to tell them about a significant situation at work. Let the mentee recount as they understand them. The mentor waits for it to unfold and for the mentee to complete their account. The mentor then augments the account using the following questions to the mentee:

1. Describe the background to the incident—time, place and location
2. Recount what happened; what did others say about what happened?
3. Describe your feelings about the situation
4. What were your concerns and thoughts at the time? Why?
5. What was most challenging about this situation?
6. What is your thinking since this incident occurred? And now?
7. What were you trying to achieve if anything? Did you achieve this? Why (why not)?
8. Did you discover any gaps in your knowledge/information as the situation transpired?
9. Who or what do you think is really responsible for the situation as it emerged? What has been done since by them? By you?
10. How did this event relate to previous experiences of yours?
11. What have you learned from this?
12. Would it make you approach things differently in the future? Why?
13. Do you feel you would handle it differently now? Better?

It is important that the mentor delves into the underpinning values and norms as well as the actions and relationships of the main players in any situation brought to them in a mentoring conversation. Otherwise, only surface issues will be dealt with which can produce a fleeting "feel good" sense which will be short lived. A mentor focusing on a double-loop learning approach to reflective practice will assist the mentee to increase their understanding and competence not only at the action level but also at the strategic, governing values realm.

## 3.9 Step 4: Reassurance

When the mentor senses that the mentee has run-out-of-steam, it is their turn to consider what they can see NOW which they might have missed previously and secondly, from the mentee's perspective what had they missed previously. The mentor needs to help clarify what they now understand from the conversation so far. Depending on the stage of disclosure and the mentor's assessment of what the mentee is feeling or what they "see", the mentor moves into summing up the conversation so far by describing the situation to the mentee using their words and phrases and only changing these where the mentor believes that there is faulty logic. Do this in a way that sounds right for the mentee to avoid sounding disingenuous. The key for the mentor here is learning to describe any gap—or difference—between the mentor's version and theirs.

## 3.10 Step 5: Problem-Solving Structure

Now the mentee is ready to begin to analyse what is going on through problem-solving. Active problem-solving approaches to dealing with issues, especially interpersonal conflict lead to a sense of control and of self-efficacy, which contribute to improved health (De Drue et al. 2004). The mentor needs to segment the approach to follow a problem-solving approach which can be broadly summarised as follows:

### *3.10.1 Stages of Problem-Solving*

a. Segment general problem area into specific problems
b. Decide which one of the problems is to be tackled first
c. Brainstorm options for tackling problem
d. Agree on preferred option for tackling problem
e. Work out steps to tackling problem using this option
f. Carry out task
g. Review what happened at next meeting
h. Decide next step, depending on progress, and agree on subsequent options

(a) *Segment general problem into specific problems*

Using "why" divide the problem into manageable proportions.

(b) *Decide which part of the problem is to be tackled first*

It is important to proceed slowly and safely through each of the above phases; working out what are safe issues to raise first? And then what are the unsafe issues, if any?

(c) *Brainstorm options for tackling problem*

Again open the process neutrally by asking open questions: for example from the narrative just described by the mentee, choose an event, action, particularly when something had gone wrong with them; and then ask them to describe further what has happened. The mentor needs to anticipate how they will respond?

The mentor picks up the mentee's response and using similar words, asks each and following questions based on content provided by them. Brainstorming is useful as it is a good process to continue the inquiry. For example, the mentor asks the mentee what they think would work. Whatever the response, the mentor needs to identify a critical point in it and build on it. The mentor then follows up by raising each issue as neutrally and matter-of-factly as possible, regardless of how they feel about it. The mentor does not engage in blame, criticise or judge the mentee. It is important to minimise the emotions in the problem-solving stage if possible. Deflection may be necessary here by offering advice as follows for example:

a. "I have suggestion" OR
b. "How have you come to that conclusion? _______________. Can we canvass some ideas about how to address these issues so that your intention is clearer in future?"

A further example of some questions suitable for this stage includes:

(a) What's happened in this situation? Name another player and ask the mentee: "what would they say has happened?" Why?
(b) What has triggered this situation? Has anything made it worse?
(c) Who/what are the drivers/inhibitors?
(d) What led to this situation initially?
(e) What are some of the influencing factors that you are concerned about here? What about the future?

The questions are asked one at a time interspersed with pauses long enough for the mentee to respond; while checking to see if the process makes sense to the mentee.

(d) *Agree on preferred option for tackling problem*

The mentor assists the mentee in developing options to address the important concerns and interests of the narrative as it unfolds. For example:

(a) What are the alternatives?
(b) What work won't get done?
(c) Is this a problem-fix; minimisation; avoidance? Why? How?

During the conversation, it is important for the mentor to normalise the situation by indicating they understand the behaviour of the mentee in those circumstances without implying agreement with it.

The mentor needs to inquire what the mentee thinks about this.

It is important for the mentee to know from the outset and to have this reinforced at different times during the session and at the commencement of each session that the mentor's goal for the discussion is to understand their perspective better, share the mentor own, and talk about how to go forward together makes the conversation significantly less mysterious and threatening.

Evaluating options needs to be fully mindful. To be valuable, the mentor has to assist the mentee draw upon their tremendous store of knowledge. Is the option useful or not? How can it be integrated into thinking and actions? Does it require a complete rethinking of approach? Role? How can this option be best connected to the work of others? Evaluation leads to an enhancement of insight.

In looking at the research evidence on evaluating options, 12 parameters are proposed by Blair and Mumford (2007), all of which are useful for consideration in mentoring as follows:

1. Risky
2. Easy to understand
3. Innovative
4. Complete description
5. Complicated
6 Consistent with existing norms
7 High probability of success
8. Easy to implement
9. Benefits many people
10. Produces desired outcomes
11. Time and effort required to execute
12. Complexity of implementation

There is always a pressure between evaluating an idea for its suitability and assessing it for its more effective way forward as it has to be tested against in whose interest is this the case.

*What's the benefit for the mentee?* The mentor asks the mentee what outcome they would want from this situation. It is up to the mentor to assist the mentee disengage from sensitive conversations so they can get back to "normal" in their working relationships. Regardless of how the evaluation works in real life, the process builds the skills of critical and creative thinking for the mentee.

## 3.11 Step 6: Implementation of the Mentoring Outcomes in Each Session

a. *Agree on preferred option for tackling problem*
b. *Work out steps to tackling problem using this option*
c. *Carry out task*

The final phase is for the mentor to ask the mentee *what is the next step?* The mentor waits for their response and again questions the mentee further before summarising agreements, disagreements and any actions for further reflection outside the mentoring conversation. The mentor needs to normalise the outcome to any commitments that the mentee makes by asking:

(a) What will happen now?
(b) Who will do this?
(c) When will it be done?
(d) When will we review it?
(e) Do we need to check in before this date?
(f) How do we keep the lines of communication open?

*A positive outcome will depend on*:

- How the mentee feels at the end of each session and from one meeting to the next;
- What the mentee says to the mentor includes non-verbal e.g. facial expression, posture, voice tone/quality.
- How the mentee presents (calm, supportive, curious, problem-solving) will greatly influence what they say.
- The mentor is maintaining high energy and directing it towards a useful purpose.

At the end of each mentoring meeting, a plan is completed specifying outcomes to date and commitments for each is to be completed prior to the next meeting.

| Meeting Plan* | | | | | |
|---|---|---|---|---|---|
| Meeting Date: | | **Start Time**: | | **Finish Time**: | |
| Mentor Name: | | **Mentee Name**: | | | |
| Outline | | | | | |
| Overarching Goals: | *Description of the broad goal/s to be addressed today* | | | | |
| Specific Objectives: | *Key elements of broad goal/s to be targeted today* | | | | |
| Specific Strategies/Activities: | List of m*ethods that could be used to approach each element* | | | | |
| Outcomes | | | | | |
| *Record specific outcomes relating to each objective from this meeting.* | | | | | |
| Commitments | | | | | |
| *Record specific commitments/follow up items that the mentor or mentee will action prior to the next meeting* | | | | | |
| Reflection | | | | | |
| *Record of the techniques or methods in each meeting that worked well, and those that could be improved in the next meeting.* | | | | | |
| Date of Next Meeting: | | **Time of Next Meeting**: | | | |

*Meeting plans are completed and reviewed at the end of each meeting

## 3.12 Reflections for the Mentor

The mentor should not assume that the mentee can see things from the mentor's point of view. How does the mentor let the mentee know if they think he/she is making an error? One example might be to ask: "In our discussion, I thought I heard you say XYZ. Is that correct?"

It is important for the mentor to consider any assumptions they are making about the mentee's intentions. For example: How is the mentor's attitude toward the mentee influencing the mentor's perception of how they are guiding them? If the mentee thinks they are overly influenced or finding the mentor judgemental, the process will not be effective.

The mentor needs to be aware of any emotional "buttons" of theirs being pushed by the mentee. Questions include: Are they more emotional than the situation warrants? What personal history is being triggered? A mentor engages with the mentee knowing what the source of any heightened emotional state they may be feeling is associated with.

The mentor needs also to ask: What might the mentor be thinking about this situation? Are they aware of the problem? If so, how do they think they perceive it? What are their needs and fears? What solution do they think they would suggest? Begin to reframe the mentor questions of them accordingly to test out some of these assumptions.

## 3.13 Great Expectations

It takes two to tango so to speak. This section will focus on the expectations of the mentor and the mentee so as to maximise the benefits of the relationship and the investment of each in it. As discussed thus far, the mentor is largely responsible for establishing a good mentoring bond and mentees can expect and trust that this will be the case. Mentoring is about mutuality—an understanding held in common usually between two people. This zone of adjacency—a zone of neither 'intense proximity' nor intense distance—would initiate a different kind of dialogue (Rabinow 2003: 43).

The mentor ultimately bears prime responsibility for the nature of the relationship that determines the value derived by the mentee. This depends on a large part of how mentoring is created as an opportunity for new learning and creativity by the skills and approaches of the mentor including their willingness to be open to expose their own work, including their learnings from inevitable limitations. Negative critique will be accepted by the mentee as they appreciate that it does not constitute the sum of the entire mentor's feedback. It is important that mentors begin their work, not in denial of their own short-comings as denial inhibits growth. The mentor needs to own and work with mentees empathically to resolved these issues if they are to move to a healthy self-interest and competition for developing their own careers, from wanting to control everything and everyone to becoming more accepting of themselves and others.

To have an authentic conversation the mentee must eventually come to the realisation individuals must be willing and capable of setting aside ways of thinking and of being, around which they have already established a personal sense of equilibrium and self-esteem. As people age, this becomes harder and harder. In some cases, it is as difficult for young adults as it is for seasoned ones to withstand change and embrace it when it affects individuals personally.

While often mentees will rely on prior experiences of success and capability, for learning to occur in mentoring, they need to be willing to endure ambiguity and chaos for real learning to occur.

When the mentoring relationship is initiated, and the conversation starts it needs to grow out of each conversant, both individually and together. It relies on each finding "what they have inside themselves" to bring to the conversation.

Ineffective mentoring can be characterised by:

(a) too much reflection by the mentor or the mentor allows the mentee to do same
(b) placing excessive focus on seemingly countless interpretations and reflections particularly on aspects that the mentee sees as insignificant. If the mentor thinks otherwise, it is important that they explain their rationale for reflecting on them
(c) mentor over-regulates the mentoring conversations and does not permit or follow through to ensure that the mentee is structuring the conversation
(d) issues discussed impact negatively on mentee's learning without them being resolved or leaving them feeling unsupported
(e) insufficient conversational space for dialogue and joint reflection
(f) lack of discussion of professional issues as required by the mentee due to mentor's out-of-date or lack of knowledge or avoidance of them
(g) lack of insight and feedback on the mentee's handling of specific situations,
(h) a mentor does not provide clear feedback—both positive and negative—to the mentee, and
(i) mentor unable to demonstrate or give an example to make things easier for the mentee to understand.

## 3.14 What Mentees Expect from Mentors

**Clear and Specific Feedback**

One of the biggest issues in professional and workplace settings is the lack of quality and timely feedback. In the absence of feedback, people are unable to establish a shared reference point. In mentoring this common reference point is essential for shared learning to occur. Further, one of the main reasons mentees seek a mentor is that they expect mentors to give them clear and specific feedback. Most seek advice and suggestions on what to do or say, depending on how they perceive the experience and wisdom of the mentor. The mentor should assist mentees gain a deeper insights into the situations that they raise to gain a more nuanced understanding of them and also anything they can read in relation to the topic. Mentors need to be prepared for this and well-read in the areas they are going to advise or offer suggestions on.

Whether at work or in mentoring, a lack of feedback contributes to a negative experience as it heightens a sense of uncertainty and ambiguity. It also makes it impossible for people to work out what is going or to solve problems. Without feedback whether that be in the form of an answer to a question, unsolicited information, opinion or advice, people will speculate, act on misperception and distrust may set in. Most people have high demand for information and communication. Even when this is forthcoming, it may not be readily understood or acted upon. To assure trust in the mentoring relationship, a mentor needs to provide prompt feedback even when there is nothing substantive to impart.

**Linking Theory with Practice**
Providing a superficial or definitive analysis of a situation needs to be supplemented by more contextualised and pragmatic thinking about it. Mentoring helps in the process of grounding information into the mentee's own situation. Mentees expect mentors will be affirmative, supportive and confirmative, characteristics vital for the acquisition of new learnings particularly in emotionally challenging situations.

**Full Engagement and Respect**
The mentor's support and encouragement are needed to maintain an appropriate level of motivation for mentees. Mentors need to appreciate that mentees are highly qualified and experienced and treat them accordingly regardless of any status or age differential between them.

**Normalising**
Mentees expect a lot from themselves too, and consequently, they appreciate mentor intervention to assist them in minimising the associated stresses and strains through, for example, normalising a reaction or phenomenon. Mentors can achieve this easily by through reflection and feedback to analyse what is happening, referring to their own experience or one they know about and assuring the mentee that this is a familiar, expected reaction in these situations.

Being given credit for positive actions, taking risks is also welcomed and experienced as affirming by mentees.

**Critical Feedback**
Giving critical feedback is tricky and mentees' appetites for this will vary: some welcoming it, others being defensive and everything in between. This can be mediated by the nature of the relationship with the mentor: how much trust, support and interest in their success they feel. It can also be mediated by how the critique is

given, if mentors rarely give feedback at all (neither positive nor negative) and suddenly provide negative feedback or only focus on the positive aspects, it is unlikely to be viewed as credible and will be dismissed. A mentor may be perceived as superficial, disinterested and unconvincing to mentees.

**Sustaining the Mentee**
Mentees look forward to their "me-time" and want the experience to be a satisfying, learning one. This does not mean that mentors should shy away from challenging mentees, giving critical feedback, asking the unaskable questions nor agreeing with everything. A satisfying, learning relationship is one where there is value for the participants and their appetite for discovery is being satiated. Often during a mentoring conversation, mentees will no doubt experience frustration, annoyance or dislike what they are hearing. Mentors should not abandon their stance because if they do, it will undermine the relationship as well as the mentor's credibility. It is important to sustain the mentee through any experience of discomfort not only to build their resilience but to use it as a window for their handling of negative feedback outside of mentoring. What both will find is that this experience will be transformative and turn out be helpful and instructive sometime in the future.

Once mentoring is drawing to a close or completed, the next step for the mentee is to develop a picture of their career over the next few years, especially their next step. Once they have developed a mental picture, the final step is developing a plan for achieving their goals. Mentees should come away from mentoring with several outcomes including a better understanding of their

a. strengths and weaknesses as well as opportunities and threats
b. changes they wish to make in their future professional life and the reasons for this
c. new activities they will take on, and
d. things they will avoid.

### *3.14.1 Expectations of the Mentor*

It is important to understand from the mentor's perspective that they do not have to be faultless—impossible to achieve in any case. Sometimes when a mentor falls short of the mentee's expectations, this forces them to draw from their own personal resources to find their own way through it. This experience can also be transformative and turn out be helpful and instructive sometime in the future and ultimately be rewarding, building their confidence in so doing.

It is important that the mentor lets the mentee have some experience of discomfort in discovering new learnings and approaches—otherwise they will not. An example of this would be to guide a mentee through reflection without filling in all the answers, even giving them "homework" to do and come back and report on their progress. This approach builds resilience and confidence and permits them to experiment with finding and scoping their own approach to resolving issues.

According to Schön (1987) this requires, among other things, becoming a reflected practitioner: "… a setting relatively low in risk, with access to coaches who initiate students into the …tradition of the calling and help them, by the right kind of telling", to see on their own behalf and in their own way what they need most to see" (p. 17).

**Ensure Active Engagement of the Mentee**

What mentees expect and what they require is sometimes not identical (Jacobsen 2001). Another way of phrasing this is through Vygotsky's term, the "zone of proximal development" (see Moore et al. (1997) for a discussion of the use of Vygotsky's theories in supervision). Sometimes it is important for gaining confidence and learning for the mentee to be afforded the opportunity for initiating and structuring the mentoring conversations, in fact, it should rarely be otherwise unless the mentee is avoiding certain issues that have surfaced through reflection and feedback.

To have a positive mentoring experience, mentees need to be actively engaged in the process and "not dragging their feet" to the sessions by frequently cancelling them or not responding well in conversations. This does not mean that they need to be on top of it all but showing that they are doing their best.

Active engagement means taking responsibility for their own mentoring even if they have been conscripted through their organisation. Mentees need to decide the topic of focus, the issues they wish to work on, new learnings, appropriate preparation, focusing on the important aspects, instead of just turning up unprepared or letting the mentor comment on whatever they think is relevant.

It is important that the mentor checks for the mentee's understanding of what is important or why certain questions are being asked or comments made. Where mentees feel the time with the mentor is too short, this is a good thing mostly. Conversations by and large should not exceed about one hour so that the mentee uses the time judiciously and realises that no matter how much time they are allocated and how good their mentor is, they will always be left with questions hanging and unfinished business. This process mimics real situations, and assists the mentee prepare and organise themselves more effectively for meetings and similar.

Mentees at times expect to give feedback to mentors. If this is the case, it needs to be accepted and acknowledged in the manner in which it is provided. A mentor should never react defensively under any circumstance. Mentees need to be aware that mentors are only human and how to approach them so as to make the most of the relationship.

**Role Modelling and the Parallel Process**

The manner in which the mentor approached the mentee needs to be aligned to how they would want the mentee to approach others in their professional situations. Any advice or suggestions given must be modelled by the mentor during the mentoring relationship otherwise their credibility will be undermined. For example, providing criticism to the mentee should be done in a way that the mentee could replicate it to another in a fairly equivalent situation e.g. their subordinate, peer or even supervisor. In so doing, the mentee will see how criticism can, in fact, be constructive. The learning here can be demonstrated through reflection either during a mentoring conversation or setting it as "homework" for personal reflection for the mentee.

## 3.15 What Does a Good Mentor Look like?

**Summing It Up**

Creative mentoring is composing mutual understanding out of what the mentee brings into the conversations. It does not always unfold logically, so the mentor needs to deal with disorder and muddled tales and riddles which are complex. The mentor and the mentee set about creating actions from this 'mess'. How?

**Focus**

(a) Taking the time to direct all attention to the mentee and their conversation
(b) Change focus as emotions, needs and concerns emerge
(c) Look on what is said, how it is said, what is not said
(d) Observe body language and tune into the tone, the pitch to search for meaning underlying the words
(e) Look "outside" the conversations to allow time to understand what is really going on; meanings that emerge so as to make sense of the total picture that is being assembled and not just one part of it
(f) Persevere even when old ground is rehashed or the mentee loses focus or appears disinterested or distracted
(g) Attend to the things that are unknown, untried, innovative or conversely the known, the tried to see if a new angle can be placed on the latter
(h) Explore differences in perspectives between the mentor and mentee
(i) Shift attention to the outer layers of meaning as the centre is conquered.

**Tapping into Experiential Knowledge and Skill**

(a) Help the mentee connect their aspirations to their professional and career goals
(b) Assist the mentee to depersonalise observations.

**Visualising**

(a) Use stories, metaphors, maps and diagrams, etc. to construct meaning
(b) Reveal the core of the matter that is the focus of the discussion
(c) Create and explore models and approaches for the mentee to use.

**Extend Warmth**

(a) Engage the mentee's curiosity by drawing analogies or comparing dissimilar themes together.
(b) Converse intelligently with the mentee, regardless of your assumptions about their intellectual competence.
(c) Use humour appropriately and assist the mentee once they feel confident to see the levity in situations.
d) Find the thread of appropriate diversion in a serious situation maintaining the substance especially in terms of outcome.

**Collaborative Enquiry**

(a) Assure the mentee is an equal conversant with the mentor.
(b) Ask questions so that they unlock the essence of the matter.
(c) Invite the mentee to question their observations and meanings not to doubt themselves.
(d) Hold an issue without rushing to solve it for the mentee.
(e) Engage multiple boundaries of the mentee: role, professional, career and personal.
(f) Build a bridge when the conversation hits a brick wall.
(g) Err on the side of supportive inquiry not advice.

**Develop Mentoring Outcomes Together**

(a) Assist the mentee put the pieces together to see the big picture.
(b) Invest in the follow up action with special meaning for them.
(c) Reconstruct if necessary.
(d) Assist the mentee to know when to work within the governing values of their context and when to question and modify these.
(e) Encourage perseverance in the mentee for a long term strategy, not a short-term fix.
(f) Encourage the mentee to engage with others outside the mentoring relationship where s/he will find ongoing support.

**Develop a Signature Mentor Approach Which Is Adaptable**

(a) Ensure ongoing growth.
(b) Adjust approach to meet the individual differences of mentees.

## 3.16 Framing Mentoring

Mentoring is not a confessional process. It is based on a principle of transcendence and reconciliation using the resources within oneself. It is important to understand that often "what we are aware of gets in the way of what we are totally unaware of".

This book hopefully clarifies for both mentors and mentees how much guidance and support is needed especially within the initial period of the mentoring relationship. Good mentoring occurs when a mentor gives advice and specific instructions on how to approach specific situations based on their own and other's tried and tested experiences or using theoretical considerations e.g. applying for a new role, a promotion, handling a conflict, providing performance feedback and the like.

The mentee is supported throughout and permitted to shape the nature of the conversations each time they meet whether in person, over Skype, telephone or otherwise. Ensuring there is space for the individual narratives gives the mentor plenty to consider in practice. It is important that mentees will have different appetites for criticism and how much they will take into account and act upon.

Some mentees need a lot of support, and others do not; A mentor needs to appreciate such individual differences. More importantly, how these can change over time during the relationship.

The experience of failure for some will be harder to bear than for others and can lead to feelings of disappointment, frustration and despair. Some mentees will need to be referred to a counsellor if mentors feel that such feelings are overwhelming a mentee. Others will be capable of turning frustrating events into self-reflection and learning from these with a mentor's guidance.

Some mentees will approach mentoring not appreciating its potential value and all should eventually depart feeling their expectations were met and at best, surprised by how much they gained from the relationship.

What is important is that all mentees need to be supported differently. What works for one mentee in a mentor's experience may not for another and so on. What is called for is for the mentor to develop a tailored, individual approach to each mentee.

## 3.17 Conclusion

The mentor needs to prepare beforehand, especially where to begin with the mentee each time they meet. It is important that the mentor learns about the mentee's own interests and the essence of what they need. By separating the issues and making this the focus as well as taking into account interests and actions, mentees are less likely to focus on personalities, which is important as there is nothing to be achieved by doing so. A person's personality cannot be changed. It is important to create an environment based on trust by building and sustaining the mentee's confidence.

What does the mentor need to do in conversing with the mentee?

(a) separate actions, impact and assumptions
(b) hold the mentee's view as a hypothesis, not a statement; be clear they are sharing assumptions
(c) inquire about the mentee's intentions

(d) anticipate and be prepared to clarify what they are trying to communicate
(e) listen for feelings, and reflect on the mentor intentions
(f) listen to any reports of past accusations to identify the mentee's feelings—start by listening and acknowledging the mentee's feelings; and then return to the question of intentions. This approach will make the mentor conversation significantly easier and more constructive.
(g) be open to reflecting on the complexity of the mentee's intention, and
(h) share the impact on their approach.

**How Can the Mentor Ensure Commitment from the Mentee?**

(a) by inviting questions and clarifications;
(b) maintaining two-way communication;
(c) acknowledging the mentee's concerns;
(d) listening for what may be difficult for them to change;
(e) following up with the mentee to help them with new approaches; and
(f) changing is seldom straightforward.

During the conversation, the mentor needs to remain conscious and observant; mindful of gaining and maintaining their own equilibrium. This is where the benefit of having a mentor lies. By the mentor choosing to remain calm and centred, they will assist the mentor to become more centred, too. This is very powerful for mentees who often comment on it later or as they conclude their mentoring relationship. It is something that most people want to learn to do for themselves. This is at the heart of mentoring-mindedness. Mentors need to appreciate that centring is not a step rather a process of how they are conversing and moving from phase to the next in a given conversation and throughout the relationship overall.

## Appendix

**Advising the mentee on having a difficult conversation with a colleague**, especially when they are obliged to give directions to a strong-willed employee, John, who insists on doing things his way and who often argues with them Quen, his supervisor. Quen is recounting this conversation with John to his mentor and seeking some guidance on how to manage it.

John arrives at Quen's office for the meeting. John's body language suggests that he's defensive—he seems to be expecting Quen's criticism… and he's ready to strike back.

What is Quen's opening?

"Thanks for meeting with me at short notice, John. I wanted a chance to share some information with you that you may not be aware of. My hope is that by having this discussion, I will get a better idea of what you consider is reasonable."

The next step for Quen is to wait and listen to John's reply. Quen acknowledges John's response and then suggests: "I am also hoping that if I am presenting you with some new information during this discussion, you might understand why I am asking you to modify your approach?"

Quen again waits and listens: How does Quen respond when a colleague believes they are treading on his/her perceived turf, even when the roles are ambiguous?

Quen's opening now is: "As I said when I asked if we could meet, I've been in my role about four months now and wanted to check in with how you see how things are going, how you feel about that, given your responsibilities? [Pose as separate questions.]?"

Quen again waits and listens [Knowing where I need to focus and where you still need my support versus where they no longer need this will be useful.] "May we talk about that?"

Quen again waits and listens: "You feel that you are ready to be independent, and I see that. May I discuss where I think we still need to work more closely together?"

Quen again waits and listens "You can let me know what you think about this agree or perhaps an alternative option. Does that work?"

**Analysis**

What's the first thing they do here? The supervisor needs to think of four to six examples of times over the last 90-days when they perceived that the person did not carry their share of the load. Be prepared to share these examples in a factual, calm manner.

What is the supervisor's objective here? It is important in this case for the supervisor to focus on the impact of the team, clients, and business. The supervisor needs to avoid language that sounds as if they are having a personal problem with them. The supervisor needs to keep their emotions in check and not let frustration with the situation seep through or dominate their interchange or what they are trying to achieve.

How might a mentee give unsolicited negative feedback to someone on their project team who is making others' tasks more difficult?

"Over the last few months, I've gone back and forth with myself if I should talk with you regarding a concern I have with the way our team is working together." *pause…*

*Enter slowly*

I don't want you/them to perceive me as being negative or being unsupportive. However, an incident happened last week that made me realise that I needed to speak with you. I am seeing something that may get in the way of us providing excellent customer service. Specifically, some of our customer orders are not being completed as timely and effectively as they could be because, during significant chunks of each day, they appear to be dealing with other things. Pause

"I have a few examples and observations that have occurred over the last 4–6 weeks, that illustrate my concerns. May I share them with you?"

*If they interrupt, stop talking and listen…*

*Then proceed with the examples. Work each example through with them.*

Be ready to discuss specific tasks or projects that they have taken on during the mentor tenure in this position in this department; focus in particular on the last 12 months.

Realise that everyone takes on more and/or different tasks during their employment.

What they want to be able to communicate effectively to the mentor supervisor is that the scope of the mentor responsibilities has become more complex or that the number of tasks they now own has increased by a large percentage.

Prepare well before the meeting.

Finally, are they in good standing with the supervisor? Was their last evaluation favourable? Is the feedback they receive positive from staff?

**What's the mentor opening?**

How could they negotiate (e.g. for a job or promotion) when they can't or don't want to compromise on one of their top priorities?

"Thank you for meeting with me today. I wanted a chance to talk with you about my position and some of the changes in responsibilities I've had in the past few years due to the resignations and new systems we've introduced." pause and enter slowly, voice even.

The first thing I want to say is that I am pleased I have been able to learn so much and been able to grow professionally in my knowledge base and skill sets. And while I am grateful to have taken on more complex tasks, and want to continue doing what I do, I also would like to see what could be done for my next step?

**Wait and listen**

Acknowledge then state: "I've identified some of the significant changes to my responsibilities since I was hired into this position and would be glad to give they a quick rundown. Does that sound like a good place for us to continue this discussion?"

The conversation proceeds. "I'm glad we were able to have this discussion. As I said, I like what I am doing and want to keep doing it. My request is to understand what my next step is. I am keen to take on more responsibilities and also engage in further training or education if that is required?" Pause and then

"Is there any other information that I could provide that would help they/they and the mentor manager make a decision on my request? When should I expect to hear back from they?"

## References

Argyris, C. (1985). *Strategy, change and defensive routines*. New York: Harper Business.
Argyris, C. (2000). *Flawed advice and the management trap*. New York: Academic Press.
Argyris, C., & Schön, D. A. (1996). *Organisational learning II*. Reading, MA: Addison-Wesley.
Bird, J. (2004). *Talk that sings: Therapy in a new linguistic key*. Auckland: Edge Press.
Blair, C. S., & Mumford, M. D. (2007). Errors in idea evaluation: Preference for the unoriginal? *Journal of Creative Behaviour*, *41*:197–222.
Brewer, A. M. (2011). Mentoring. In S. Roffey (Ed.), *Positive relationships: Evidence-based practice across the world*. New York: Springer.
Cunningham, J. B., MacGregor, J. N., Gibb, J., & Haar, J. (2009). Categories of insight and their correlates: an exploration of relationships among classic-type insight problems, rebus puzzles, remote associates and esoteric analogies. *Journal of Creative Behaviour, 43*(4), 262–280.
De Dreu, C. K. W., van Dierendonck, D., & Dijkstra, M. T. M. (2004). Conflict at work and individual well-being. *International Journal of Conflict Management, 15*, 6–26.
Hartley, R. (2004). Young people and mentoring: Towards a national strategy, big brothers big sisters Australia, Dussledorp skills forum and the smith family. http://www.thesmithfamily.com.au/webdata/resources/files/tsf_Mentor_May04.pdf.
Jacobsen, D. M. (2001). Building different bridges: Technology integration, engaged student learning, and new approaches to professional development annual meeting of the American educational research association in Seattle, WA http://files.eric.ed.gov/fulltext/ED453232.pdf
Koestler, A. (1964). *The act of creation*. New York: Macmillan.
Losch, A. (2009) On the origins of critical realism. *Theology and Science*, *7*(1), 85–106.
Moore, D., Monaghan, E.J., & Hartmann, D.K. (1997). Values of literacy and history. *Reading Research Quarterly*, *32*: 90–102.
Rabinow, P. (2003). Anthropos today. *Reflections on modern equipment*. Princeton and Oxford: Princeton University Press.
Rogers, C. R., & Sanford, R. C. (1984). Client-centered psychotherapy. In H. I. Kaplan & B. J. Sadock (Eds.), *Comprehensive textbook of psychiatry* (Vol. 4, pp. 1374–1388). Baltimore: Williams and Wilkins.
Salovey, P., & Rodin, J. (1984). Some antecedents and consequences of social-comparison jealousy. *Journal of Personality and Social Psychology, 47*, 780–792.
Schon, D.A. (1987). *Educating the reflective practitioner: Toward a new design for teaching and learning in the professions*. San Francisco: Jossey-Bass.
Watson, J. C. (2002). Re-visioning empathy. In D. Cain (Ed.), *Humanistic psychotherapies: A handbook of research and practice*. Washington, DC: American Psychological Association.

# Chapter 4
# The Burden of Unburdening in a Mentoring Relationship

*The light dove cleaving in free flight the thin air, whose resistance it feels, might imagine that her movements would be far more free and rapid in empty space.*
Immanuel Kant Critique of Pure Reason (1900, p. 6)

**Abstract** Everyone has secrets, some are trivial while others are life-changing regardless of who instigates, preserves, or reveals them and under what circumstances. This chapter focuses on the challenges of the burdens that are imposed upon people and the process of unburdening in mentoring. Trust is an important element in this process. Techniques for encouraging transparency and disclosure are discussed using a case study.

Like the light dove, what impedes us also provides the way forward. Mentoring is about solving problems and overcoming hurdles that block our path. What sustains us is the search for new ways of thinking about things. This search can be intensified at different phases of development and crossroads. At these junctures, people seek support just as the dove can only fly because of the invisible support of the air that holds and bolsters her. Mentees in taking flight seek from within their own resources or others and if fortunate, may find a mentor to assist them to navigate the byways and crossways. As stated previously, mentoring typically involves a more experienced person, usually one acting as a guide or an interventionist for the other, less experienced person.

Conversation like air, a dialogue, is the main tool of mentoring through which a relationship is forged and hopefully sustained, principally on trust. Two people converse together with one exploring, listening, observing and assisting the other through reflection as well as providing feedback, giving guidance, support and encouragement (Hartley 2004). The other committed to reflection, exploration and following up. The relationship, prescribed or informal, is established in a range of contexts including personal, professional and organisational. Regardless there is a pattern to these conversations, unique to the participants involved, which will be explored further throughout the following chapters.



A.M. Brewer, *Mentoring from a Positive Psychology Perspective*,
DOI 10.1007/978-3-319-40983-2_4

Mentoring is essentially contradictory in that it requires the effort of one person to divulge personal and at times, previously never disclosed information so as to attain genuine openness between them. The degree of openness attained influences the mentoring outcomes. In mentoring, there is a twofold burden of denial and disclosure, often experienced as an internal push-pull tension for one or other. The mentor, recognising that disclosure requires effort and inspiration, needs to find a way to assist the mentee in releasing tension in the hope that this triggers disclosure for analysis and development. Of course, once the initial disclosure occurs, it can release a floodgate, and a mentor needs to be well prepared for this. Depending on the nature of the disclosure and its magnitude, the mentor may need to refer the mentee to a counsellor or other specialist still maintaining the elements of mentoring, if appropriate. For example, if the mentee disclosed suicidal thoughts, the mentor may consider with the mentee calling in specialist assistance while not stepping away from the relationship. To pass the mentee onto someone else in this situation, could exacerbate the suicidal depression and reinforce to the mentee that each time they attempt to reach out they are abandoned.

Without an assurance of a high degree of openness for the issues that the mentee brings to mentoring, the mentor cannot assess the situation and allow the *flow* of development to begin. Transparency versus suppression is at the core of the contradiction and struggle in mentoring. While understanding is the hallmark of successful mentoring, acquiring it, is no mean feat. By the time information is exchanged in any relationship, it is screened, concealed, filtered, selected and reformulated by each conversant to suit their purposes, even if unintentionally. Information will undergo further recycling throughout the mentoring relationship. Herein lies the challenge for the mentor to work through this labyrinth, sift through the words so as to assist the mentee who may be experiencing confusion in trying to make sense of it all. This chapter outlines a distinctive set of challenges for both the mentor and mentee in this process.

From the beginning of the relationship, the mentor strives to create 'safe learning' context, by investigating what is working well and what is not for the mentee. The best approach for the mentor is to create a narrative framework, by which the parts of it can be completed as the relationship develops. Explanatory competence is crucial for the mentor.

It is employed during the process of conversing when the mentor reconstructs situations for the mentee by putting into words the chain of events that comprise the difficult situation(s) they experience; ensuring that the mentee can explicitly appraise the situation as well as tackling their emotional, pragmatic and idealistic responses to it both then and now. Explanatory competence is also concerned with identifying communication breakdowns. A case study serves to exemplify the mentoring relationship and the techniques discussed in this paper.

## 4.1 Unburdening

To engage with a mentor requires willingness, and if paid for by the employer an obligation, for the person to be open with the mentor about their aims, aspirations, and difficulties. Opening up may create some unease about expressing aspirations and work difficulties, previously held private. This discomfort may be intensified where the mentor assumes that they will be able to address problems by the person simply talking about them. If the mentor becomes frustrated by slow progress and shows this, it will outweigh any benefits of mentoring. Teasing out the techniques to facilitate disclosure is important.

### 4.1.1 Denial and Disclosure

As mentioned in Chap. 1, a successful mentoring relationship is essentially paradoxical in that it requires the effort of one person to divulge personal and at times previously undisclosed information so as to attain genuine openness between the mentor and mentee. The degree of openness attained influences the mentoring outcomes. In the mentoring relationship, there is a twofold burden of denial and disclosure, which may present as a push-pull tension within the mentee. The process of disclosure and the effort it requires to achieve this, while not always apparent to others, is intensified if the mentee is essentially a private person. The mentor, recognising that disclosure requires effort and inspiration, needs to find a way to assist the mentee in releasing the tension so that disclosure triggers reflection and new learning to instigate further self-revelation for the mentee. Ultimately, greater openness with a mentor frees the mentee from the tension of secret-keeping, although the initial exposure can be taxing for them. Even if the information to be disclosed is not so secret, mentees will feel a degree of vulnerability in opening up to someone else, especially if the mentoring relationship is prescribed rather than naturally emergent between confidants.

Mentees not only state their view of things but also defend their position. As information is socially constructed in terms of the 'before and after', it is then incorporated into the mentoring conversation. Sometimes after expressing their interpretation of events or people, a mentee will struggle to reinforce their position with the mentor. Alternatively they may "pour unguent" on what they have previously revealed, so as to recover it, tone it down, or to appear less forceful and more accommodating in the eyes of the mentor. It is here that the mentor recognises the strength of the dire need for affirmation. Internal emotional struggles such as these will be intensified the stronger the need is or, the more political the situation is that surrounds the mentee, especially in institutional and professional settings. A mentor needs to remain vigilant for such indicators as they assist in the marking out the course of the exchange. Without assuring a high degree of openness, the mentor cannot assess and provide constructive feedback to the mentee. This is at the core of the contradiction and struggle in mentoring: transparency admonishes concealment and vice versa.

## 4.2 The Challenge of Secret-Keeping

The challenge is to shed light on information that the mentee is bound to be harbouring even unconsciously. People are inclined to keep confidences private in varying propensity for different reasons, ranging from discretion through to power (Perrow 1970a, b, 1993). Holding on to a secret affords a person both subjective and objective control over others who do not have similar access to this information or something else. Secrets, if revealed, vary from that which pertains to the mentee only with serious ramifications for them personally, to that which will affect others acutely.

There are different types of secrets which have to be concealed for various reasons:

1. Shadow secrets: information about the mentee which could contradict the image they represent professionally or personally.
2. Strategic secrets: information which allows the mentee to control others and lead them in the direction they desire.
3. Inside secrets: information known by an inner circle in which the mentee is a participant. Creates the in and out groups. For the in group, bonding is increased.
4. Entrusted secrets: information used to maintain the mentee's role with key people.
5. Free secret: information confided in the mentee by another, not related to the mentee and one that cannot be disclosed while still maintaining the role.

Disclosure of such secrets would not affect their performance.

## 4.3 Accidental Disclosure

Circumstances often tempt people, mentee or otherwise, to reveal information, sometimes when they least expect it. The enticement to reveal should not be underestimated, as divulging a secret can release tension with the mentee experiencing the immediate liberating effects of being unencumbered by it any longer. Any immediate relief, however, may be countered by a sense of disloyalty, loss of face, bewilderment and so on.

To prevent accidental revelations from occurring requires continual control by the mentee and a huge amount of effort. If they are determined not to disclose private information, even in situations where they may be lured to do so, intentionally, or otherwise, it requires strong emotional containment to avoid an accidental utterance such as using the wrong word in a sentence which might allude to the secret or the fact that there is one. This containment is a burden as it potentially saddles the mentee directly and indirectly with guilt, responsible or not. This knowledge is distressful and impacts the mentee's well-being (Lane and Wegner 1995; Pennebaker 1990).

## 4.4 Customs Governing Secrets and Transparency

Rendering the containment of information more complex are the norms governing secrets, which vary according to circumstances. In some cases, the norms for non-disclosure are clear-cut and upheld by legislation such as part of board membership, national security; in trade and commercial settings; or in the investigation of crime; or in other cases; for example, by institutional governance through regulations such as in the confessional relationship with a Catholic priest. Within families, relationships and amongst friends, social and familial norms vary about secret-keeping as well as the pressures to uphold this.

Clouding the matter further is a continuing propensity for people to share personal information or that known about others e.g. online, social media and televised "tell-alls". In the former, people assume a degree of anonymity and increased candour. As they become less guarded and distant from the person(s) concerned, people reveal information about others that under normal circumstances, they may feel more inhibited about doing so. The norms governing information in these contexts are uncertain and difficult to decipher.

The social norms of the disclosure become ambiguous since people disclose information according to circumstances. In situations where they feel anonymous, people are inclined to be expansive such as conversing with "a stranger at a bus stop" or posting information on social media; and may be less forthcoming when they understand the direct impact of revealing it to themselves and others e.g. in the case of victim impact statements about cyber-bullying.

The mentor armed this knowledge, affording a sense of confidentiality and working through the ramifications of the potential disclosure helps reassure the mentee.

## 4.5 The Effort to Contain and Disclose Private Information

As previously stated, an act of secret-keeping is contrived deception, requiring effort for the secret-keeper not to succumb to any enticement, real, convenient or imagined, to disclose it. The secret-keeper may feel devious as it involves continual covering up, potentially resulting in further duplicity, with an additional drain on their resources.

While it takes effort to contain private information, the struggle to disclose it should not be underestimated. The longer the information is undisclosed, the harder it becomes for the person to reveal it as they have usually embellished it with a web of deception over an extensive period of time. The process of making it known may also be upsetting for the mentee due to a dual sense of loyalty and betrayal. In opening up, the mentee thinks that they risk letting down anyone they may have been "protecting", including themselves. In the mentee's eyes, they (as protector) switch to become turncoat and fear others will see it in the same way. This is premised on that keeping a secret pertains to a significant matter which, if revealed, would have ramifications, in a negative way, for those "protected" by it, although this is not always immediately apparent.

The tension of initially holding and then revealing a meaningful secret is intensified when it is associated with powerful relationships, including interpersonal struggles and a revelation that will lead to a turning point for the mentee and others. Even if these are only presumed, the burden for the mentee is potentially immense. Additionally, the mentee may be the sole source of the information or be complicit with others. If significant ramifications are the consequence of revealing previously withheld information, this provides the challenge in a mentoring relationship—an issue which is not always out in the open.

## 4.6 The Challenges of Mentoring

Challenges exist for both the mentee and mentor, albeit each different in nature, in both intensity and consequences. In a professional or organisational relationship, professional practitioners, management and employees are hostages to the prevailing culture.

### *4.6.1 Challenges for the Mentee*

The first challenge lies in mustering the effort needed to make a full or even partial disclosure of privileged information to a third party. Even when a mentee confides "all", it is erroneous to assume full disclosure. Tacit (unspoken) knowledge, while recognised, may not be easily articulated by the mentee, regardless of their formal position elsewhere. The mentee may not fully appreciate that the mentor, if part of the same institution or profession, is also subject to this tacit knowledge and influenced by it. Mentors may not always fully acknowledge this either to the mentee or be aware of it themselves.

The second challenge is that under these conditions, opening up by the mentee, that is, sifting through the issues and seeing things for-what-they-are requires a regurgitation of the "facts", which often tumble out in an opposite direction to what is intended by the mentee or expected by the mentor. This process, in particular, requires reflection, analysis and re-ordering of things to place them into perspective.

The mentor needs to be able to employ explanatory competence to identify and overcome communication breakdowns, and to gain and restore understanding through redressing gaps in verbal and contextual meaning. Interpretation is not a straightforward matter to unravel, and the logic of the mentee and mentor may be at odds.

The third challenge is that often mentees are concerned about the loss of face: they need to appear strong and open as opposed to weak and secretive. This sense is heightened if the mentee is seeking promotion or referral within the institution or profession, acting as a force against disclosure.

The fourth challenge is the effort to overcome the strongly-held aversion to disclosing private information when it is governed not by law but rather by organisational norms. In this case, mentees are concerned about how this might appear in terms of professional or organisational loyalty and betrayal. The mentee cannot move forward while remaining loyal to the culture that bars them from revealing information that they need or feel should be spoken about.

## *4.6.2 Challenges for the Mentor*

### 4.6.2.1 The Worldviews of the Mentor and Mentee

How does the mentor handle the difference between how they perceive the mentee's world view when a mentee may not perceive it as particularly problematic? For example, a mentee may describe a situation at work and believe they are not contributing to the situation adversely. They may see everyone else as the "problem" and distance themselves from it. Moreover, the discussion of any difference in perceptions about this situation may be difficult if a solid rapport has not been established between the mentor and mentee. Trust is essential for such a discussion to ensue and for it to be beneficial to the mentee. A mentee's world view has been developed and ingrained over years of experience, and it is not easy to unravel. A further difficulty for the mentor is that discussing a mentee's possible negative contribution to situations might disrupt their self-image and cause them distress which may evoke frustration, anger or anxiety from them. The mentee may feel that the mentor is criticising them and deliberately distorting the situation rather than trying to guide the mentor to understand it and find a way to deal with it. Their normal reaction to criticism may be either verbal or nonverbal displays of hostility, negative mind-reading or self-blame.

Apart from trust, patience and skilful questioning is required to achieve the desired outcome. A mentor needs to listen and validate the mentee's perceptions followed up by finding a way to reframe the situation so that the mentee can begin to feel comfortable about questioning it.

#### 4.6.2.2 Stereotyping

In mentoring, a mentor is confronted by impressions formed about the mentee and by the mentee such as snippets of stories or information they reveal. Both can lead the mentor consciously or unconsciously to stereotyping, characterising them in some way, leading to biased judgment that is erroneous. This can lead the mentor to cut off the mentee either by giving their assessment, not paying attention to what is being said and short-circuiting the mentoring process. It is important to use only relevant, appropriate evidence, avoid typecasting the issue or the mentee, and the people that the mentee is referring to.

#### 4.6.2.3 Safe Learning for the Mentee

A further challenge for the mentor is to create and demonstrate a safe 'space' for the mentee to trust and open up to them. The crux of disclosing is that there is a tension for the mentee between the relative protection of "keeping quiet" (internal reality) and the feared consequences of revealing things as they see them (external reality). The second part of this challenge is for the mentor then is to rebalance these realisms, attempting to integrate them where possible. In both cases, the mentoring relationship becomes a haven, and while restorative initially, it ultimately becomes an impediment if used as an ongoing crutch.

#### 4.6.2.4 Cues to Elicit Trust

Ensuring the mentor is providing appropriate cues for eliciting trust and disclosure is also a challenge. This can be taxing for the mentor due to people's inconsistent strategies for disclosure. A mentee's "decision point" of whether or not to make information known is often based on their perception of situational cues at a given point in time (John et al. 2009). The mentor, therefore, needs to remain vigilant in observing and managing cues with the mentee such as eye contact, fidgeting, and posture.

#### 4.6.2.5 Dissolving a Mentor-Mentee Relationship

Finally overcoming the risk of the mentoring relationship becoming a permanent prop for the mentee needs to be dealt with.

#### 4.6.2.6 Seeking Help Beyond the Mentor

It is important that mentors identify and observe their reactions to limit personal biases encroaching on their mentoring of the mentee. Furthermore, when mentors are not able to resolve such conflicts on their own, they need to seek external advice from a peer or superior. These actions might not be possible for a mentor with blind spots. The crucial step to avoid these outcomes is to create a safe environment for mentees to confide any concerns with an appropriate third party.

## 4.7 How Does All This Work in a Mentoring Relationship?

Confidentiality is the hallmark which preserves the well-being of the mentoring relationship. The mentor must assure privacy and confidentiality of the information disclosed by the mentee—a basic obligation for safe 'learning'. This creates an ethical relationship which inhibits the mentor passing on information to others. All mentoring relationships need to be governed by protocols and confirmed to each party in the relationship prior to the commencement of the process. If the mentoring relationship is emergent—that is, comes about informally, it is obligatory for the mentor to clarify protocols and to ensure that both have some agreement that information divulged by either one is not passed on to a third party without permission.

The mentor commences creating 'safe learning' by requesting the mentee to describe their work situation and listens carefully for cues about what is working well and what is not, with the idea of creating a narrative framework. Practically speaking, the dialogue initially focuses on tangible examples which the mentee considers are important and troublesome. In listening to these experiences, the mentor aims to elicit as factual a version as possible from the mentee and uses each account to develop a simple narrative. To achieve this, reflective and open questioning is employed which involves summarising using the mentee's own vernacular. The mentor observes any difficulty that the mentee may be having in dealing with specific issues or situations, making these explicit or making note to investigate these further.

Deeper investigation of specific difficulties is postponed until a time when the mentor can piece together enough of a narrative to provide a wider context, and a certain degree of trust has been established within the relationship. It is then that the mentor's focus is on what the mentee sees as troublesome, embarrassing, or poignant, and together they attempt to uncover the reasons for this. What begins to occur is the transition from the factual aspects reported initially by the mentees towards their subjective evaluations and reactions, and in so doing, the unburdening of private information and secret thoughts.

Once disclosure flows, the focus is increasingly moved to the mentee's emotional position especially the aspects of the situation(s) that lead to distress. Again a chain of events is constructed around the emotional aspect of the narrative, prompting reflection by the mentor on how and why distress is part of their story.

Sensory and auditory insight by the mentor is crucial as is their observation. Through these techniques, a mentor can label what is going on and invite the mentee to evaluate them. Notions of conflict and power are introduced to see how the mentee responds, followed by further reflection on how they see failure, e.g. not getting a promotion, having had their career development arrested, or their decisions blocked by political maneuverings.

The ongoing experience of safe 'learning' for the mentee is further extended throughout the relationship, without fear of consequences, shame or loss of face. With appropriate timing, the mentor assists the mentee as they work out the links between their experienced drawbacks and invites reflection on the similarities and differences. Mutual disclosure is an advantage here as it benefits both the mentee and mentor, enabling them to identify their common experiences, important for making explicit, tacit issues (see Fisher et al. 1991). It is also a way for the mentee to receive guidance by way of example, and this adds to their learning.

## 4.8 Techniques for Encouraging Disclosure and Transparency

Teasing out the mentoring techniques to facilitate disclosure is important. Mentees open up to specific cues that engender trust (e.g. using linguistic cues by selecting simple words rather than long-winded alternatives); employing grammar, syntax, and vocabulary to suit the situation; using the broader context so that each conversation is linked to making up a coherent whole; and using sensory acuity, shifts or changes in the way a person looks or sounds (Alter and Oppenheimer 2009). This situation is likely to develop when the appointed meeting place is congenial and free from interruptions (Joinson and Paine 2007), and the mentee can confirm that their mentor is someone of integrity (Andrade et al. 2002). Further, the mentee needs to know that the benefits of disclosure outweigh any personal disadvantage of non-disclosure (Paine et al. 2006).

Explanatory competence is a crucial aptitude for the mentor. It is employed as the mentor reconstructs situations for the mentee by creating a narrative around the chain of events that comprise the difficult situation(s). The process is developed in such a way so that the mentee can explicitly appraise the situation as well as tackle their response to it both then and now. Explanatory competence is also concerned with identifying communication breakdowns, and being able to restore understanding through redressing gaps in verbal and contextual meaning provided by the mentee.

Mutual disclosure encourages further self-disclosure and interpersonal trust (Turner et al. 2007) as well as diminishing anxiety (e.g., Greenberg and Stone 1992). The trust engendered by the mentor enhances the quality of relationship (Collins and Miller 1994), and often improves outcomes (Fisher et al. 1991).

Despite these benefits, self-disclosure is also inherently risky. Mentees fear giving up the protection of privacy for fear of enhanced scrutiny and potential criticism (e.g., Jourard 1971; Derlega and Berg 1987; Matsushima and Shiomi 2001).

## 4.9 A Mentoring Case Study

The following case study serves to exemplify the mentoring relationship and the techniques described thus far.

Sandra is a 49-year-old semi-professional, who is married with three young adult children and started up her own successful business. She decided to seek a coach to mentor her through some difficult decision points in her life, both familial and work-related problems. Mentoring by the author commenced with Sandra early in 2011. Meetings were organised in groups of 10 sessions initially and then on an as needed basis. When things were going well, Sandra did not meet.

Formal mentoring was initiated with a problem diagnosis, using a self-report questionnaire followed by two sessions providing situational examples by Sandra. As the mentoring relationship developed, Sandra revealed that her relationships with her partner in life and business, two of her sons, and her best friend (whom she employs in her business) were problematic for different reasons. Sandra expressed feelings of rejection by her partner, competition from her best friend, frustration with her younger son and overall a sense of low control and experienced conflict.

The first transition occurred when the conversation moved from Sandra's factual descriptions of events and relationships, toward her interpretation of these. At this point, her emotions became the focus of reflection. Sandra was confused about her feelings as they were inconsistent with how she wanted to feel. For example, she felt sneaky in situations when she did not reveal information to her partner about her every move. She felt confused by the conflict between an employee and her best friend who was also employed in her business. Her relationship with her mother-in-law affected her intensely despite the fact that she was in her late eighties. A slip-of-the-tongue revealed this when she mistakenly said: "I'd like to be able to suffer her more than I do" and used the word "suffocate" instead of "suffer".

Initially, Sandra was encouraged to state things as she saw them, and typically she described interpersonal experiences between herself and members of the family or with her staff. She was invited to describe them in detail through questioning and non-verbal cues such as nodding understanding. We explored her actions, others' reactions; who initiated, who responded; interspersed with appraising each in turn.

After constructing the narrative as presented, the second transition occurred through requesting Sandra to suggest why people acted and reacted the way they did in the various situations. Much time was devoted towards elaborating a detailed analysis of the various situations, both family and work and making connections between these two spheres. For example, by describing a work situation involving her staff and her best friend, Sandra started to appreciate that she was responsible for the way they took advantage of her. By linking this to an upset with her mother-in-law, she was able to see the similarity between the two situations. In both cases, Sandra liked to retain control by taking on tasks which others could have done for themselves (including her aging mother-in-law) and then felt used by them. At times as a mentor, the author feigned misunderstanding to enable Sandra to recount the story from another angle so.

The third transition of reflection occurred when the focus turned to Sandra's emotional experience and how she dealt with rejection. She began to acknowledge her own needs for appraisal from others and compliments as well as her distress when these were not forthcoming. Sandra had kept her needs and distresses secret and not shared them with anyone including those closest to her. She felt challenged by the assertive individuals around her and threatened by potential conflict with them. By disclosing her needs and emotions, so, Sandra might gain some insight into what is happening and would be able to unburden to deal with the tension in relation to this. While difficult, this became important for her in dealing with issues of control and conflict both in her professional and personal spheres. Sandra appreciated that not declaring her goals and needs were preventing her emotional and professional development, further adding to her emotional burden. She learnt to model open communication and deal with the issues through mentoring.

## 4.10 Conclusion

A mentoring relationship potentially provides a release for mentees by permitting them a safe 'space' to unburden their serious concerns as well as enabling them to release the emotional tension associated with withholding this information over time and in so doing provides them with an opportunity for positive learning and development.

Mentors are responsible for working out which parts of their understanding differ from that of the mentee. While it is rare to think of uncovered information as a "hidden agenda" in mentoring, there may be things that go unsaid or unobserved, essentially unrecognised by both parties in mentoring. Hidden information may be a barrier to achieving a mutual relationship with the mentee.

## References

Alter, A. L., & Oppenheimer, D. M. (2009). Uniting the tribes of fluency to form a metacognitive nation. *Personality and Social Psychology Review, 13*(3), 219–235.

Andrade, E., Kaltcheva, V., & Weitz, B. (2002). Self-disclosure on the web: The impact of privacy policy, reward, and company reputation. *Advances in Consumer Research, 29*(1), 350–353.

Brewer, A. M. (2011). Mentoring. In S. Roffey (Ed.), *Positive relationships: Evidence-based practice across the world*. New York: Springer.

Collins, N. L., & Miller, L. C. (1994). Self-disclosure and liking: A meta-analytic review. *Psychological Bulletin, 116*(3), 457–475.

Derlega, V. J., & Berg, J. H. (Eds.). (1987). *Self-disclosure: Theory, research, and therapy*. New York: Plenum Press.

Fisher, R., Ury, W., & Patton, B. (1991). *Getting to yes: Negotiating agreement without giving in* (2nd ed.). New York: Penguin Books.

Greenberg, M. A., & Stone, A. A. (1992). Emotional disclosure about traumas and its relation to health: Effects of previous disclosure and trauma severity. *Journal of Personality and Social Psychology, 63*(1), 75–84.

Hartley, R. (2004). *Young people and mentoring: Towards a national strategy*. Retrieved from http://www.dsf.org.au/resources-and-research/126-young-people-and-mentoring-towards-a-national-strategy.

John, L. K., Acquisti, A., & Loewenstein, G. F. (2009). *The best of strangers: Context dependent willingness to divulge personal information*. Retrieved from http://ssrn.com/abstract=1430482.

Joinson, A. N., & Paine, C. B. (2007). Self-disclosure, privacy and the internet. In A. N. Joinson, K. Y. A. McKenna, T. Postmes, & U. D. Reips (Eds.), *Oxford handbook of internet psychology* (pp. 237–252). Oxford, UK: Oxford University Press.

Jourard, S. M. (1971). *Self-disclosure: An experimental analysis of the transparent self*. New York: Wiley.

Kant, I. (1900). *Critique of pure reason* (J. M. Meiklejohn, Trans.). New York: The Colonial Press.

Lane, J. D., & Wegner, D. M. (1995). The cognitive consequences of secrecy. *Journal of Personality and Social Psychology, 69*(2), 237–253.

Matsushima, R., & Shiomi, K. (2001). The effect of hesitancy toward and the motivation for self-disclosure on loneliness among Japanese high school students. *Social Behavior and Personality, 29*(7), 661–670.

Paine, C. B., Joinson, A. N., Buchanan, T., & Reips, U. D. (2006). Privacy and self-closure online. In *Extended abstracts of the conference on human factors in computing systems* (pp. 1187–1192). New York: ACM.

Pennebaker, J. W. (1990). *Opening up: The healing powers of confiding in others*. New York: Morrow.

Perrow, C. (1970a). Departmental power and perspectives in industrial firms. In M. Zald (Ed.), *Power in organizations* (pp. 59–89). Nashville: Vanderbilt Press.

Perrow, C. (1970b). *Organizational analysis: A sociological view*. Belmont: Wadsworth Pub. Co.

Perrow, C. (1993). *Complex organizations: A critical essay* (3rd ed.). New York: McGraw-Hill.

Turner, R. N., Hewstone, M., & Voci, A. (2007). Reducing explicit and implicit outgroup prejudice via direct and extended contact: The mediating role of self-disclosure and intergroup anxiety. *Journal of Personality and Social Psychology, 93*(3), 369–388.

# Chapter 5
# Blame

*Self-reverence, self-knowledge, self-control—these are the only way to sovereign power.*

—Tennyson

**Abstract** Understanding blame and its sources are the topic of this chapter as well as the role that power and control play in blaming. Mentors will appreciate how to assist the mentee deal with blame and the development of personal and professional boundaries.

When people engage in blaming, they do so as a response to a set of circumstances which have unexpectedly changed for them. The change may be overt and dramatic e.g. either they have been harmed in terms of reputation, change of status or role or injured in some way or seen harm or injury to others. The change may be less overt but equally significant to them in terms of someone acting disingenuously or failing to act according to agreed expectations, explicit or implicit. The aggrieved party responds by looking to blame either the person who is the instigator of the action, or someone or something else as a proxy. Why? Is it because they feel that someone should provide reparation to the harmed or injured parties or be admonished for delivering harm or failing to be accountable or meet the agreed terms of the "social contract". What if the action, such as the harm or injury or the inaction, was caused accidentally rather than deliberately? Would the aggrieved party's evaluation change as a consequence? When it comes to the process of blaming, mentoring assists by holding the mirror up to the mentee to show how various contributing factors of an event come into play and how fraught it is with implicit behavioural norms and power relationships.

Some people are quick to blame, and few never do so. The reason is that people respond to issues using different sets of assumptions. One set of assumptions may be about a 'just worldview' and seek reparation, another may focus on 'accountability based on risk' and seek compensation, another on 'victim blame' and provide latitude to the instigator and yet another based on 'prosocial behaviour' and so on. There is also a further difference when a group instigates a situation. Even so, an individual may be singled out as a substitute for the group and become the target of the aggrieved party's claim.



A.M. Brewer, *Mentoring from a Positive Psychology Perspective*,
DOI 10.1007/978-3-319-40983-2_5

The focus in this chapter is working through some key dimensions of blame that will assist the mentor in working with the mentee along an agreed path. Understanding the role of blame in a person's life is important for self-regulation, professional and personal development and ultimately a degree of satisfaction with outcomes. Mentoring can assist the mentee develop an awareness and reinforce a person's self-esteem in meeting both professional and personal standards. The mentor becomes a source of a "second opinion" in regard to the mentee's coping strategies and feelings, and if successful can rebuild feelings of control over their social or physical environment through the mentee taking appropriate action. Learning to handle criticism from others in the mentoring relationship is a key process.

## 5.1 What is Blame?

Blame is externalised as an "… act of attributing a personal failure to another person or event" (Fast and Tiedens 2010, p. 97). It can arise due to a sense of unfairness or bitterness as an aftermath for something going wrong. People perceive blame and feel its emotional effect such as frustration (Quigley and Tedeschi 1996) leading to anger, outrage, and guilt (discussed in the next chapter). Blame is also internalised and result in a person's "inner critic" engaging in self-admonishment.

In both cases blame is a form of "social judgment is a symbolic act, one that holds tacit implications for the self. As such, people treat evaluations of others as evaluations of themselves … and manage their judgments of others to affirm and retain flattering self-images" (Dunning's 2012, p. 496). There is a tendency for people to review their past actions and effectively bestow culpability retrospectively.

In its two forms, internalised or externalised, blame is either constructive or destructive depending on the context. If a mentee is engaging in self-blame, and this is unwarranted, then it is destructive. Blame needs to be attributed where it belongs. If a mentee is blaming others per se, and it is warranted, it is destructive. In each case, the converse is true depending on the situation.

In considering blame in mentoring, it is about moving the mentee away from blaming others or self-blame. It is essential that mentees do not become stuck in a blaming mindset. Not only is this unproductive for the mentee longer term but also in the short term, it inhibits the mentor's ability to learn what is really causing the problem and inhibits both to do anything meaningful to consider and eventually attribute it to where it belongs.

In every crisis, macro or micro, people look for those to blame; that is they look to attribute the responsibility for the accident, the disaster, the unfair policy, the governing regime to someone else.

## 5.2 Reasons and Sources of Blame

Attributing culpability for an action or an event outcome is central both to the law (Hall 1947) and to moral judgment (Weiner 1995) and if a forerunner for most legal recourse. Being found blameworthy legally has serious consequences (Inbar et al.

2012, 52). So while one person may not be culpable legally or otherwise, it is important to question: what part did I contribute to this outcome? What could have been done differently?

Blame is a powerful form of post hoc rationalisation. People either blame others for why things are as they are or turn it in on themselves. In blaming others they often perceive themselves as the good person who is trying to do their best and failed through no fault of their own. They may acknowledge that they participated in the event, however, were not responsible for the outcome. Legal decisions around who is blameworthy consider this too (Gray and Wegner 2011, p. 516).

Turning blame inwards is another matter. Emotions can be differentiated in terms of feelings, thoughts, appraisals, action tendencies, and actions (e.g., Frijda 1986; Roseman et al. 1994). Most people experience blame as a powerful emotional blow. It is rationalised by seeing the fault lies with other's shortfalls, mistakes or wrongdoings or as a performance deficit, a failure, a lack of responsibility or inaction by them.

When things go amiss in life, most people look for reasons why. Sometimes it is not apparent, and the next thing people question is who is responsible? And following that who is accountable? The closer the mishap affects a person, the more they will seek answers to these questions to avoid cognitive dissonance. It is not so much to blame another rather they seek explanation. Depending on how readily forthcoming the information to their questions is will depend on the extent of their evaluation of the situation.

The absence of information may lead a person to attribute blame as a way of making sense of the situation. A list of sources of blame follows.

### *5.2.1 Sources of Blame at Work Include*

(a) Feeling powerless e.g. a sense of being blocked by another before the desired goal is attained and motivation is sapped.
(b) Lack of role clarity.
(c) Poor definition of responsibility and accountability.
(d) Oppositional role responsibilities interfacing with another.
(e) A colleague relying on allies to enhance their position.
(f) Competing for the sake of competing.
(g) Perceiving something out of context.
(h) Poor performance criteria.
(i) Interdependence and shared performance resources.
(j) Poor channels of communication.
(k) Information overload.

A second reason for blame is that people expect that events proceed in a fair and reasonable way. The greater this expectation, the more people are likely to blame something or someone when things go awry (Dalbert 2009). Depending on the outcome of the event, people will develop a reason or justification for it based on their experience of similar issues or incidents events. If they are personally harmed or injured or someone else is they will expect to be recompensed. Another source of blame surrounds less implicit harm such as professional reputation or personal integrity which could occur directly as a consequence of an event or indirectly. In this case also, people seek to be recompensed.

Often people blame the person at the centre of the incident or a close colleague, supervisor for not taking greater responsibility. Blame often takes the form of why did they put themselves in that situation? In other words, the victim is responsible for their predicament because, in a fair world, they are in control of the situation and should have known about how to avoid it. For people who believe the world is unfair, there is no inconsistency and, therefore, no need to blame the victim (Van den Bos and Maas 2009).

If the blame cannot be pinpointed, a mentee may engage in self-blame. The form of this may start with "why me?" and then gather intensity to the point where they feel guilty characterised by how did they come to be in that situation? Why did they put themselves in that situation?

These are questions that a mentee may voice and a clear marker for the mentor to be alert to for critical reflection analysing their beliefs about blame in relation to the circumstances, which trigger "disorienting dilemmas" (Mezirow and Taylor 2009). These conundrums consequently deepen critical self-criticism. They are important opportunities for the mentor to initiate reflective discourse with the mentee, so as to transform and expand understandings of their needs, goals and interests and those of others.

The professional or workplace culture also guides people in the event of a mishap in terms of what they should or should not do as well as what they can and cannot do. The culture will be shaped by regulations and policies in place governing specific events such as fraud, workplace health and safety, discrimination and harassment. In events outside this the work culture provides some guidance depending on how its values and beliefs have been articulated and strengthened. A mentor can assist the mentee to identify these norms and values as a way of dealing with issues of blame.

People have a sense of both in their lives either through their formal institutional memberships or through socialisation (particularly norms that establish role expectations and obligations in a given society) and use both according to their knowledge and attitudes that are, in the case of the latter, attuned to their beliefs, motivation and experience. Aspects of one's national culture that provide order and control (i.e., social norms and rules), and those that provide a valued personal identity (i.e., heritage and history). In the main if someone transgresses a workplace policy, e.g. a teacher takes a class on a field trip while, under the influence of alcohol and an accident occurs, this results in greater blame. People perceive situations as less fair and expressed higher intent to address the wrongdoing when the consequences were high in severity and when a person who should have known better is responsible (Nicklin and Williams 2009).

When people work professionally, guided by clear implemented policies and norms they are more likely to comply and if they do not, they will be deemed irresponsible and their supervisor may be also held accountable. Given that self-regulation involves monitoring and formative feedback, it is more useful for mentors to monitor actions rather than inactions, decisiveness rather than indecision (Coats et al. 1996; Wegner 1994). It is important that mentees understand how each contribute to these respective outcomes as disapproving versus approving, culpable versus laudable.

Credit is bestowed for achieving positive outcomes based on role responsibility, and approval is afforded a person for overcoming the temptation to do the wrong thing: e.g. avoiding lying, covering up or scapegoating others. Both involve effort and taking control of the situation by the main actor in the situation. Both instances accord with a Kantian view that is, an action is not praise or blameworthy unless it is done intentionally by the person either by enacting the responsibilities of their role or taking control of the situation and acting in the best interests of the wider group (Kant 1785/1996).

## 5.3 Self-regulation and Apportioning Blame

Blame stems from social relationships and is based on reciprocal evaluations and judgements of the self and others (Mallea et al. 2014). A person's belief system provides a yardstick by which they can choose, act and evaluate themselves and others in relation to this. Organisations wish to encourage people to do the right thing according to their job description, follow the rules and policies of the employer but also to act pro-socially (i.e. on behalf of others and/or for the public good). Thus although caring for others is always positively considered, there is a discretionary aspect of caring which lies outside a mandatory duty of care. This is particularly true when a person is not responsible for employees who do not directly report to them or distant familial relationships compared with the most obligatory nature of a manager's or a parental duty of care. Outside of a duty of care which defines particular responsibilities, a person's proximal relationships at work and in professional circles require stronger obligation from them in terms of their well-being although it is up to a person's judgement about how they respond. For example in a situation where things go wrong for a friend or colleague (e.g. a friend does not help another friend out of a tricky situation while travelling together, or a supervisor does not sponsor a direct report for promotion when there is every reason to do so) others will bestow judgement as not living up to their social obligations (Haidt 2003). In the example above, blame is attributed the friend and supervisor who are judged as having failed to assist or open up an opportunity when they could have done so for the 'injured' party. In situations where there is a conflict between the self-interest of a person and interest of a group (a social dilemma), a specific belief will motivate people to act in people's best interests (Frank 1988; Ketelaar 2004).

When attributing blame, people believe those culpable of wrongdoing or failing their responsibilities need to be penalised in line with the severity of the harm to the victims and the ongoing impact.

## 5.4 Identifying with the 'Victim' and the 'Offender'

Blame is felt vicariously by those who may be in no way directly affected by the transgression or harm. The reason for this is that in some way they identify with the victim, both directly and indirectly. (e.g. Hatfield et al. 1994), as well as how people may experience positive and negative feelings as a result of their social identity or association with successful or unsuccessful others (e.g. Cialdini and de Nicholas 1989; Tajfel and Turner 1986; Tesser 1988) or may experience vicarious dissonance from the acts of others (Norton et al. 2003) For example, if a young girl is run over by a hit-and-run driver, other parents of similar aged daughters in particular; parents or the community, in general, will empathise with the affected parents and may feel outraged by the event.

Self-blame could also be a projective identification with the offender and a fear that deep down a person may have done or could engage in similar actions.

## 5.5 Power and Control

People either experience a sense of control over their professional and personal situations or wish to do so. In both cases, real or expected events and decisions intercede and jeopardise a person's perceived control and sense of self-efficacy e.g. redundancy, the "glass ceiling" and other missed opportunities. To counteract this, people need to engage in self-preservation to regain a sense of control and a feeling of well-being and to minimise anxiety—positivity if you like (Shepherd et al. 2011).

Control is an important motivator (Deci and Ryan 1987). People are motivated to reach or maintain a sense of general control over themselves now as well as future events and outcomes. People require (a) acceptance and approval from others; (b) draw on their status, power, and the control of resources; and most importantly (c) predictability and order (Hogan and Holland 2003). These motives, if they are appropriately directed towards group goals, assist people to form positive relationships with others as well as helping them make sense of their contribution to a situation, professionally or otherwise. Further, people try to make sense of their world as a way of anticipating theirs and other future actions. This set of expectations is employed so that they can ascertain what might happen and be ready to control events and activities as they unfold so that they are able to achieve worthwhile outcomes.

However, when a person's control is frustrated, people seek to remedy this. Whereas primary control means the ability to control desired outcomes directly, secondary control is described as re-gaining control more indirectly (Skinner 2007). For example, if a person has the authority to direct a project this is primary control. If however a person is a member of the team they rely on their 'horizontal' influence to shape outcomes, hence secondary control. If a workplace mentor is being employed, a mentee will trust them to assist them in certain situations, hence the notion of vicarious control.

Sometimes a mentee's personal sense of control is undermined by either a direct or indirect threat or fear of intimidation. One approach to handling anxiety about being intimidated is for the mentor to ask the mentee: why they may be feeling this way? If there no tangible evidence of a threat, then it is important that the mentor assists the mentee through bolstering their self-affirmation. For example, this process is achieved by getting the mentee to focus on their strengths and achievements and using this knowledge to deal with the current threat. In extreme situations that individuals compensate the negative thinking with positive thinking as a way of reducing cognitive dissonance. However, this compensatory effect may be short-lived. People who have experienced shock and upset (e.g. returning war veterans) often find a way to reduce their anxiety referred to as "fluid compensation" (Park et al. 2012). Research has shown that people employ self-efficacy unconsciously. For example people with high self-esteem automatically compensate for the "gap" by acknowledging it and then engendering their positive qualities (and repress their weaknesses) following failure feedback (Helgeson et al. 2006)—demonstrating outward benefit.

## 5.6 Blame as a Form of Entrapment

Blame is complex to understand because you need to unravel the cause-effect relationships between variables that are difficult to tease out in everyday interactions (Bradbury and Fincham 1990). Blame can have detrimental effects depending on how it attributed both in measure and how public it is.

It fundamentally damages trust and respect and undermines relationships, values and beliefs. It has a deleterious effect upon workplace cultures as it affects the attitudes of everyone. Often mentees describe their workplace culture as a "blame culture" characterised by tight hierarchical control, micromanagement and low trust. Once this type of culture takes hold, it is hard to dissolve. Changing the leader and not the team will not achieve a turnaround or the opposite. Attempting to refresh the culture with the existing group rarely works as it is hard to overcome distrust. The lesson here is to ensure that the workplace or team culture is consultative, based on fairness and open communication.

## 5.7 Women and Men

The "think manager-think male" (TMTM) notion resonates in work situations. For example, when a woman does not perform well, her "gender" may be held responsible (Ryan and Haslam 2005, 2007). One explanation apart from "victim-blaming" is that women are often selected to lead in difficult times, not because they are expected to redress the situation, rather they are seen to be decisive, work well with people. They are often easy targets to take the blame for organisational failure (Ryan et al. 2011). In Australia, this has frequently occurred with female political leaders both at the State and Nationally. Alternatively if a woman is selected for a role over a man blame my come in the form of attributing the woman's promotion to being provided with an unfair advantage due to her gender. This claim might find support amongst others. Similar examples are cited in regard to team performance where often women are blamed for letting the team down (Haynes and Lawrence 2012).

## 5.8 Dealing with Blame Through Mentoring

Cognitive dissonance studies have shown that "getting people to act contrary to their attitudes (when they believe they have freely chosen to do so) is a powerful way to change beliefs and attitudes, including low self-esteem" (Rizvi and Linehan 2005). A mentor encouraging a mentee to reconsider their position when they feel justified in blaming another (whether this is appropriate or not) is a powerful instigator for attributing the sentient to where it belongs regardless of the legalities of any situation. The example used here is an individual and their work group.

[Before continuing to read on here, you may wish to refer back to table in Sect. 1.1 of this book, where some of the changes that trigger blaming are outlined].

A person's life is interrupted when a change or an incident occurs (e.g. losing their job) changing the nature of how they see things including perceptions around key relationships and indeed the context. The intensity of the change is dependent on the meaning the person assigns to it and how significant it is in altering their life. For example, loss of employment needs to be considered in the context of the person's e.g. age, prospect for future employment, financial reserves, number of dependents, labour market opportunities, expected loss of employment as well as the level of personal and professional disruption they experience as a consequence. It may also change whether or not they can continue to function as they expected to do prior to this event. Regardless of the nature of the change, a person's usual routines are interrupted in some way. The affected person has to adjust to meet the demands being placed on them due to this incident. The incident is perceived to be dislocating in terms of self-concept depending on the degree they identified with their work or professional role; perceptions of others, their roles and relationships, changing boundaries, communication patterns, norms, intentions and values.

Understanding these aspects and teasing them out in mentoring is important in understanding the complexity of blame for the mentee who finds themselves in such a situation.

In the face of a blame-inducing incident, people will initially question their own part in it and self-concept. The mentee's understanding of who they are and how they relate to others and their social worth may become confused. What is concealed prior to the event may become clearer or not as the case may be. The incident such as redundancy may produce a marked shift in roles, depending on the gravity of the issue for people. Some will welcome the "nest egg" others will not. There will be a shifting of power with some people jockeying to influence the situation and particularly, the outcomes. Often, conflicts will arise intensifying the blaming. These conflicts limit a person's capacity to diagnose what is going on and to adjust to an incident. Thus, assessment of the nature of the changes to roles by the mentor is critical as it offers an understanding into one aspect of the chaos and conflict for the mentee thus releasing anxiety for them.

### 5.8.1 *Personal and Professional Boundaries*

The mentee's boundaries including tasks, social and psychological need to be understood as these may be perceived as significantly altered. Boundaries are used by the mentee to manage internal and external interactions (McLendon and Petr 2005) and allow a balance of connection and independence with others especially at work. A psychological boundary is one that serves as an injunction/expectation for when and how colleagues can interact (Hartmann 1991). Subsystems and coalitions within the mentee's professional sphere or workplace lead to a significant change following an individual's loss of job or redundancy. Blame is often a response to ward off a pending change or a sign to understand what lies beneath it.

The impact on the routine and functioning of the mentee (Myer and Moore 2006) is an example of the way boundaries can be altered following an incident. The more a person's daily routine is altered by an incident, the more existing boundaries are affected.

Another example that a mentee may bring to mentoring is where their work group experiences a situation involving some group members and not others. For example, some of the members may be made redundant or become incapacitated due to a workplace accident but not the mentee. These incidents not only severely disrupt work group boundaries but also the mentee's boundaries such as a sense of autonomy. In both cases, a mentee may experience "survivor guilt" and find this very troubling. If a mentor senses this level of anxiety or the mentee raises it during mentoring, this information helps both understand the complexity of the incident and work together to develop interventions to reinstate a sense of stability and a way forward for the mentee.

Boundary ambiguity is associated with a disturbance in the usual or expected unfolding of actions or events (Manning 2009). In crisis situations, boundary ambiguity can become exacerbated by past encounters and relationships that have been unproductive (Manning 2009). The greater the experience of nonconformity in boundaries, the more severe the impact on the people involved in it. Reconsidering boundaries assists the mentee develop a sense of order around the situation of uncertainty e.g. in the case of the threat or loss of employment. Boundaries can be made more permeable or rigid depending on the mentee's perception of the incident and the manner in which boundaries are used (Carroll et al. 2007).

### 5.8.2 *Communication*

Closely related to the concept of boundaries involves the flow and exchange of information preceding the event, during it and post. In many cases, blame may be directed at the failure of adequate communication not only in terms of the nature and frequency of communication but also the quality of listening and sharing of information. In the aftermath, situations, communication patterns are modified because of uncertainty about the situation (Tjersland et al. 2006), disagreement about what should have been done and actions now required (Coombs 2012), and the desire to establish control (Lalonde and Roux-Dufort 2013). Communication patterns will become chaotic during an event which induces blame.

How the mentee describes a situation of change or crisis and who is to blame is significant. The description may focus on directly observed facts, their hearsay from others, or they may provide an obviously embellished account of what went on. For the mentor, it is important to work with the mentee to ascertain how chaotic the account is compared to the event, whether or not there is a desire to assign blame by the mentee or from others towards them. The aim is to establish a sense of control as the mentee attempts to cope with the situation.

The mentor needs to be attentive to changes in the way the mentee is communicating to detect some of the emotions they are experiencing associated with this event. Another issue concerns the trustworthiness of communication or a tendency to embellish excessively the severity of situations (i.e., created unwarranted catastrophes).

The nature of the incident can be instrumental in the type of change in communication patterns. For example, sexual harassment may result in the exchange of information with only selected members of a work group. Communication might also be altered due to the fact that some work group members are no longer available or are not able to communicate. Blaming may be a way to desensitise their feelings about this issue. While mentoring, the mentor needs to consider the type of information exchanged or not exchanged. Confessions may be made, demands placed on others, fears expressed, and declarations proffered that would not otherwise have occurred. At other times, information may be less forthcoming as so that people protect themselves from further being identified with the incident and its possible negative effects on them personally or professionally. Identifying the changes in communication patterns is an important part of understanding the mentee's response to such an incident.

### 5.8.3 Norms

A norm is a guide or a custom for action (Fehr and Fischbacher 2004). Norms also govern expectations about how work is to be conducted as well as how a person responds to specific situations. Norms around conversational topics in an operating theatre amongst male and female surgeons and nurses or gossip amongst professionals are examples of this. Such norms provide structure and consistency in a professional setting. When all members comply with the norms, everyone understands what is going on. However, when norms are breached in some way by one or more members, the sense of co-operation is undermined. The person perceived to be responsible for the breach is less believed and marginalised. These changes not only change co-operation within the group but also can reverberate to the wider situation as people gossip about it. In other words, the adjustment to change may cause work group members to interact or react quite differently, positively or negatively.

When an incident affects work group processes, people can become distracted and focus on things tangential to work or the incident. Assessment of changes in work group norms assists mentees to understand better observed actions within the work group. Interventions can then be tailored to help people regenerate norms that can help them to adjust as well as others to work together to resolve the situation if possible.

### 5.8.4 Aims

Work gives people direction and to engage in prosocial actions. When things do not proceed according to intentions, people experience unexpected uncertainty. For example, when the economy is stable, a small-business is likely to develop goals that provide security and stability for staff including additional rewards and benefits. In periods of financial downturn, the goals may have to change and consequently, are no longer perceived by staff as secure, predictable, realistic, or obtainable. Because of the uncertainty, staff may become resistant, voice their concerns and blame management. The lack of uncertainty regarding long-term goals can precipitate individual work group members to doubt their individual competence, the competence of other work group members, and/or the work group's competence to sustain itself financially and can lead to greater stress and disarray in the functioning of the work group. This issue may be brought to mentoring for discussion.

It is important for the mentor to note that following a change at work especially if unexpected, mentees may engage in less logical thinking and more towards dealing or not with their emotions. When all is going well, people may engage in a logical process to resolve issues of concern. When things are not going well, they may resort to blaming through fear of uncertainty without reviewing what part they played in bringing the situation about. The mentee may become too short-sighted and/or unrealistic to see things clearly and seek out a mentor as a result.

The mentoring relationship serves to hold the mentee together during the immediate peak of a crisis over an issue. The mentor assists the mentee to deal with the emotional highs and lows before working on specifics. Working through a realistic assessment of the impact of an incident should include exploring the reality of how the mentee is affected. This approach is aimed at assisting the mentee to regain a sense of security and stability.

### *5.8.5 Values*

Values provide a stimulus for the mentee's attitudes and actions. They may be experiencing a misalignment of values personally and professionally. The values that a person considers important may be altered by the perceived uncertainty of an unexpected change or incident. Values may be altered as perceptions of mentee's needs change especially in response to change (Schmidt and Welsh 2010). For example, a person may decide that they are investing too much time into their work triggered by a personal or professional change in their life which has brought on a mounting pressure between the demands of paid work and their personal and family life. A mentee who previously prioritised work ahead of personal life may rebalance their priorities and invest more time in their personal life. This change leads to an adjustment in their personal value set which may not align with the expectations of their employer as far as available time spent at or for work.

As with the previous characteristics, assessment of changes to values gives mentors important information to work with the mentee towards resolving issues. Examining the changes in values helps mentors to assist people to balance, actively and rationally their individual needs and collective values and determine whether work group decisions are logical in light of their values and are not solely emotional responses to the stress of the incident. A problem-solving approach that ways the costs and benefits of decisions in light of the work group's circumstances, values, and goals can be very beneficial.

The above factors are interrelated and overlap to some degree. However, understanding the changes that take place in each of the characteristics is critical for providing crisis intervention services to people.

## 5.9 Conclusion

Blame often ensues due to a lack of clarity about goals, roles, responsibilities, delegations and lack of information and resources. Good planning is an optimal method to prevent everyone pointing the finger at each other. Blame is often illogical. Often a person blames others for similar faults that the evaluator has e.g. people in glass houses shouldn't throw stones. Applying a double standard could also be interpreted as blame when used to disenfranchise one of two equally guilty parties. This approach is especially true when the disingenuous person fails to see that the standard he or she is applying to others is equally applicable to him or herself. Blame can be contrasted with disingenuous. In both cases, individuals content the integrity of one over others. There are two ways to do so: lifting oneself up (as in pretence) or knocking down someone else (as in blame).

One way to manage blame both at the individual and collective levels is through open and reflective questioning. It is important to interrogate what occurred? Why did it occur? What outcome were the mentee and mentor aiming for and expected? How can they ensure that this outcome is not repeated? What lessons are to be learned from this?

## References


Bradbury, T. N., & Fincham, F. D. (1990). Attributions in marriage: Review and critique. *Psychological Bulletin*, 107, 3–33.

Carroll, J. S., Olson, C., & Buckmiller, N. (2007). Family boundary ambiguity: A 30-year review of theory, research, and measurement. *Family Relations, 56*(2), 210–230.

Cialdini, R. B., & De Nicholas, M. E. (1989). Self-presentation by association. *Journal of Personality and Social Psychology, 57*, 626–631.

Coats, E. J., Janoff-Bulman, R., & Alpert, N. (1996). Approach versus avoidance goals: Differences in self-evaluation and well-being. *Personality and Social Psychology Bulletin, 22* (10), 1057–1067.

Coombs, T. W. (2012). *Ongoing crisis communication: Planning, managing, and responding* (3rd ed.). Thousand Oakes, CA: Sage Publications.

Dalbert, C. (2009). Belief in a just world. In M. R. Leary & R. H. Hoyle (Eds.), *Handbook of individual differences in social behaviour* (pp. 288–297). New York: Guilford.

Deci, E. L., & Ryan, R. M. (1987). The support of autonomy and the control of behaviour. *Journal of Personality and Social Psychology, 53*, 1024–1037.

Dunning, D. (2012). The relation of self to social perception. In M. R. Leary, & J. P. Tangney's (Eds.), *Handbook of self and identity* (pp. 481–501). New York: Guilford Press.

Fast, N. J., & Tiedens, L. Z. (2010). Blame contagion: The automatic transmission of self-serving attributions. *Journal of Experimental Social Psychology, 46*(1), 97–106.

Fehr, E., & Fischbacher, U. (2004). Social norms and human cooperation. *Trends in Cognitive Sciences, 8*(4), 185–190.

Frank, R. H. (1988). Passions within Reason: the strategic role of the emotions. New York: Norton.

Frijda, N. H. (1986). *Emotions*. Cambridge: Cambridge University Press.

Gray, K., & Wegner, D. M. (2011). To escape blame, don't be a hero—Be a victim. *Journal of Experimental Social Psychology, 47*(2), 516.
Haidt, J. (2003). The emotional dog does learn new tricks: A reply to Pizarro and Bloom. *Psychological Review, 110*(1), 197–198.
Hall, J. (1947). General Principles of Law (2nd Ed.) Indianapolis: Bobbs-Merrill.
Hartmann, E. (1991). *Boundaries of the mind.* New York: Basic Books.
Hatfield, E., Cacioppo, J., & Rapson, R. (1994). *Emotional contagion.* New York, NY: Cambridge University Press.
Haynes, M. C., & Lawrence, J. S. (2012). Who's to blame? Attributions of blame in unsuccessful mixed-sex work teams. *Basic and Applied Social Psychology, 34*(6), 558.
Helgeson, V. S., Reynolds, K. A., & Tomich, P. L. (2006). A meta-analytic review of benefit finding and growth. *Journal of Consulting and Clinical Psychology, 74*, 797–816.
Hogan, J., & Holland, B. (2003). Using theory to evaluate personality and job performance relations: A socio-analytic perspective. *Journal of Applied Psychology, 88*, 100–112.
Inbar, Y., Pizarro, D. A., & Cushman, F. (2012). Benefiting from misfortune: When harmless actions are judged to be morally blameworthy. *Personality and Social Psychology Bulletin, 38* (1), 52–62.
Kant, I. (1785/1996). Groundwork of the metaphysics of morals. In M. J. Gregor & A. Wood (Eds.), (Trans.). *Practical philosophy: The Cambridge edition of the works of Immanuel Kant* in Cambridge. Cambridge: Cambridge University Press.
Ketelaar, T. (2004). Ancestral emotions, current decisions: Using evolutionary game theory to explore the role of emotions in decision-making. In C. Crawford & C. Salmon (Eds.) *Evolutionary Psychology public policy and personal decisions.* (pp. 145–168). Mahwah: Lawrence Erlbaum Associates.
Lalonde, C., & Roux-Dufort, C. (2013). Challenges in teaching crisis management: Connecting theories, skills, and reflexivity. *Journal of Management Education, 37*(1), 21–50.
Manning, M. (2009). The effects of subjective norms on behaviour in the theory of planned behaviour: A meta-analysis. *British Journal of Social Psychology, 48*(4), 649–705.
Mallea, B. F., Guglielmob, S., & Monroe, A. E. (2014). A theory of blame. *Psychological Inquiry, 25*(2), 147–186.
McLendon, D., & Petr, C. (2005). Family-direct structural therapy. *Journal of Marital and Family Therapy, 31*, 327–339.
Mezirow, J., & Taylor, E. (Eds.). (2009). *Transformative learning in action.* San Francisco: Jossey-Bass.
Moore, D., Monaghan, E. J., & Hartmann, D. K. (1997). "Values of literacy history" *Reading Research Quarterly*, 32: 90–102.
Myer, R. A., & Moore, H. B. (2006). Crisis in context theory: An ecological model. *Journal of Counselling and Development, 84*(2), 139–147.
Nicklin, J. M., & Williams, K. J. (2009). Reactions to others' mistakes: An empirical test of fairness theory. *The Journal of Psychology, 143*(5), 533–558.
Norton, M. I., Monin, B., Cooper, J., & Hogg, M. (2003). Vicarious dissonance: attitude change from the inconsistency of others. *Journal of Personality and Social Psychology, 85*(1), 47–62.
Quigley, B. M., & Tedeschi, J. T. (1996). Mediating effects of blame attributions on feelings of anger. *Personality and Social Psychology Bulletin*, 22, 1280–1288.
Park, C. L., Mills, M. A., & Edmondson, D. (2012). PTSD as meaning violations: Testing a cognitive worldview perspective. *Psychological Trauma Theory Research Practice and Policy, 4*, 66–73.
Rizvi, S. L., & Linehan, M. M. (2005). The treatment of maladaptive shame in borderline personality disorder: A pilot study of opposite action. *Cognitive and Behavioural Practice, 12*, 437–447.
Roseman, I. J., Wiest, C., & Swartz, T. S. (1994). Phenomenology, behaviours and goals differentiate discrete emotions. *Journal of Personality and Social Psychology, 8*(2), 206–221.
Ryan, M. K., & Haslam, S. A. (2005). The glass cliff: Evidence that women are over-represented in precarious leadership positions. *British Journal of Management*, 16: 81–90.

Ryan, M. K., & Haslam, S. A. (2007). The glass cliff: Exploring the dynamics surrounding the appointment of women to precarious leadership positions. *The Academy of Management Review* Vol. 32, No. 2 (Apr., 2007), pp. 549–572.

Ryan, M. K., Haslam, S. A., Hersby, M. D., & Bongiorno, R. (2011). Think crisis-think female: The glass cliff and contextual variation in the think manager-think male stereotype. *Journal of Applied Psychology, 96*(3), 470.

Schmidt, C. K., & Welsh, A. C. (2010). College adjustment and subjective well-being when coping with a family member's illness. *Journal of Counseling & Development*, 88: 397–406.

Shepherd, S., Kay, A. C., Landau, M. J., & Keefer, L. A. (2011). Evidence for the specificity of control motivations in worldview defense: Distinguishing compensatory control from uncertainty management and terror management processes. *Journal of Experimental Social Psychology, 47*(5), 949–958.

Skinner, E. A. (2007). Secondary control critiqued: Is it secondary? Is it control? Comment on Morling and Evered (2006). *Psychological Bulletin, 133*, 911–916.

Tesser, A., & Collins, J. (1988). Emotion in social reflection and comparison situations: Intuitive, systematic, and exploratory approaches. *Journal of Personality and Social Psychology*, 55, 695–709.

Tjersland, O., Mossige, S., Gulbrandsen, W., Jensen, T., & Reichelt, S. (2006). Helping families when child sexual abuse is suspected but not proven. *Child and Family Social Work, 11*, 297–306.

Van den Bos, K., & Maas, M. (2009). On the psychology of the belief in a just world: Exploring experiential and rationalistic paths to victim blaming. *Personality and Social Psychology Bulletin, 35*(12), 1567.

Wegner, D. M. (1994). Ironic process of mental control. *Psychological Review, 101*(1), 34–52.

Weiner, B. (1995). Lessons from the past. *Psychological Inquiry, 6*(4), 319–321.

# Chapter 6
# Guilt

*My guiding principle is this: Guilt is never to be doubted.*
—Franz Kafka

**Abstract** People feel a sense of guilt when they feel they have breached a standard which they or others value. The Nature and Timing of Guilt is discussed. Guilt is also associated with shame, envy, and self-pity. Is guilt always negative? How do mentors assist mentees discuss issues around guilt and support them in this process?

While the quote above is taken out of context, its tenet holds as reading this chapter will show. Guilt, regardless of context, is self-limiting. Many constraints are self-imposed. These are the cognitive and emotional impediments that have taken hold over time, based on self-limiting, often rigidly held assumptions and attitudes about the way "I am". Mentoring mindedness seeks to address these by "unpicking" and understanding them. Reflection and feedback is important in this process, questioning these assumptions and attitudes to penetrate the underlying guilt. The mentor and the mentee work to enhance the latter's self-awareness as a way of encouraging them to achieve their aspirations and overcoming perceived fault.

Guilt is an emotion limited by internal censoring rather than by external influences. However, it is primarily a reactional stance by a mentee to the internal sentients, often perceived as being externally imposed. Moreover, a person may have experienced guilt for so long that it is now a deep-seated part of their self-concept. It may also act as a self-preservation stratagem which impedes their development as they continue to respond to its negative rather than positive components. All emotions develop as a response to an external or internal impetus. Emotions are useful in some situations and become impediments in others. All emotions serve some function at the time when they occur. Emotions become dysfunctional when they no longer serve the mentee's purpose, prolonged and block personal development (Izard 1977). When emotions become dysfunctional, they undermine the opportunity for realistic self-assessment. It is at this point of dysfunctionality that a person may decide they need assistance, not realising the part that guilt as an overriding emotion may be contributing to their predicament.

 
A.M. Brewer, *Mentoring from a Positive Psychology Perspective*,
DOI 10.1007/978-3-319-40983-2_6

The need for seeking a mentor is an overarching desire to fulfil one's expectations fuelled by a sense of trepidation that this is unlikely to happen. The apprehension is a deep-seated linked to a sense of self-guilt which is two-edged. It contains (a) the initial source of anxiety or felt guilt, for example, unfulfilled expectation about career aspirations or an experience of a significant failure combined with (b) feelings of embarrassment about feeling guilty. In addition to unfulfilled ambitions or disappointments, self-guilt also emanates from difficult conversations with colleagues and wide-ranging, troublesome situations.

Guilt is further related to an array of other emotions such as fear of being "found out" that one is not up to the current role held or being considered a "failure" in it. When frustration and anger with self occur to the point of not coping, a person is potentially paralysed. In mentoring the person may present in a heightened emotional way, either angry or easily intimidated by being overly apologetic or who continuously seeks unnecessary permission before they voice a viewpoint or take any action. Being excessively apologetic is a coping mechanism (Witvliet and McCullough in Post 2007) in dealing with the distress of self-sabotage even though it may not be recognised by the mentee in this way. This outcome is often the result of a very empathic person or someone who does not have clear professional or personal boundaries (Witvliet and McCullough in Post 2007) (see Chap. 5).

Mentoring creates a positive learning space to allow guilt and related emotions to surface and become the focus of reflection, without the mentee feeling that they are further evaluated. Talking about such feelings with a mentor and analysing their linkages to perceptions and difficult situations liberates mentees to work on developing a plan of action to assist in neutralising any negative feelings and to learn to respond appropriately to these in the future.

Mentoring is a positive process in that the mentee realises their power through learning—not only single loop learning but also through double-loop discovery (see Chap. 10). This form of learning encourages mentees to take risks while being supported by a mentor who is there to assist the mentee deal with stumbling blocks that are part and parcel of risk taking when trying out new strategies in situations where they are struggling. The ensuing trust forged between the mentee and mentor yields positive benefits both inside the mentoring relationship and beyond it both with others and in the longer term. The mentoring capital that develops for the mentee creates an inner reserve that the mentee draws from time and time again as they face new challenges.

## 6.1 Defining Guilt

Most people feel guilty at some stage. It can be short-lived or a prolonged sense that they carry with them throughout their life. There is a positive function to feeling guilt morally and ethically which will be discussed in this chapter. While it may serve a useful function at first, if prolonged it is usually felt as a negative experience and at its extreme, a burden leading to self-torment and even guilt-proneness (Tangney et al. 2007). As stated previously with few exceptions, everyone feels guilt following a failure to fulfil expectations, although it may be experienced differently from person to the next.

Researchers have attempted to distinguish guilt from shame. For example, shame is an emotion that engulfs the complete self, whereas guilt is associated with a specific misdemeanour (Lewis 1971). Shame is rarely shared compared to guilt. For example, a person may feel guilt for not doing enough to achieve an outcome such as completing a project on time and consequently feeling frustrated and disappointed due to not meeting their own expectations and those of others. This feeling is likely to be discussed. On the other hand, a person who brings disfavour onto their team or their organisation's reputation may feel shame and this is unlikely to be shared. Sharing one's feelings with others helps the mentee to cope.

Guilt and regret are also often confused. Regret is a way of redirecting guilt into sorrow sometimes on behalf of others. A sense of regret means that the person feeling remorse may even support the 'wounded parties' (Imhoff et al. 2012) and value it. However, most people turn the regret inwards and engage in self-pity. These aspects will be explored in this chapter.

## 6.2 The Nature and Timing of Guilt

Guilt like all emotions surfaces acutely and intensifies over time. Most people are motivated by the right thing to do in any situation based on their moral judgments and not always what is in their best interests. The issue is how intentional is this capacity? For example, a person stands up for someone being bullied at work even though this may be personally detrimental in terms of time investment, being seen as an informer and setting the victim ahead of the group.

However, if a person witnesses bullying and does nothing about it, it is assumed that they have chosen self-interest or imprudently think they are protecting the organisation's reputation over their legal and moral obligations as well as the rights of affected individuals. Non-reporting is regarded as morally agnostic when a person ignores evident wrong-doing intentionally, knowing the consequences. Guilt eventually arises if the 'non-reporter' eventually realises the impact of their actions on others, especially if in due course, someone becomes seriously disheartened, aggrieved or leaves the organisation. The 'witness' may cope by dismissing this knowledge and rationalise that they are powerless to do anything about it by being plagued by "what if..?" questions. People are more likely to respond to a situation requiring immediate action to resolve a problem quickly as opposed to one that is hidden and requires a longer term fix.

Feeling and expressing guilt for any wrongdoing is seen as worthy by most people. People, acting wrongly and not expressing any signs of guilt for their actions, are more likely to be blamed rather than understood. Introducing victim-impact statements into our legal system is an example of the perpetrator taking responsibility for their actions as well an opportunity to express remorse. In these situations, guilt is more likely to have a positive influence on motivation in reforming behaviour and future actions. While the perpetrator may not be praised for accepting responsibility and proclaiming their guilt, the victims and the community will feel more inclined to see that justice has been levelled. Others may be deterred from wrongdoing due to potential public censure and embarrassment (Cohen et al. 2012, p. 355).

Experiencing guilt is linked with regret and shame. Research shows that when people experience guilt they are more likely to think, feel, and act ethically (Tangney and Dearing 2002; Tangney et al. 2007, 2009, 2012).

As suggested above, guilt shapes people's attitudes and actions as in assuming responsibility for one's actions. Further, a person may feel guilty about not turning up to work on time even though no one notices it. If so their guilt may function to redirect their future actions and decisions about punctuality and strengthen their future resolve to arrive on time. In this case, guilt has a positive influence on motivation.

Feeling and expressing guilt is a way of manifesting a duty of care[1] to others and an attempt to restore genuine bonds that may have been broken. Psychologically, guilt is sensed when there is a disconnect between what the person believes is right including the morally correct thing to do and their subsequent actions if these fall short of the former. For example feeling guilty about not working back late when the organisation is under pressure or not fulfilling the requirements of the project to your best efforts. How deep the guilt is felt will depend on its nature, whether the person dwells on it, what the reasons for it will influence whether the experience worsens, is overcome or suppressed. In some instances especially if the issue becomes public, such as failing a performance deliverable, guilt is associated with public embarrassment or shame.

Psychological guilt is also experienced when a person(s) from a similar ethnic background violates the rights of a group from a different one. Collective guilt is a despairing feeling experienced when people perceive they or others (whom they identify with in some way e.g. ethnic, religious) is responsible for wrongly harming another, even when they are not personally responsible and had no connection with their actions (Gunn and Wilson 2011). An example is the historical mistreatment of Aboriginal Australians (Zimmermann et al. 2011). If there is no apology and no recompense, even in this situation some of the Australian population will feel psychological and social guilt for the past and current situation.

People's response to psychological guilt varies from a sense of "feeling bad"; owning up to their actions and either apologising on behalf of others or themselves e.g. I accept that my actions are discriminatory and issue an apology; I violated the rules and will recompense my team; or confessing to a misdemeanour and seeking a penalty.

[1]Generically and legally.

### 6.2.1 *Guilt and Shame*

Guilt and shame are activated when a person knowingly acts against what they know to be 'right' and cannot justify their actions to themselves even as a post hoc rationalisation. If this is the case, they can feel ashamed, embarrassed and confused. However, they will either struggle to alleviate their dissonance and guilt or seek to make amends. A mentor may assist the mentee to come to terms with this. For example, this can occur where a manager has treated a subordinate badly without reason. If the situation is not managed it may lead them to feel defensive, and this could exacerbate the situation (Tangney and Tracy 2012; Tangney et al. 2005). A person may feel guilt after offending her supervisor (action-focused), and feel shame when acting disloyally towards them. While guilt encourages accountability and an apology at times aimed at re-establishing relationships, shame tends to lead people to act in the opposite way. They may seek to run away from the situation or exit altogether so as to minimise further embarrassment and stigma. Mortification and guilt (but not shame) are emotions that people can use to help them restore stability in a situation while simultaneously inhibiting further indiscretions and encouraging them to make amends (Tangney and Tracy 2012).

### 6.2.2 *Envy*

Envy, generalised or specific, is also a reason why a mentee may decide to embark on mentoring. Envy occurs when a person feels aggrieved because they perceive they have been treated unfairly. This unfair treatment could be direct and specific or generalised in that they were dealt an unfair hand by life. Envy then involves a process of social comparison (Ortony et al. 1988). Mentees may be experiencing envy about why others are being promoted, and they are not or about a specific peer whom they compete with has now been made their supervisor through a highly sought after promotion. Envy is experienced more intensely the closer it is to the mentee both in relational and skill terms because the opportunities were there for them to achieve also and believe that they should have attained the role. Envy is more intensely felt, when they dislike the person they were competing against (Smith et al. 1996).

The mentee may only have a tacit understanding of the part envy plays in this situation. They may not be able to admit their own feelings of envy as it would be admitting to their weaknesses not only in not getting the job but also in feeling envy itself. If the mentee does not accept feeling envious, s/he will seek to cover it up both to themselves and others by making excuses such as they were not interested in the role, too many other commitments to take on such a senior role or blame political manoeuvrings behind the scenes (Salovey and Rodin 1984). Such tactics to suppress envy while relieving self and social damage can lead to longer-term self-destruction such as not applying for the next promotion and thereby curtailing not only career advancement but also career development.

Moreover, a mentee may not have expressed the felt envy to anyone else, and so if it is discussed with a mentor for the first time, it is a deeply significant and confronting moment for the mentee. It is one issue that a mentor might wish to probe as the relationship develops and their mentee's trust is gained. They may have been suppressing this view up until their meeting with the mentor where this is first raised and struggling with their emotions about it.

It is healthy to use others as a benchmark for both performance and achievements. The reason for this is that most people engage in some form of social comparison with peers or others at some stage so as to learn from them in some way. Much of this occurs without any sense of resentment, an emotion underlying envy. Learning by social comparison is natural from a very young age, where peers become the benchmark for action and then performance.

Most people strive for self-improvement and this requires a yardstick for self-assessment. Peer comparison is often used for the purpose of judging one's performance or outcomes against another. It is often competitive but not necessarily. Even if it is, this should not be viewed as necessarily negative. On balance, people's definition of success and failure are constructed by comparing their own performances to those of others.

Most people compete in some way: from the time they first enter school until they retire. Competition necessitates self-comparison with others: what they have attained and how they perform. Outside of these domains, people strive to compete for resources whether this is in the form of opportunities and access to resources. Being competitive relies on an individual's capability and talent as well as their accumulated resources such as knowledge, access to income and so on. Sometimes these are inherited biologically, familial and others have been competed for by staving off others.

When a person compares favourably to others on a given dimension, it is typically met with a positive affective response. And so people learn to feel rewarded when they compete favourably with others which in turn increases the likelihood that the strategy worked and is likely to be repeated.

People's response is to strive hard to enhance one's chances or appeal so as to achieve an improved future outcome (Buss and Dedden 1990). Most societies are successful because of this go all-out behaviour. When people compete and do not achieve the desired outcome, some are not daunted by defeat and invest even more effort to achieve the desired outcome. Others "give up". People, who are outperformed, feel okay if the outcome is fair. If not, competing and losing may lead to them to feeling resentment. Both emotions are characterised as envy (Smith and Kim 2007). A second response is to render the competition less attractive or appealing.

Gaining insight into envy assists a mentee conceptually to identify what they are trying to achieve and how this relates to their sense of hurt. If well-founded, the mentor can assist the mentee to develop a course of action to redress both deficits in their actions and emotions. Dealing with the underlying issue rather than a surface one helps the mentee come to terms with it and readjust for next time.

Superiority is far more negative emotion. It is a form of self-satisfaction in relation to others. It may target another's misfortune, termed 'schadenfreude' (Smith et al. 1996) e.g. not getting a job, losing out on a project, failing an exam and so on. How open should a mentor be in pointing out to a mentee that they detect the mentee's triumphalism? Through an appropriate questioning and problem-solving approach discussed in earlier chapters, particularly Chap. 3, it is skilfully handled by the mentor and should be. Peers and supervisors would be well aware of a person's high-handedness. This posture is a sign of emotional immaturity and potentially a reason why a mentee's career is or will stagnate.

### *6.2.3 Guilt and Self-pity*

Expressions of self-pity are not often forthcoming in mentoring. However, there are signs that can alert the mentor about this such as the ways that mentees use to cope in difficult situations, such as escape, physical or mental, preventing them from going to great lengths to conceal their guilt. Self-pity, rumination and projection confusion blocks coming to terms with the issue as these intensify felt-distress and throw any attempts to analyse the situation into chaos. People become self-absorbed and focus on the emotion rather than the issue at hand. Self-pity leads to disengagement by personalising issues, becoming defensive, intensifying negative rather than positive emotions.

Mentoring provides the way out of guilt through engagement with a trusted mentor and assists the mentee to re-engage with the problem at hand. The mentor and mentee discover and learn not only about the things that are self-undermining but also how to build a strategy to meet these challenges. Mentoring forms a positive relational resource as a result.

## 6.3 Positive Guilt

Guilt, like envy and unlike superiority, is often associated with regret, tension, and remorse (Tilghman-Osborne et al. 2010). However feeling guilt can be associated with positive outcomes and has been linked to expressing empathy and compassion (Flynn and Schaumberg 2012). Psychological guilt can also be social that is interpersonal, derived from the knowledge of having caused inexcusable harm to another or, in a more general sense, of not having behaved selflessly and lacking consideration for others.

Feeling guilt after the event demonstrates a degree of empathy (Basile and Mancini 2011, p. 98). Experiencing an event where someone is disadvantaged or penalised through no fault of their own e.g. a colleague is made redundant; a group struck by a natural disaster and not doing anything about it even if they are not the perpetrator nor within their control to prevent it, can lead to experienced guilt. When such events occur, guilt may be experienced collectively: a group-based emotion experienced (Caouette et al. 2012) even though they may not be responsible for the harm at all.

Individually, guilt may be expressed both with consequences for the person experiencing it or not. A person may reveal a secret which has dire consequences for others and feel guilty about being the source of such feelings or not spending sufficient time with a person, who subsequently commits suicide.

Under these circumstances, guilt is a positive emotion providing there is an examination of it as it could lead to altruistic actions from others when people go over what might have been done differently. Other-oriented employees tend to empathise with and feel responsible for other people, tendencies that leave them prone to anticipating feeling guilty if they let others down (Eisenberg 2000). Philanthropic giving is an example of this whereby people examine the situation of their own against others and decide to make a difference often assuaging guilt over their fortunate circumstances. This form of altruism may also be an example of "collective guilt" not essentially negative nor labelled, where others are encouraged to give to a worthy cause based on their feelings of feeling "better off" than others less fortunate. Guilt serves a prosocial function by inhibiting damaging actions and inducing people to apologise and make restitution for wrongdoing (Ciarrocchi and Murray-Swank 2007) Becoming a mentor could be another example of this.

Guilt is thus something a person feels if they link their actions to a misadventure or wrongdoing, relative to a local moral order. Guilt need not ensue in such situations (there is no direct, automatic link involved), but there is at least a normative reason to feel guilt. Other emotions can also accompany the experience of having acted wrongly. One can be angry with oneself, be embarrassed, or self-disgust. For example, if I act wrongly toward person A, who then, because of this commits a crime, B against person C, then I would not normally be seen as responsible for—hence guilty of—B. Guilt relations are thus not causal (for if A causes B, which causes C, then A is also the cause of C), but normative (Hollis 1977). "Cultivating feelings of anticipated guilt, other-orientation strengthens the association between core self-evaluations and job performance." (Grant and Wrzesniewski 2010, p. 110).

## 6.4 The Role of Guilt in Influencing Others

People who are successful at influencing others are highly attuned to the needs of their followers, prioritising others' interests ahead of their own (Choi and Mai-Dalton 1998; Conger and Kanungo 1994). Increasing a sense of moral purpose is a strategy used by 'influentials' to bring value and alignment of the various competing interest groups together. For example, this could include the overarching mission of an institution, a team working within that organisation and the individual staff. Responding to a higher order is something that most humans find deeply motivating. It is also a way of eliminating guilt about being selfish when a person's goals can be aligned with something wider than themselves (Carpenter et al. 2006). However, guilt may still be present in the form of dissonance between the institution's principles and those of the people working for an organisation which is being publically rebuked because of its actions, products or services e.g. church, government, schools, university staff.

A sense of guilt decreases the negativity of any dissonance if people find some way of dealing with the criticism and also assuaging the discontent (Polman and Ruttan 2012, p. 131) Mentors can assist mentees experiencing intense guilt by assisting them develop strategies to show empathy and improve their conflict handling skills resolving conflicts. If these skills are developed, mentees are less likely to deepen the conflict and bring about some resolution even if there is no substantive change taken by the institution (Cohen et al. 2012). Mentees can bolster their influencing skills by assuming a stronger sense of responsibility for their action or collusion in actions that led to a conflict e.g. making a difference which may be related to a sense of guilt about "the way things are" (Schaumberg and Flynn 2012, p. 327).

## 6.5 Revealing Guilt to a Mentor

Social emotions are influential in creating and sustaining and at times, terminating relationships. Emotions are central in ensuring socially appropriate behaviors and compensating for inappropriate ones.

The experience of guilt, whether it is a feeling of worthlessness, incompetence or inappropriate, is discomforting. It is important to appreciate how a sense of guilt relates to the core of their self-concept. A mentee's guilt can lead to inadvisable actions and decisions which in turn exacerbates other relationships and life outside of work.

There are feelings that the experience of guilt may be harbouring: not only disappointment and shame as suggested above but also aggression. Mentors need to understand the source of feelings presented. Feelings that surface readily are often symptomatic of underlying ones. The origin may lie in the knowledge of a failure to keep a promise with oneself or with others, a breach of contract if you like—legal e.g. a duty of care; psychological or a social one, or a combination of these. To illustrate, when a person decides to improve their performance or to apply for promotion and they are unsuccessful will inevitably feel disappointed (in some cases it may be undisclosed relief). A sense of social shame if others become aware of it could ensue. Social shame is demotivating as some may feel so embarrassed that they become "stuck". There is much evidence, developed over a long period, to show this. Guilt is experienced psychologically (Izard 1977; Lewis 1971) and socially (Tangney and Tracey 2012) because it is rooted in human connectedness.

Shame is fleeting if it is addressed swiftly. For some people, feelings of shame have occurred in early career (or earlier) and pervade most decisions they subsequently make. Mentees may not be aware of such feelings as if they have masked these by incorporating them into their self-concept. Even if they are aware they will feel a sense of anxiety about it; or the fact that they have poor self-esteem and feel different to others or worse act out at work through inappropriate behaviour such as anger. Guilt and its associated emotions of shame and embarrassment can prevent mentee's professional and personal development as well as career aspirations.

Mentoring assists mentees deal with these negative aspects of guilt through the mentor working with them to take a more objective stance: for example, by considering a hypothetical situation which has parallels to the one under focus. Using this approach, frees up the mentee from the negative emotions of the situation and allows them to concentrate on the problem or issue at hand. As with other emotions, guilt can escalate needlessly and if so needs to be addressed quickly (Hale and Clark 2013, p. 24). Shame emotions often lead people to recoil from the problem at hand (in the hope that they will just go away), feelings of guilt prompt people to engage problems (hoping they can be solved) (Lewis 1971; Tangney et al. 2007). Guilt-proneness acclimatises mentees to the effects of their actions on others (especially any negative ones), which prompts them to act in more socially responsible ways (Tangney et al. 2007).

Mentees who have been abused, victimised, harassed or overlooked at work can feel guilty about it seeing it as their fault and subsequently, immense shame. Regardless of whether these emotions are imposed and subsequently promoted through poor self-concept or the result of someone else's actions, overwhelming them can dampen their professional life. Mentoring can provide a process from being freed from the negative spiral of emotions. Mentors can assist mentees to learn how to accept responsibility for their actions and put their guilt into perspective. Further mentoring provides an opportunity to learn that such emotions are normal in that no one is immune from them rather it is how they are dealt with. This fundamental release of guilt and blame allows mentees to liberate themselves from the negative effects of guilt, shame and embarrassment.

## 6.6 How to Assist Mentees Deal with Guilt

It can now be seen that guilt contains at least four elements:

1. acknowledging past or present wrongdoings;
2. responsibility assuming ownership of one's equal part in creating conflict situations; and
3. increasing one's sense of selfhood, and
4. enhancing relational attachments with others (based on Nahon and Lander 2013).

Empathy is important for the mentee to develop through emotional-sharing, perspective-taking (see worldview in Chap. 1), self-processing as well as understanding and controlling one's emotions—developing emotional intelligence or EQ if you like.

Mentoring is principally judgment-free for mentees so that they can share their goals and motivations with their mentor as well as any sense of guilt that they might be experiencing. The link between guilt and future actions is important within the mentoring relationship in terms of whether the mentee will feel exposed or not either in the long or short term (Tangney et al. 2007). However like all emotions, feeling remorseful is contradictory. In excessive doses guilt if unchecked can lead to self-destruction with dire consequences in some cases. In other cases, guilt serves inoculate mentees from future limitations if they have engaged in reflection and deep learning as a consequence. Guilt helps people learn to problem solve: what went wrong, why and how can this be avoided in the future.

Within the framework of positive mentoring, the mentor assists the mentee in engaging actively in reflecting on their predicaments, attitudes and related emotions. The mentor needs to be aware of how the mentee presents. Are they passive or frustrated? A mentor needs to demonstrate interest and curiosity in the mentee so that this may influence the mentee's own level of engagement. In other words, the mentor is using their engagement with the mentee as a way of understanding how they cope in everyday life (Fredricks et al. 2004). Appreciating the nature of guilt may lead to showing more empathy and being sensitive to other's needs. This approach is particularly valuable for learning in mentoring.

The second strategy used by the mentor is to work out what situations are triggering an emotional response in the mentee. Understanding the degree of intensity of an individual's negative reaction to a situation, a person or a relationship varies from highly controlled, concealing embarrassment or indifferent to a low sense of control, manifested by anxiety (Compas 2009). If these feelings are severe, the mentee may not cope well because of escalating and seemingly competing demands of the situation (i.e., individuals have to manage not only the event but also their own reactions). This predicament can divert energy away from dealing directly with the task and toward emotion regulation (Boekarts 1993). Being able to cope well results in a person being able to focus and engage in the problem at hand to try to solve it rather than the extraneous factors surrounding it. Re-engagement usually involves renewing their effort to focus, marshal their reflective capacity, and other signs of mastery (Dweck 2006). The opposite of reengagement is giving up or abandoning the demanding role or career.

The mentor needs to draw heavily from the mentee's reflections to understand what is going on (Connell and Wellborn 1991). Reflective questioning by the mentor is paramount at this time. A mentee's appraisals of their capacity to build relationships, their sense of self-efficacy, and autonomy (self-determination) are necessary to engage in problem-solving and decide a way forward (Elliot and Dweck 2005; Osterman 2000; Su and Reeve 2011).

Today due to media in all its forms there is tendency towards sensationalising or catastrophising events to ensure they do not go unnoticed. Similarly, when mentees have to deal with issues that disturb them, they often, seem more vivid or shocking. If so, this can intensify the sense of harm or shame in their own minds. For example, a mentee once stated: "When something bad happens, I feel like nobody will like me" or another in regard to their self-assessment of their capability: "I feel totally stupid" or "they make me feel that I don't know what I am doing"; and another emphasising self-blame and guilt "I feel like it's all my fault".

## 6.7 Conclusion

The genesis of guilt lies in a person's values system and the extent that it aligned to and can be reconciled with the other values systems that they interface with. Personal guilt emerges from the disruption of one's values and their discrepancies with the person's actions. The conundrum for mentoring in relation to guilt is to what extent the mentee's values and actions align with other values systems rather than assuring a greater proximity between their own value systems and actions (Nahon and Lander 2012, 2013). A further question to ask for mentors is one about gender differences if not in experiencing guilt in expressing it. Are there gender differences, more likely in some people's gendered experience to struggle with this in mentoring and perhaps become defensive or not (Nahon and Lander 2008, 2011).

Experienced guilt is an emotional response to this dilemma. It is experienced when a person feels they have transgressed in some way. All people are aware of this emotion, especially its negative effects. In some cases guilt, shame and embarrassment are normal responses to people in specific circumstances. If "found" guilty (including self-inflicted guilt), people can feel a sense of shame which involves deeply negative feelings about oneself. Guilt can be experienced secretly —and often is. However, it leads to embarrassment if the actions or feelings contributing to the guilt become known to others. To feel otherwise would be deviant in itself. It is when these emotions do not work themselves out that the person becomes incapacitated.

However, there is a positive side. Learning about emotions and how to deal with them through mentoring evokes, refines and develops approaches and, therefore, becomes a meaningful experience which transfers to other spheres of life: professionally, socially and psychologically. Most people come to mentoring hoping not only to develop insights into how to progress their personal and professional journeys and along the way, and through candour discover some "facts" about concerns that will assist them in their journey. Mentees may expect to be uplifted from their current patterns of thinking.

Guilt can impede building self-confidence (see Chap. 2) and introduce confusion into the mentoring relationship preventing the mentee from deriving value from it.

# References


Basile, B., & Mancini, F. (2011). Eliciting guilty feelings: A preliminary study differentiating deontological and altruistic guilt. *Psychology, 2*(2), 98–102.

Boekarts, M. (1993). Being concerned with well-being and with learning. *Educational Psychologist, 28*, 149–167.

Buss, D., & Dedden, L. (1990). Derogation of competitors. *Journal of Social and Personal Relationships, 7*(3), 395–422.

Caouette, J., Wohl, M., & Peetz, J. (2012). The future weighs heavier than the past: Collective guilt, perceived control and the influence of time. *European Journal of Social Psychology, 42* (3), 363–371.

Carpenter, D. D., Harding, T. S., Finelli, C. J., Montgomery, S. M., & Passow, H. J. (2006). Engineering students' perceptions of and attitudes towards cheating. *Journal of Engineering Education, 95*(3), 181–194.

Choi, Y., & Mai-Dalton, R. (1998). On the leadership function of self-sacrifice. *The Leadership Quarterly, 9*(4), 475–501.

Cohen, T. R., Panter, A., & Turan, N. (2012). Guilt proneness and moral character. *Current Directions in Psychological Science, 21*(5), 355–359.

Compas, B. E. (2009, Summer). Coping, regulation, and development during childhood and adolescence. *New Directions in Child and Adolescent Development*, (124), 87–99.

Conger, J., & Kanungo, R. (1994). Charismatic leadership in organizations: Perceived behavioural attributes and their measurement. *Journal of Organisational Behaviour, 15*(5), 439–452.

Connell, J. P., & Wellborn, J. G. (1991). Competence, autonomy and relatedness: A motivational analysis of self-system processes. In M. Gunnar & L. A. Sroufe (Eds.), *Minnesota symposium on child psychology. Self processes in development* (Vol. 23, pp. 43–77). Chicago, IL: University of Chicago Press.

Dweck, C. S. (2006). *Mindset: The new psychology of success*. New York, NY: Random House.

Eisenberg, N. (2000). Emotion, regulation, and moral development. *Annual Review of Psychology, 51*(1), 665–697.

Elliot, A. J., & Dweck, C. S. (Eds.). (2005). *Handbook of and motivation*. New York, NY: Guilford.

Flynn, F., & Schaumberg, R. (2012). When feeling bad leads to feeling good: Guilt-proneness and affective organisational commitment. *Journal of Applied Psychology, 97*(1), 327–342.

Fredricks, J. A., Blumenfeld, P. C., & Paris, A. H. (2004). School engagement: Potential of the concept, state of the evidence. *Review of Educational Research, 74*, 59–109.

Grant, A. M., & Wrzesniewski, A. (2010). I won't let you down or will I? Core self-evaluations, other-orientation, anticipated guilt and gratitude, and job performance. *Journal of Applied Psychology, 95*(1), 108–121.

Gunn, G. R., & Wilson, A. E. (2011). Acknowledging the skeletons in our closet: The effect of group affirmation on collective guilt, collective shame, and reparatory attitudes. *Personality and Social Psychology Bulletin, 37*(11), 1474–1487.

Hale, M. A., & Clark, D. A. (2013). When good people have bad thoughts: Religiosity and the emotional regulation of guilt-inducing intrusive thoughts. *Journal of Psychology and Theology, 41*(1), 24–35.

Hollis, M. (1977). *Models of man*. Philosophical thoughts on social action models of man: Cambridge University Press.

Imhoff, R., Bilewicz, M., & Erb, H. (2012). Collective regret versus collective guilt: Different emotional reactions to historical atrocities. *European Journal of Social Psychology, 42*(6), 729–742.

Izard, C. E. (1977). *Human emotions*. New York, NY: Plenum Press.

Lewis, H. B. (1971). *Shame and guilt in neurosis*. New York: International Universities Press.

Murray, K. M., Ciarrocchi, J. W., & Murray-Swank, N. A. (2007). Spirituality, religiosity, shame and guilt as predictors of sexual attitudes and experiences. *Journal of Psychology and Theology*. 35(3) (Fall 2007): pp. 222–234.

Nahon, D., & Lander, N. R. (2008). Recruitment and engagement in men's psychotherapy groups: An Integrity model, value-based perspective. *The International Journal of Men's Health, 7*(3), 218–236.

Nahon, D., & Lander, N. R. (2011). Emerging perspectives on masculinities and men's lives: Challenging the "myth of the emotionally defective male." In M. E. Harrison & P. W. Schnarrs (Eds.), *Growing our field: Emerging perspectives on masculinities and men's lives. The 18th annual American men's studies conference proceedings* (pp. 20–30). Harriman, TN: Men's Studies Press.

Nahon, D., & Lander, N. R. (2012). PTSD and the common good: Working with men from an Integrity model perspective. In P. W. Schnarrs & J. P. Marino (Eds.), *Men, masculinity and the common good in an era of economic uncertainty* (pp. 154–164). Harriman, TN: Men's studies Press.

Nahon, D., & Lander, N. R. (2013). Working with men in groups from an Integrity model perspective. *Journal of Men's Studies, 21*(2), 162–177.

Ortony, A., Clore, G. L., & Collins, A. (1988). *The cognitive structure of emotions*. Cambridge: Cambridge University Press.

Osterman, K. F. (2000). Students' need for belonging in the school community. *Review of Educational Research, 70*, 323–367.

Polman, E., & Ruttan, R. L. (2012). Effects of anger, guilt, and envy on moral hypocrisy. *Personality and Social Psychology Bulletin, 38*(1), 129–139.

Salovey, P., & Rodin, J. (1984). Some antecedents and consequences of social-comparison jealousy. *Journal of Personality and Social Psychology, 47*, 780–792.

Schaumberg, R. L., & Flynn, F. J. (2012). Uneasy lies the head that wears the crown: The link between guilt proneness and leadership. *Journal of Personality and Social Psychology, 103*(2), 327–342.

Smith, R. H., & Kim, S. H. (2007). Comprehending envy. *Psychological Bulletin, 133*, 46–64.

Smith, R. H., Turner, T. J., Garonzik, R., Leach, C. W., Urch-Druskat, V., & Weston, C. M. (1996). Envy and schadenfreude. *Personality and Social Psychology Bulletin, 22*, 158–168.

Su, Y.-L., & Reeve, J. (2011). A meta-analysis of the effectiveness of intervention programs designed to support autonomy. *Educational Psychology Review, 23*, 159–188.

Tangney J.P. & Dearing R. (2002). *Shame and Guilt*. New York: Guilford.

Tangney, J. P., Mashek, D., & Stuewig, J. (2005). Shame, guilt, and embarrassment: Will the real emotion please stand up? *Psychological Inquiry, 16*, 44–48.

Tangney, J. P., Stuewig, J., & Mashek, D. J. (2007). Moral emotions and moral behaviour. *Annual Review Psychology, 58*, 345–372.

Tangney, J. P., & Tracy, J. L. (2012). Self-conscious emotions. In M. R. Leary & J. P. Tangney (Eds.), *Handbook of self and identity* (pp. 446–478). New York: Guilford.

Tilghman-Osborne, C., Cole, D. A., & Felton, J. (2010). Definition and measurement of guilt: Implications for clinical research and practice. *Clinical Psychology Review, 30*(5), 536–546.

Witvliet, C. V. O., & McCullough, M. E. (2007). Forgiveness and health: A review and theoretical exploration. In S. G. Post (Ed.), *Altruism and health: Perspectives from empirical research* (pp. 259–276). New York: Oxford University Press.

Zimmermann, A., Abrams, D., Doosje, B., & Manstead, A. (2011). Causal and moral responsibility: Antecedents and consequences of group-based guilt. *European Journal of Social Psychology, 41*(7), 825–839.

# Chapter 7
# Silence and Giving Voice to the Mentee

*Heard melodies are sweet but those unheard/ Are sweeter (Keats).*

**Abstract** Silence is complex and refers to a lack of sound through to people either not being permitted to voice their opinion or feeling that this is the situation. This chapter will differentiate between silence and pause, deliberate and inadvertent silence. Ways of using silence positively in mentoring is outlined and the use of silence as a form of influence.

Today since we live in a global community of networked interactions, most people expect to stay in touch with others, personally, professionally and socially around the clock. While the incidence of interactions is high, the nature of the communications may be different depending on the channel used. Communications are increasingly more superficial and fleeting. More people know a lot more about us too, although not necessarily in a profound way.

From early childhood to senior years, people are communicating with each other using multiple personal channels. In fact our culture of blogging, tweeting, and texting, "being in touch" is highly desired and valued. Being out of touch is rare today. When people feel "out-of-touch" or when they do not receive a response to their email, text, tweet or blog, they are seen as being "unfriended", unpopular and some discomfort is likely to ensue. A lack of communication is often viewed with suspicion or disdain in that people feel that information is being kept from them.

Silence on the communication channels is not welcome. It is perplexing on the one hand in that people query why there is no response or unnerving in the same way that people are anxious about having nothing to talk about, an inadvertent silence. In business meetings, interviews and other social gatherings. Mostly unintended silence is dreaded, especially so when people are meeting each other for the first time, for example they are concerned about, "what will I say?" characterises their trepidation. Silence is not always fraught, however. It can take on different shades and tones—helpful at times, or awkward rather than fearful, at other times.

In mentoring, silence takes on special significance. It is important for mentors to understand how silence is structured outside of the mentoring relationship and how

 
A.M. Brewer, *Mentoring from a Positive Psychology Perspective*,
DOI 10.1007/978-3-319-40983-2_7

the effects of this, often not acknowledged by the mentee, spill over into the mentoring relationship and potentially impede it. For example, silence produces an "unequal relationship, in which the silencer compels the speaker to shut up, stratifies the relationship, thus undermining equality and mutual respect" (Kramer-Moore and Moore 2012, p. 81)

Equally, silence can positively build the mentoring relationship with the mentee, negotiating conversational pauses and the like; which facilitates the conversation.

Silence in workplaces and professional relationships is used in a range of ways including by the high-ranking to muzzle less influential colleagues or workers, forcing them into an unspoken submission. This process initiates a culture of silence. In other cases, silence is used to suppress any form of opposing voices in regard to issues, outcomes or events.

While the political implications of silencing, being silenced and speaking out are significant; so too is the personal impact. Although silence can be protective in specific contexts e.g. "keeping the peace" it can be less so when the only possible alternative to expressing a viewpoint is self-defeating (Kramer-Moore and Moore 2002, pp. 154–158). This situation is similar to being captured and incriminated where the person's best defence is to remain silent, drawing strength from this position.

As previously mentioned, others find being in the presence of others and not having anything to say, or fearful of not being able to find their voice as terrifying. There are numerous reasons why people become silent, apart from socio-political, cultural or gender reasons. People often state that speaking up might put them in a position of feeling/being disloyal, becoming too emotionally engaged, exposing themselves, maintaining a boundary with others, not wanting to engage in gossip or trying to appear enigmatic to defend against real or imagined potential threats, or to exert some control over the situation.

A further dimension is being given "the silent treatment" as a form of social rejection, either in a given context where people are not included in the social discourse or more generally, when they are not included in the communications. The experience of rejection may result in various adverse psychological consequences such as isolation, low confidence, anger and despair (Eisenberger et al. 2003).

When the silent member fails to respond to others, this can promote their feelings of anxiety; fear of being judged negatively; concerns about their being perceived as stupid, wrong, inadequate, and so on for what they said; and suppressed or overt hostility. Silence can lead to negative feelings given that it is often equated with being snubbed, criticised, and so on. A person who continuously presents as silent is seen as either withholding information, ignorant or weak. Whatever the reason their silence often frustrates others especially when they encourage them to participate actively and misunderstand the reasons for their continuing silence. If others' attempts to encourage participation are genuine and it does not produce the desired outcome, then the silent one becomes a target of derision or is simply overlooked.

Appreciating silence and voice in all nuances and purposes is the aim of this chapter.

## 7.1 Defining Silence

As the title of this chapter suggests there is a distinction to be made between being silent; feeling or being silenced intentionally by whatever means; equally between voicing and not voicing. In all instances, power is an important element in whether a person feels they can voice or not and even when they are speaking, they may not be voicing. For example, not being able to voice or being silenced (both are different) suggests a loss of power for the person.

Being silent takes many forms, from having nothing to say through to a shared understanding that need not be voiced. People use silence to listen, not to respond, not to intervene in a conversation for various reasons e.g. to contribute to a negative discussion; none of these actions are passive. Most are intentional.

Silence can be intended either for a moment or throughout a conversation (Kurzon 2007). When it is intended, it is an exercise of influence either by preventing others knowing the views of the silent one or attempting to compel others to cease speaking.

Both voice and silence are used within the interactions between mentees and mentors. Often, at least initially, mentoring conversations reflect the stance of the mentee in how they use voice and silence in everyday conversations, intentionally and otherwise. In everyday conversations, both voice and silence are navigated and sometimes are enforced either by a speaker, the context or both. The experience of each will depend on the standing of the mentee. For example, an early career mentee may experience 'being silenced' by colleagues more than a mentee who is a chief executive officer. Women as a group may be silenced on speaking out about norms that are taken for granted in their workplace which impede or discriminate against them in some way. The word 'impede' is used significantly here as often it is translated into impediment, meaning that there is a flaw and it lies with women rather than in how the context has been socially constructed. Silence under these circumstances is tantamount to marginalisation.

Silence is not uncomplicated. It needs to be understood for its diverse value and energy rather than its seemingly uncommunicative and passive nature. Whatever form it takes, silence has communicative power; it is not only reflective. However, it is always private even when displayed in a shared context e.g. people sitting together not talking. When public, it is both interpersonal and personal. In some contexts, silence is a form of respect e.g. observing a minute's silence. However, silence and not answering back may be due to a person's position.

In mentoring, even when the mentee is relaying an incident, they may be voicing some aspects and not others. Conversing is not equivalent to voice (Hirschman 1970).

Silence takes on different meanings and structures depending on the context and the nature of the relationship and interactions: who, why, what, when, where and how? It can:

(a) connect people if perceived as yielding to their needs or demands.
(b) assume consent or affirmation e.g. when no one dissents from announced decision.
(c) preserve and restore relationships as it can signify warmth and understanding in a way that words cannot.
(d) used to avoid further exacerbating a situation e.g. during gossip conversations.
(e) separate, if perceived as out-of-place, stilted or unexpected.
(f) disrupt relationships in situations where silence is perceived as avoidance, dissent or dissatisfaction. This negative connotation can be exacerbated specifically when speaking out is perceived a futile or risky (Argyris 1976).
(g) suppress information suggesting a lack of transparency.
(h) "speak volumes" by no one commenting.
(i) promote deeper thinking by providing a meditative context, representing understanding and acceptance.
(j) create a vacuum if participants do not perceive it positively, for example, not participating in prayer in a religious setting.
(k) express dissent as it can be confusing and even intimidating (based on Jensen 1973).

## *7.1.1 Silence and Pause*

A conversation is always punctuated with pauses; most of these go unnoticed in everyday conversations, as one or other conversant reflects momentarily, searches for words to respond to questions from the other as they each negotiate the conversational cycle. Pauses are noticed if questions are left hanging or extend beyond a few seconds or so. A pause is then perceived as silence although not necessarily negative; it gives the other pause to reflect too.

**Implicit and Explicit Silence**

In all forms of verbal interaction, silence is implicit and part of any channel of communication even, as previously stated in emails and social media, and is powerful in understanding the psycho-social dynamics of the workplace (Blackman and Sadler-Smith 2009, p. 570.) Not only is silence understood in a verbal sense that is speaking or not but also beyond where it intentionally directed to create an enduring pause, which becomes a backdrop for understanding both verbal and non-verbal communications.

Through the explicit use of silence, people anticipate and reinforce meaning and use it in a similar way as one would punctuate a sentence: a comma here, a full-stop there.

Philosophers such as Merleau-Ponty (1962), Heidegger and Wittgenstein (Overgaard 2006) all discussed the meaning of silence and how it lent significance to conversations. Silence varies in form and meaning from "*being silent*" and fully engaged or not to not exhibiting the usual signs of "being present" in the dialogue. There is also someone becoming silent as a result of "*being silenced*", directly or indirectly regardless of how others perceive this. Different interpretations can be formed by being silent or silenced. Silence takes two further forms discussed as follows.

#### 7.1.1.1 Deliberate Silence

Deliberate silence is when people choose to reserve their opinions and concerns either about a specific topic under discussion or more generally e.g. during gossip or not wanting to exacerbate a situation. If the silence is understood in those terms then, a little discomfort is experienced. However if the silence is unexpected or when active engagement is warranted, then it is seen as abrupt and may be misunderstood.

Out of the long list of silent forms mentioned at the beginning of this chapter, three types of silence are worthy of closer examination. These are differentiated by the intention of the silent conversant: (a) defensive silence, (b) acquiescent silence and (c) pro-social silence (Dyne et al. 2003). The first two types are evident of distrust by the silent party or others whereas in contrast, pro-social silence defined by Dyne et al. (2003) as withholding information or opinions with the intent of not adding to the negative tone of a conversation or where the silent person's power may lead to a situation of arresting control from others. In being silent, the intention is to show consideration for the other conversants. It is positive silence, mindful of others e.g. allowing others to proffer their views, not joining into criticism; not reporting someone's failure and so on. By comparison, pro-social silence demonstrates a concern for others rather than a distrust or fear of any adverse outcome from proffering one's opinion.

When conversants silence themselves, it is a form of impression management (Snell et al. 1988); or to withhold information for various reasons including the speaker believing it is irrelevant, low interest or disinterest or discourteous or too confronting (Fivush and Edwards 2004). These are all relevant in mentoring especially when a mentee feels that the mentor may find the story too difficult to listen to, e.g. in cases of harassment, violence or loss, and try to protect the mentor by not revealing it. Where they may be grieving and sense the mentor is too and so on.

There are cross-cultural interpretations of silence too which could vary depending on the purpose, the sub-culture and the situation. The higher authority the silent person has or the more outgoing they are, the more prosocial silence is valued by others as they understand the silence is respecting or protecting them in some way. These three forms will be detailed as follows.

Another form of silence is characterised by 'don't rock the boat' which is also a premeditated suppression of relevant ideas, information, or opinions. This silence is exercised as a form of self-protection usually to guard against "getting it wrong" or fear of a pending disagreement. Even though the silence appears to be inactive, it is an active withholding of relevant information for self-protection based on the fear that the consequences of speaking up could be personally damaging or at least, unpleasant (Pinder and Harlos 2001). Fear is usually the driver of this type of silence (Morrison and Milliken 2000) as well as for emotional protection (Dyne et al. 2003); and to avoid being in the position of being the one bearing bad news (Rosen and Tesser 1970), or an opportunity for others to voice (Detert and Burris 2007; Gephart et al. 2009). Mentees will use inactive silence when they disagree with specific recommendations of a mentor, all the more reason for mentors to desist from proffering advice. Mentees will become even more guarded if they believe other alternatives are superior to what is being suggested so they think that withholding their views is the best personal strategy. It is likely that they also use this ploy in their professional relationships too, especially with peers and supervisors. Mentees, being silent in this way, often believe they would rather 'suffer in silence' than 'rock the boat'.

Yielding silence refers to an inexpressive withholding of relevant ideas, information, or opinions, based on an acceptance of "that's the way things are here". Mentees may not speak up at work due to their belief that their opinion is neither needed nor valued by their supervisors and senior management (Morrison and Milliken 2000). It is a form of compliance further facilitated by a culture where conformity is expected; risk-taking is penalised, especially if the outcome is ineffective and dissent is bottled-up. The mentee may present in this way to the mentor. People who have given up hope for improvement or opportunities and are not willing to exert the effort to speak up, get involved, or attempt to change the situation are often perceived as agreeable (Harlos 2001; Dyne et al. 2003). Actually they are more like automatons although may be seething underneath.

Both these defensive forms of silence inhibit the mentee from building social capital professionally and in their workplaces. However, there are many circumstances under which silence is valuable and appropriate. For example, pro-social silence refers to "withholding work-related ideas, information, or opinions with the goal of benefiting other people or the organisation, based on altruism or cooperative motives" (Bell et al. 2011, p. 135) and is instrumental in building social capital. The reasons for engaging in prosocial silence are various including people understanding when to speak and when not to in the interests of being positively aligned with others; avoiding complaining and trying to become more accepting of things going wrong, change or other disruptions at work without grumbling. Others who use this form of silence not only value affiliation, but are also interested in maintaining social capital (Adler et al. 2008) and protecting social identity (Ashforth and Mael 1989).

However, there are some instances where prosocial silence can miscarry especially in regard to not understanding the moral and ethical purpose of the context (Knoll and van Dick 2013; Umphress and Bingham 2011) where people put the reputation of the institution or themselves ahead of what is the morally right and ethical thing to do such as not exercising a duty of care, not reporting wrongful or criminal behaviour. Mentors need to understand this could occur in some institutional contexts more than others where the culture is purportedly cohesive and there are attempts to protect the reputations of management or their institutions. If the pro-social behaviour is used in this way, it will rebound with negative publicity for all.

Being silent when people know it is not in any one's interest to do so is another form of silence whereby people sometimes withhold information to gain an advantage. The withholding of or providing insufficient or distorted information, with the purpose to mislead, disguise, or confuse is negative. Silence could also be used as a form of unvoiced protest (Van Dyne and Ellis 2004) Information withholding based on opportunism is seen as an action that depletes a productive workplace (Gruys and Sackett 2003). While it is a form of opportunism, it also differs from the accepted standards of action especially in a group context (Brinsfield 2013). It also depletes social capital.

#### 7.1.1.2 Inadvertent Silence

This form of silence is unintended and occurs without purpose. It is largely due to communicative incompetence brought on by anxiety over a situation, cultural shock or an unexpected turn of events. It is a silence that is dreaded by both speaker and audience when a person fails to articulate their views as expected.

## 7.2 Knowing Silence in a Mentoring Relationship

As can be seen in this chapter so far, silences have their own dynamic. Each one has been distilled for the purposes of a mentor understanding how it can be employed in their conversations with mentees. Each silence identified below forms a subset of one of the others, and selected to illustrate their effects, as follows:-

(a) Natural silence as in any conversation
(b) Intentional silence to solicit a response or seek clarification or to get the mentee to refocus
(c) Time out as in "taking a breather" allowing the mentee to regain composure, for example, to signal respect and empathy for a situation that they may be recalling
(d) Invitational silence to allow the mentee the space to take the lead and equalise the power between them
(e) Facilitative silence without destroying the effect of silence is achieved through reflective questioning (see Chaps. 2 and 3).

(f) Awkward silence as the mentor or mentee has lost direction or following a disclosure and feeling embarrassed
(g) 'No response' silence which may be used to take control of the dialogue or by one to resist the relationship developing or block the content.
(h) Compassionate silence similar to meditative silence to give acceptance and understanding of another's situation which is different to (c) above.

Silence is a typical and valuable element of mentoring (based on Knapp 2008). Accommodating, comfortable silence gives the mentee time for reflection or gathering their contemplations and feelings. It provides the time and stillness for deeper feelings to emerge and be considered by them (Knapp 2008). A mentor needs to understand and use it strategically for this purpose.

Silence is also demonstrated by a mentor's unflappability, especially when being told something about which the mentee feels embarrassment. Silence is used to facilitate the inpouring of additional information, or encourage a further response from the mentee (Knapp 2008). When used with concentration and eye contact, it solicits a further response and conveys the mentor's genuine interest (Levitt 2001). For example, when mentees self-disclose, they may experience hesitation, apprehension, or difficulty confiding their concerns suitably and coherently. The mentor can acknowledge by gesturing and remaining silent, in effect, encouraging mentees to proceed slowly, reflecting and assembling their thoughts as they go. Throughout this phase, the mentor maintains appropriate eye contact and focus. This demonstrates the mentor's openness not only for receiving further information but also as an expectation that the mentee will say more. In that sense, silence can be instrumental in not only encouraging self-reflection but also self-direction (Duba 2004). This is achieved by the mentor using silence as an "open question" to the mentee to take a risk in disclosing something that is sensitive or embarrassing. Without silence, mentees will not interpose to convey an important piece of information.

Silence, as in pausing, encourages mentees to take their time and think as well as understand how they feel about things. It permits the mentee to organise and prioritise their ideas—a sorting out process (Knapp 2008). Most of all, silence facilitates the generative process for reflection from both the mentee and mentor strengthening their rapport and ultimately their relationship (Ladany et al. 2005). For example, as the mentee feels more relaxed with the mentor, silence becomes a normal part of the process and is not perceived as awkward or undermining (Ladany et al. 2005).

Mentors learn to accommodate silence as part of the ebb and flow of the conversation. When it is adapted in this way, the mentor is attentive, allowing silence to take its natural course. If silence is contrived, the mentor needs to use it purposively e.g. allow the mentee space to collect their thoughts, feelings or both. There are conversational circumstances that are highly appropriate for its effective practice in mentoring (Ladany et al. 2004). Only through authentic focus is the mentor able to call how and when to introduce it. Too early in the mentoring relationship could mean that it is off-putting for the mentee.

It is important that mentors and the like learn how to navigate the relaxed as well as the challenging aspects of the practice of silence in mentoring (based on Duba (2004). When it is mostly uncomfortable, the mentor should desist and use open questions until the mentee feels more relaxed. Silence has an important place in mentoring and mentors need to be able to accommodate it comfortably.

As previously discussed, silence can be beneficial or stressful. Understanding how to use silence effectively to engage and sustain relationships as well as those silences which hamper it. The most important aspect of using silence is for the mentor to be at ease with it even if this defies the mentee in the early stages. Once there is trust between the mentor and mentee, employing silence for whatever purpose is likely to be understood and accepted but more importantly, used to facilitate the mentoring outcomes both within the relationship and beyond it.

The other issue in considering silence is the behaviour during a period of silence which is influenced by how the mentees understand silence i.e. not speaking, refusing to speak or quietness.

Some mentees will present as disinclined to dialogue and prefer to listen. This may be one of the reasons for seeking a mentor as they realise they need to become a more active contributor professionally, in the work place or socially.

One of the traps in any conversation especially in mentoring is not permitting the silence to go its full length and rushing to fill a perceived void, thereby not giving the mentee a chance to toy with it (Mearns and Thorne 2000). This does not mean that a mentor should let it go on to the point where the mentee is discomforted by it.

When a mentee falls silent, there are a number of explanations. There may be some confusion about the content of the conversation or the relationship itself or they are using it for reflection. Or the content may lead to a feeling of guilt or despondency and if so, they are likely to be more passive during the silence. If frustrated and even angry, they may be more active which can be detected by their posture and non-verbal behaviour.

Another trap is for the mentor to become distracted; look at phone or watch, nod off or lose the thread of the conversation. Remaining actively present with the mentee is vital during silence.

Interpersonally, silence in a mentoring relationship may imply withdrawal and withholding positions that allow the individual to step out of the 'moment' or the mentoring relationship. However rather than viewing this negatively, it could be one of positive solitude for reflection and a more thorough critique of the discussion. Often in our busy lives, there are not enough periods of quietness or retreat for reflection.

Quietude usually involves the absence of words. It is far from solitary and engages the mentee to exist "in-the-moment" so as to focus without using words. Engagement between the mentor and mentee may occur:

(a) through gentle eye contact rather than through direct gaze
(b) by averting their gaze from each other or avoiding eye contact
(c) by focusing on an object in the room
(d) using gesture to show that an issue is

    i. under consideration e.g. putting a hand under chin,
    ii. gathering thoughts,
    iii. reflecting back.

This form of silence facilitates the mentee becoming calm for reflection. A mentor needs to understand how to use this—speaking quietly, allowing a mentee time to reflect, a restful meeting space. For example in responding to a question, the mentee should be encouraged to continue through quietness in reflecting on the circumstances of the issue they are discussing. Not expressing them here is meaningful and needs to be further explored. See Fig. 7.1.

| SILENCE | NATURE | CLARIFICATION |
|---|---|---|
| Inexpressible | Tacit knowing (inexpressible) | Information associated with skills or 'know how' that cannot be 'spelled-out' (cf. explicit: the knowledge that can be spelled out and formalised) |
| | Intuitive knowing (emotional realisation) | Subjective, emotionally recalled based on symbols or cues (e.g. purposive questions; associations) |
| Expressible | Perception (nascent) | Ah- ah moment (preceded by a 'feeling of knowing' or 'tip-of-the-tongue' experience) |
| | Knowing (dormant) | Suddenly remembered after prompting |
| Silenced and will not be shared | Silenced voice | By self or other's actions |
| | Acquiescent silence | Purposively withheld by self for the purposes of (a) personal power; (b) submission; or (c) concern for others. Under these circumstances, silence is influential. |
| | Intimidated silence | Enforce silence in response to an assertive other or norms perceived in context. |

**Fig. 7.1** Based on Blackman and Sadler-Smith (2009, pp. 572–577)

## 7.3 Silence and the Inner Quiet

The mentor also needs to silence their own inner voices and not let them take over, that is, to listen to what the mentee is saying. Both conversation and inner voices camouflage the inner quiet essential for listening to the mentee, producing an internal busyness which the mentor needs to be aware of. "In the [mentor's] inner world, just as with the [mentee], the responses which matter most are those that need time and space to surface out of the unconscious. I think [the mentor] need[s] to listen slowly" (Parsons 2009, p. 264). Listening deliberately diffentiates the mentoring conversation from the everyday one. Deliberate listening depends on a quiet that is not silence (Reis 2009). The quiet mentor may not speak although their posture indicates deep engagement, listening deliberately before commenting. This form of quiet is extremely powerful for the mentee's reflection and learning.

In understanding their own inner voice, the mentor assists the mentee coming to terms with their internal voice or what has been termed the inner critic (Earley and Weiss 2010). Mentees like all of us are sabotaged by listening to the inner critic e.g. by striving for perfections at work, for feeling guilt-ridden, not taking risks, baseless fears of not being popular, of failing, not taking a break, feeling ashamed or unworthy of respect and so on.

Mentoring assists mentees to come to reflection on their "inner chatter" which may be actively depleting them of thinking. Reflection is necessary so that mentees are able to become open to new ideas and learning. When their inner voices are silenced and dysfunctional assumptions are corrected, mentees are able to interpret meanings differently or rethink their assumptions so the way they see the world can be more beneficial for them and self-satisfying.

Releasing the inner voice provides the mentee with a newfound freedom which is essential for understanding self constraints and employing more effectively skills that will lead the mentee to increased flexibility to listen to more appropriate internal messaging. Inner freedom assists the mentee to decide what is valid criticism and needs to be acted on and what is does not. The inner voice needs to be replaced by an internal navigator who works out good risks, minimises pitfalls and so on. The mentor and the mentee together replace the inner critic with a more realistic voice (based on Earley 2012).

## 7.4 Tacit Knowledge as a Form of Silence

In all spheres of life, there is knowledge held of which people are unaware until it is drawn to their attention and voiced. The outcome of becoming aware of tacit knowledge is that people who hold it can call upon it more actively. Tacit knowledge is likely to emerge during mentoring much to the surprise, often of the mentee, because they did not know they "had the knowledge".

Tacit knowledge is rarely spelled out. When it is, it can be viewed with scepticism, especially if there is no evidence basis for it. At other times, it forms part of "dare-not-speak-its-name" category. The former is disaggregated into that which cannot be literally spoken (tacit knowing and intuitive knowing) and that which might surface in conversation following deliberate reflection and the latter ('silenced') into repressed, withheld and suppressed voice (see Fig. 7.1).

## 7.5 Silence and Influence

Whether a person is silent or not, depends on perceptions of intrapersonal and interpersonal processes operating in context and how the person interprets and responds to these. A mentor needs to consider these processes not only for the mentoring relationship and conversations but also for assisting the mentee's diagnosis of situations.

### *7.5.1 Silence, Power and Assertiveness*

In any group, there are people who tend to be assertive and give their views openly, others remain reticent, while others will observe the group before speaking up. Most people new to a group take the time to become acquainted with members and sense their way into the relationships before weighing in too prominently. This process occurs regardless of gender, age and cultural background. People who exercise influence and immediately assert their rights in a new situation, tend to be risk takers and self-focused. Such people are often "thinking out loud" as a means to draw connections amongst the information at hand (Pavitt and Johnson 1999). This "thinking out loud" serves to influence others to a larger or lesser extent depending on the person's evidence, verbal style or position power in relation to them.

Interpersonal processes such as a defined agenda, the use of questions rather than statements, voting and so on introduces a more collaborative process and assists in equalising the influence of individuals in any conversation. The nature and orchestration of the interaction plays a central role in the readiness of individuals to express themselves and the nature of those expressions and in some cases, this may be best done other than meeting face-to-face (Bonito and Sanders 2011). Such processes minimise the importance of individuals and persuasive processes such that only deliberating carefully on the decision at hand, matters. An important part of this process is the composition of the group; their expertise and experience, and capability for problem solving and decision making (see Moreland and Levine 1992). Clearly, influence combining both intra- and interpersonal processes is important in understanding, overcoming or introducing silence.

### 7.5.2 *Converting Silence to Resilience*

The negative implications of being silenced, either directly or by a workplace or professional culture, are obvious. There is also a deep contradiction in what mentees discuss with mentors in regard to "being silenced" or their own inability to voice at work or with professional colleagues. Mentees often have highly demanding roles, many of these are linked to a profession such as law, accounting, medicine and health, the sciences and education for example both in public and private organisations. However, this phenomenon not only exists in the professions but also in most occupations such as customer service, project management, administration and manual labour. On the face of many of the roles in these fields have inherently high control vis-à-vis their clients or students but not necessarily within their workplace, nor their organisational or professional hierarchies. In fact, it may be quite the opposite.

Many mentees discuss the issue of either being intimidated, embarrassed, insulted and marginalised or being negatively affected by the allocation of work schedules. If this occurs on a frequent basis, it is considered as bullying (Einarsen et al. 2003) When mentees experience these negative effects associated with their work or role, they also discuss the pressure they feel, coupled with a lack of control over their situation, often with little support. Such effects have been well attested to by Karasek and Theorell (1990).

Seeking a mentor is almost the last resort for getting support to deal with these situations. Mentees often report to me about how their formerly high self-confidence diminished as a consequence of the effects of being intimidated, embarrassed, insulted, or marginalised. They begin to experience feelings of inadequacy, fearful of doing or saying the wrong thing which ultimately make them feel uncertain in other facets of their work and even outside of work. They often became confused about what is expected of them, silent and do not contribute in meetings leading to being eroded by their power in front of colleagues and co-workers including those junior to them. Seeking alternative roles is not an option in many cases due to contractual obligations or finding another role.

There are, of course, a number of options open to mentees including seeking assertiveness training, reporting persistent harassment and bullying, neither of which may improve the situation. These options need to be considered seriously. In the case of reporting bullying, this is almost mandatory but not without its consequences for the "whistle blower". One way a mentor can assist in this situation is to diagnose carefully the situation confronting the mentee through structured problem-solving so that they can build their capacity " to adjust to adversity, maintain equilibrium, retain some sense of control over their environment, and continue to move on in a positive manner" (Jackson et al. 2007, p. 3). For the mentee, it is important that they have considered carefully, by way of planned preparation, their initial options and some evaluation of these as they play an important role in influencing interaction and decision making. The mentoring conversation is a way of preparing for these situations outside of mentoring by considering with the mentee the following issues:

(a) the mentee's contribution,
(b) the process (e.g., group composition; evidence quality; behaviours and/or cognitions that typically unfold during group interactions), and
(c) the outcomes (e.g., participation), such that inputs are not often considered and/or accounted for.

The capacity to be heard is one of the principal ways in which mentees attempt to pursue their particular interests.

From the perspective of positive mentoring, a mentor demonstrates to the mentee that they can become stronger as a consequence of such negative workplace and professional experience as it might assist them in developing a more resilient stance and a way for modelling this for others.

## 7.6 Conclusion

In mentoring, silence is positive when it indicates reflection, or when used effectively by the mentor to ensure there is sufficient pause for the mentee to consider an issue and respond.

Mentors can inadvertently silence the mentee by demonstrating a disregard for their circumstances, misunderstanding, misinterpreting or showing disbelief in regard to the incidents relayed by them, or simply by being unfocused and unmindful (Pasupathi 2001). Importantly, when the mentor and mentee collude by focusing on parts of the evidence and not others or failing to address issues by asking relevant questions then a certain fiction is created and reinforced (Cue et al. 2007). How silence and voice are employed in mentoring is significant: what is voiced and attended to as in everyday life becomes privileged over what is not. What is silenced is ultimately ignored, overlooked and forgotten.

1. The ability to listen effectively. Mentors need to engage in listening as a major form of engagement with mentees. When mentees demonstrate their ability to listen, this will add to their acceptance by the mentee. Many mentors become focused on what they are going to say next rather than listening to the mentee. If this is the case, the non-verbal behaviour will be evident to the mentee that the mentor is not really listening and, therefore, interested in what they have to say. Practising this in everyday conversations on listening closely is important. Listening is empowering. Listening allows you to attend to not only what is being said, what is not being said, and nuances of non-verbal behaviour including feelings through facial expressions. Most people are not influenced by another's words rather by their actions.
2. Being minded about the mentee's feelings. Silence places the mentee in the foreground. Using silence to listen carefully to not only what people say but also

the manner of their expression, reveals much as to what is going on. Intuition is very important in this and should not be ignored.

3. Self-control. Silence is a proxy for self-control when feeling out-of-control, not only leading to a semblance of being in control, and through rehearsal it can become a measured response in some situations. Silence used for this purpose should not be over-played.
4. Intelligent silence: In life when facing a new challenge, making silence your first response gives a person the opportunity to reflect before they act, increasing the likelihood that what is said and done will be effective and make sense to others. A mentee needs to be supported by using this approach. Equally a mentor needs to model it throughout the mentoring conversation. Mentors need to resist the urge to leap into rescuing the mentee and assist them to work it out for themselves. The wisest action for the mentor is often creating the space for a mentee to think through their willingness to listen and ask questions.

## References

Adler, P. S., Kwon, S. W., & Heckscher, C. (2008). Professional work: the emergence of collaborative community. *Organisation Science, 19*, 359–376.

Arygris, C. (1976). Theories of action that inhibit learning. *American Psychologist, 31*, 638–654.

Ashforth, B. E., & Mael, F. (1989). Social identity theory and the organisation. *The Academy of Management Review, 14*(1), 20–39.

Bell, M., Özbilgin, M., Beauregard, T., & Sürgevil, O. (2011). Voice, silence, and diversity in 21st century organizations: strategies for inclusion of gay, lesbian, bisexual, and transgender employees. *Human resource management, 50*(1), 131–146.

Blackman, D., & Sadler-Smith, E. (2009). The silent and the silenced in organisational knowing and learning. *Management Learning, 40*(5), 569–585.

Bonito, J. A., & Sanders, R. E. (2011). The existential centre of small groups: Member's conduct and interaction. *Small Group Research, 42*, 343–358.

Brinsfield, C. (2013). Employee silence motives: Investigation of dimensionality and development of measures. *Journal of Organisational Behaviour, 34*(5), 671–679.

Cue, A., Koppel, J., & Hirst, W. (2007). Silence is not golden: A case for socially shared retrieval-induced forgetting. *Psychological Science, 18*, 727–733.

Detert J. R., & Burris, E. R. (2007). Leadership behavior and employee voice: Is the door really open? *Academy of Management Journal, 50*(4), 869–884.

Duba, J. D. (2004). Using silence: "Silence is not always golden." In L. Tyson, R. Pérusse, J. Whitledge, J. Duba, P. Neufeld & J. DeVoss (Eds.), *Critical incidents in group counseling* (pp. 265–270). Alexandria: American Counseling Association.

Dyne, L. V., Ang, S., & Botero, I. C. (2003). Conceptualizing employee silence and employee voice as multidimensional constructs. *Journal of Managerial Studies, 9*, 1359–1392.

Earley, J. (2012). *Activating your inner champion instead of your inner critic*. Larkspur, CA: Pattern Systems Books.

Earley, J., & Weiss, B. (2010). *Self-therapy for your inner critic: Transforming self-criticism into self-confidence*. Larkspur, CA: Pattern Systems Books.

Einarsen, S., Hoel, H., Zapf, D., & Cooper, C. L. (2003). The concept of bullying at work: The European tradition. In S. Einarsen, H. Hoel, D. Zapf, & C. L. Cooper (Eds.), *Bullying and emotional abuse in the workplace* (pp. 3–30). London: Taylor and Francis.

Eisenberger, N. L., Lieberman, M. D., & Williams, K. D. (2003). Does rejection hurt? An FMRI study of social exclusion. *Science, 302*(5643), 290–292.

Fivush, R., & Edwards, V. J. (2004). Remembering and forgetting childhood sexual abuse. *Journal of Child Sexual Abuse, 13*, 1–19.

Gephart, R. P., Van Maanen, J., & Oberlechner, T. (2009). *Organizations and risk in late modernity organization studies, 30*(2–3), 141–155.

Gruys, M., & Sackett, P. (2003). Investigating the dimensionality of counterproductive work behaviour. *International Journal of Selection and Assessment, 11*(1), 30–42.

Harlos, K. P. (2001). When organizational voice systems fail: More on the deaf-ear syndrome and frustration effects. *The Journal of Applied Behavioural Science, 37*(3), 324–342.

Hirschman, A. O. (1970). *Exit, voice, and loyalty: Responses to decline in firms, organizations, and states Cambridge*. Mass.: Harvard University Press.

Jackson, D., Firtko, A., & Edenborough, M. (2007). Personal resilience as a strategy for surviving and thriving in the face of workplace adversity: A literature review. *Journal of Advanced Nursing, 60*, 1–9.

Jensen, J. V. (1973). Communicative functions of silence. *ETC: A Review of General Semantics, 30*, 2249–2257.

Karasek, R. A., & Theorell, T. (1990). *Healthy work: Stress, productivity, and the reconstruction of working life*. New York: Basic Books.

Knapp, H. (2008). *Therapeutic communication: Developing professional skills*. Los Angeles: Sage Publications.

Knoll, M., & van Dick, R. (2013). Authenticity, employee silence, prohibitive voice, and the moderating effect of organisational identification. *Journal of Positive Psychology, 8*(4), 346–360.

Kramer-Moore, D., & Moore, M. (2002). *Life imitates art–encounters between family therapy and literature*. New York: Solomon Press.

Kramer-Moore, D., & Moore, M. (2012). *Destructive myths in family therapy: How to overcome barriers to by seeing and saying a humanistic perspective*. Chichester: Wiley-Blackwell.

Kurzon, D. (2007). Towards a typology of silence. *Journal of Pragmatics, 39*, 1673–1688.

Ladany, N. Friedlander, M., & Nelson, M. L. (2005). *Critical events in psychotherapy supervision: an interpersonal approach*. American Psychological Society.

Ladany, N., Hill, C. E., Thompson, B. J., & O'Brien, K. M. (2004). Therapist perspectives on using silence in therapy: A qualitative study. *Counselling and Psychotherapy Research: Linking research with practice, 4*(1), 80–89.

Levitt, D. H. (2001). Active listening and counselor self-efficacy: Emphasis on one microskill in beginning counselor training. *Clinical Supervisor, 20*(2), 101–115.

Mearns, D., & Thorne, B. (2000). *Person-centred therapy today*. London: Sage.

Merleau-Ponty, M. (1962). *Phenomenology of perception* (C. Smith, Trans.). London: Routledge.

Moreland, R. L., & Levine, J. M. (1992). The composition of small groups. In E. J. Lawler, B. Markovsky, C. Ridgeway, & H. Walker (Eds.), *Advances in group processes* (pp. 237–280). Greenwich, CT: JAI Press.

Morrison, E. W., & Milliken F. J. (2000). Organizational silence: A barrier to change and development in a pluralistic world. *Academy of Management Review, 25*(4), 706–725.

Overgaard, S. (2006). The problem of other minds: Wittgenstein's phenomenological perspective. *Phenomenology and the Cognitive Sciences, 5*(1), 53–73.

Parsons, M. (2009). Reply to commentaries. *Psychoanalytic Dialogues, 19*, 259–266.

Pasupathi, M. (2001). The social construction of the personal past and its implications for adult development. *Psychological Bulletin, 127*, 651–672.

Pavitt, C., & Johnson, K. K. (1999). An examination of the coherence of group discussions. *Communication Research, 26*, 303–321.

Pinder, C. C., & Harlos, K. P. (2001). Employee silence: Quiescence and acquiescence as responses to perceived injustice. In K. M. Rowland, G. R. Ferris (Eds.), *Research in personnel and human resources management* (Vol. 20, pp. 331–369). New York: JAI Press.

Reis, B. (2009). Performative and enactive features of psychoanalytic witnessing: The transference as the scene of address. *International Journal of Psycho-Analysis, 90*(6), 1359–1372.
Rosen, S., & Tesser, A. (1970). On reluctance to communicate undesirable information: The MUM effect. *Sociometry, 33*(3), 253–263.
Snell, W. E, Jr., Belk, S. S., Flowers, A., & Warren, J. (1988). Women's and men's willingness to self- disclose to therapists and friends: The moderating of instrumental, expressive, masculine and feminine topics. *Sex Roles, 18*, 769–776.
Umphress, E., & Bingham, J. (2011). When employees do bad things for good reasons: examining unethical pro-organizational behaviours. *Organisation Science, 22*(3), 621–640.
Van Dyne, L., & Ellis, J. B. (2004). Job creep: A reactance theory perspective on organizational citizenship behavior as over-fulfillment of obligations. In J. A. M. Coyle-Shapiro, L. M. Shore, M. S. Taylor, & L. E. Tetrick (Eds.), *The employment relationship: Examining psychological and contextual perspectives* (pp. 181–205). Oxford: Oxford University Press.

# Chapter 8
# Attachment and Loyalty

*Glassed with cold sleep and dazzled by the moon*
*Out of the confused hammering dark of the train*
*I looked and saw under the moon's cold sheet*
*your delicate dry breasts, country that built my heart: …*
Judith Wright Train Journey (1953)

**Abstract** The focus in this chapter is on the importance of relationships for people, individually and collectively and how relationships are the DNA for an inspiring and indeed, creative life and community. Delving into the key concepts of attachment and loyalty reveals the risks and value of both.

## 8.1 Why Attachment?

A question that is often asked is how effective is mentoring and how do you know it is effective. What makes a difference in mentoring is the mentor's capacity to engage with the mentee: namely the mentor's capacity to gain rapport and engender trust. Warmth, empathy, and genuineness as well as interpersonal actions, such as self-disclosure, intentions and response modes are important (Sexton and Whiston 1994). All these elements facilitate the mentee's capacity to invest in the mentoring relationship and form a connection with the mentor.

One of the most significant theorists on the nature of human connection was Bowlby (1980). He identified three principles for effective attachment: first, proximity suggests accessibility for the mentor and mentee; secondly, security suggests confidentiality and that thirdly, during further exploration the mentor will support the mentee throughout the process, exploring personal possibilities. A mentor is working on ensuring that the relationship is shaped by these principles over time which leads to enhanced learning for the mentees.

To form and sustain connections with others, relies on trustworthiness or loyalty. In seeking out a mentor, the mentee has something to tell, learn or both. The mentee needs to establish trust with the mentor so as to present their position, describe their relationships, and discuss their needs and so on. It is important that the mentees



A.M. Brewer, *Mentoring from a Positive Psychology Perspective*,
DOI 10.1007/978-3-319-40983-2_8

considers and reflects on their current and past relationships where these experiences may have troubled them.

The nature of their relationships outside of mentoring may be initially reflected in their relationship with the mentor. Exploration of past relationship experiences and recurring patterns within them helps mentees focus on how they perceive, select and interpret these; their expectations of others and strategies for managing them (Mikulincer and Shaver 2007). Such exploration potentially leads to beneficial change. Of course, this depends on the mentor's capacity to assist the mentee address their issues of concern and develop strategies for change, where desired.

It is important for the mentor to appreciate the relationship needs with others as well as the purposes others serve, differ throughout the life span (Consedine and Magai 2006; Magai 2008). What older adults require in their relationships changes (Carstensen et al. 2011) as life's priorities change: work connections may be less important than community engagement for example. Further, they may be expecting less from others and willing to give back more. What they are exploring are more meaningful interpersonal relations. This is contrast to adults, at earlier stages of their careers who may be seeking promotion, salary and tangible benefits.

People connect with others in different ways and a mentor needs to appreciate this: some people feel very confident in building professional relationships and less so with non-professional ones while the reverse may be true for others. Some people feel insecure and lack confidence in their ability to forge strong relationships with others believing others are always right and the "problem is with me". In other cases, people feel a heightened sense of self-possession and see others as not being able to live up to their personal or relationship expectation. In both cases, individuals may be perceived as aloof although, in the former, it is for entirely different reasons. There are others who are simply anxious and fearful of connecting especially professionally as they do not feel they can measure up to expectations or because they have witnessed others being intimidated and wish to avoid the same experience for themselves (Bartholomew and Horowitz 1991).

In presenting to a mentor, some mentees will prefer to maintain distance with the mentor, while others will want reassurance. The mentor's challenge is to facilitate those at the extreme ends of 'distance' and 'closeness' to a more balanced approach in their relationships while maintaining or developing a sense of personal and professional autonomy. The risk is that those seeking closeness will become overly dependent on their mentors and present as needy whereas as those wanting to remain 'detached' will not develop an easy professional rapport with their mentors (see Merz and Consedine 2012; Merz et al. 2009). The mentor is working with the mentee to strive for a secure attachment which is positively correlated with measures of well-being in both cases (Merz and Consedine 2012).

People who feel they cannot live up to other's expectations or lack confidence in relationships may present as less optimistic about their future career and opportunities. Often these are people who are high maintenance, depend on others for providing them with feelings of their own self-worth rather than seeing their own intrinsic worth (Foster et al. 2007). They try to please others as they fear rejection.

Mentors will require heightened sensitivity to these issues and also how they work in building relationships with these type of mentees (Mikulincer and Shaver 2007).

Mentees who fear relationships often have low self-worth which goes unrecognised due to their emotional stoicism (Collins and Feeney 2000) and are less likely to trust others (Consedine and Magai 2006). They draw on themselves for providing their emotional needs as they are suspicious of others; while reacting defensively to external displays of emotions (Laan et al. 2012). Mentees like this find that "life is especially difficult" (Mikulincer and Shaver 2007, p. 43).

Attachment requires being open to revealing issues that weigh on them. In seeking out a mentor, the mentee may be confronted with loyalty to the other being traded for fairness for themselves. Implicitly mentees are weighing the value of loyalty to the group i.e. the employer or the profession relative to what they perceive as fairness and equity to themselves. In any situation, fairness suggests that all persons and groups be treated equally. And yet most people would concede that the world is unfair.

Mentoring often constitutes a sense of disloyalty for the mentee due to a conflict between competing concerns that the mentee might have in regard to the reason for seeking a mentor. It might also present a deeper conundrum of putting the interests of self ahead of those of others e.g. the employer, the profession, the supervisor, the team. Not only in this sense but also in others, the mentoring relationship mirrors the social and psychological nature of relationships that the mentee and mentor have independently of each other.

By contrast, loyalty suggests partiality which may be lead to preferential support for some although not all. If this is the case, people will start to trade loyalty off against fairness. The next transaction they consider is what is in their best interests, whether they are the recipients of special favours or not; and is considered a moral decision. This consideration may take place for a specific situation or a generalised one. While most people value fairness, loyalty complicates this equation in the case of perceived obligations (Baron et al. 2013), and affiliations (Rai and Fiske 2011) where each lessons people's preference for loyalty versus fairness (Shaw et al. 2012).

Often confiding in a mentor leads to a relationship where power is delayed due to the mentor's perceived expertise and experience. The mentor needs to be mindful of this, always working towards empowering and not discouraging the strength-building process.

At all times, a relationship with the mentor needs to be established by a warm rapport, trust and confidence. When mentees confide in mentors about sensitive issues concerning actions and relationships at work, often they feel they are betraying their supervisor's loyalty and those of the organisation (Ingram and Bering 2010). The notion of betrayal and divided loyalties needs to be addressed.

More generally, relationships forged by the mentee with the mentor and other colleagues are influenced by both generalised and relationship-specific perceptions of self and those reflected by others (Pierce and Lydon 2001). Both the mentee and mentor will experience the highs and lows of their relationship that reflect the nature of their relationships with others. Each set of relationships that the mentee has, for example, influences their interpreting and responding towards their other relationships in the wider social world (Bowlby 1973). The mentoring relationship is a co-operative construction and reconstruction of meaning applied by the mentee, based on perceived reciprocation and exchange. Both the mentee and mentor need to be loyal to the relationship and to each other within the parameters of mentoring.

The focus in this chapter is the nature of the loyalty connection between the mentee and mentor and how this influences the learning, especially the learning to trust, and other outcomes for the mentee especially in terms of their ongoing relationships with others. Much of what is discussed in mentoring is associated with the quality of independent relationships with a focus on the key attribute of loyalty. This assumption of loyalty is derived from an expectation that mentees, outside of mentoring, are committed to their supervisor, professional body, and others in exchange for benefits. If those benefits are not forthcoming, in the mind of the mentee, this throws the affected relationships into disarray and has ramifications for all their other relationships too. The mentee starts to question their loyalty ties, their trust in others and even their selfhood. This was a fundamental question for Hirschman (1970): what motivates people to become and sustain commitment in their relationships with their employer, management and others. This commitment or loyalty is both positive and negative and can lead to tension and contradictions which people need to unwind and explore.

## 8.2 Why Loyalty?

Loyalty is an enduring issue in all human relationships, from the time of a person's first friendships through to their life-forming relationships such as personal, professional and business partnerships. All of these relationships are underscored by a contract either legal or social (implicit or explicit) or both. There needs to be a sense of integrity as discussed in Chap. 6 Guilt. What facilitates each of these relationships is both an emotional reliability (see Durkheim 1965) as well a rational one. In both the emotional and rational elements of these relationships, there are psychological and social dimensions present.

Loyalty requires that there is both an attitudinal and a behavioural dimension and the two need to be aligned to avoid cognitive dissonance (Festinger 1957). The attitudinal dimension is a commitment to abide by the values, beliefs and interests of the other party—person, group, or institution. For example, a person shows loyalty to their profession and may or may not demonstrate similar loyalty to their supervisor. For loyalty to ensue, commitment is followed up with actions to demonstrate that they accept and follow these values and interests. To do otherwise results in dissonance for the mentee. If this is the case, it leads to distress for the mentee and is often a reason for seeking a mentor to assist them to navigate their way around this. The attitude and actions in one domain need to be fairly consistent across multiple life domains.

Loyalty in mentoring requires a perception by the mentee that this relationship is a unique bond with the mentor and it is highly valued. This value will be demonstrated by both who seek to preserve and endorse it by observing confidentiality, privacy and care.

## 8.3 How Relevant is Loyalty Today?

It may be time to reconsider how relevant or useful the concept of loyalty is. As workplaces become more flexible and, markets less regulated, loyalty to employees and employer is less relevant and less apparent today. It is the professional ties, the fulfilment of the work itself, peers and supervisor who are more influential in shaping a person's experience at work and therefore, their loyalty.

In today's work and professional settings, some people are rewarded and acknowledged for loyalty while others may be overlooked. If this is the case, it can lead to inequity, disparity and undermine relationships at every level in the workplace.

Moreover, blind loyalty is a form of suppression and disregards the reality that loyalty in some relationships is undeserving. To be loyal to those that are perceived as undeserving is disingenuous. Some people and indeed some positions warrant institutional authority, even though the incumbents might not be worthy, consider personal loyalty as their due and do not feel the need to reciprocate which undermines their significant relationships especially with those of less influence.

Are people loyal? The answer is it depends. Most people in most spheres, professional or personal, refer to loyalty in a way that suggests that they value it. Are people truly loyal or conform out of habit or wish to avoid rocking the boat? Compliance through habit certainly exhibits elements of loyalty.

Loyalty depends on people's experience and how rewarded or acknowledged they were for showing commitment to a person, a goal, a client or a customer. What people require from their various situations, work and personal, is more layered than it has been in the past. Career cycles are shorter than in the past. People are more likely to engage in multiple careers with increasing responsibilities.

Loyalty and choice are important. Loyalty may be more related to the experience of the opportunities afforded by the employer e.g. further education, training, networking, international travel and work rather than the employer relationship per se.

The failure to appreciate the complexity of loyalty is something that mentors need to consider. Compliance or experience could be masking low loyalty. Understanding loyalty that reflects personal attachment such as expressions of trust and preference are more meaningful. Even when loyal, mentees will have difficulty explaining their attitudinal loyalty.

While choice is a factor in militating against loyalty. Today people have many more choices in terms of their work and professional relationships and dealings. Frequently, the number of choice options is greater than the person's ability to maintain loyalty relationships with all the relevant stakeholders, especially when there are mixed loyalties which are unclear and uncertain. For example, people can be simultaneously loyal to a supervisor, team, organisation or brand, profession or professional reputation. Individual employees depend on their organisation or profession to provide them with resources (e.g., facilities, equipment) and support (e.g., training and development) to perform their role (Yim et al. 2008). When the attitudes of the person align with organisation or profession, there is a connection and this is similar in the mentoring relationship when there are two similar referents coming together and both recognise it.

People connect through what is often described today as the X factor. Howard and Gengler (2001) referred to an emotional infectivity which they described as a flow of emotions from one person to another, generating a wave effect, not unlike the "Mexican" wave. As such, a mentor's emotional stance elicits an expressive response from the mentee. This affect is researched in area of customer loyalty, whereby positive feelings lead to loyalty and investment (based Yim et al. 2008).

People need to align actions and attitude so they relieve any distress when these are askew, according to cognitive dissonance theory (Festinger 1957). Another way to describe this is to understand what is going on and what may be contributing to feelings of discomfort for mentees. Awareness of what is going on is quite complex in most workplaces and professional settings. The reason is that actions from colleagues, supervisors and subordinates are aligned to multiple targets depending on each group's and individual's interests, values and expectations. Cognitive dissonance triggers this evaluation or re-evaluation of what is going on (Sluss et al. 2012). Most people who achieve benefits from a relationship, whether it be their supervisor, general medical practitioner or mentor, feel grateful the emotional appreciation for benefits received, accompanied by a desire to reciprocate, which leads to loyalty. If successfully done through a mentoring relationship and well-articulated by the mentor, it can lead to a transference of this learning to other relationships.

The mentor, by means of regular meetings over a period of time providing individualised attention to the mentee, becomes a significant relational-other (Hennig-Thurau et al. 2002). It is through this, that a mentor influences mentees by providing feedback, moderating their expectations and assists them with their plans. Mentors need to recognise their potential influence and not abuse it.

## 8.4 The Riskiness of Loyalty in Mentoring

Loyalty is viewed as a binding relationship between two people in either a social, emotional or legal sense. A loyal relationship sometimes prevents one person from seeking other more expedient interests and relationships.

The notion of loyalty can mean one person sublimating their needs for the other e.g. followers submitting to the instructions of a leader, one partner supporting the other and foregoing personal benefits as a consequence. Loyalty based on personality can also make for an unhealthy situation and potential abuse. A mentee may simply transfer their compliance from one situation to the mentoring relationship. This is a risk in mentoring relationships where mentees become overly dependent on the mentor. One way to mitigate this risk is to ensure that the duration of a mentoring relationship extends for no longer than 12 weeks at at time without a break.

The more educated and professional the workforce, the less likely that loyalty will automatically flow. Loyalty develops and evolves "just as a seed grows into a tree" (Hill 2003: 258). If the organisation is established along democratic lines with well-articulated values, engagement processes including inclusivity, the need for loyalty is diminished.

In all cases, loyalty on the part of one person for the other may be exchanged, borne out of self-interest or subjugated benefits. If loyalty is attained through domination, then the faithfulness is not sincere but endured out of fear through the threat of penalty, withdrawal of rewards, conflict or reprisal. If loyalty is reciprocated and exchanged, then there is steadiness between the mentee and mentor, both benefiting in some way and both feeling a sense of trust and respect between them. The process will lead to a strong sense of self is what drives human action and is critical for an autonomous and efficacious life. People who are too insecure and lack confidence in their ability to forge strong relationships with others or who are anxious and fearful of connecting with others, need to come to terms with this. This is a key learning outcome of a mentoring relationship.

A person's concept of self-worth comprises a set of meanings which they draw on in a social role or situation, defining what it means to be who one is in that role or situation (Burke and Tully 1977). Trust and confidence are linked. If a mentee feels confident and assured, it follows that they will act accordingly engendering trust in others who are more likely want to relate to them in some way. Accordingly a strong notion of self is important for sustaining loyalty in these relationships.

a. Personal loyalties
b. Team loyalties
c. Professional loyalties
d. Employer loyalties

In each of the above sets of loyalties, the mentee needs to be encouraged to question the values and integrity of each as well as their own perceptions of self, including whether this is the position they value and aspire to become or one that others have imposed upon them.

## 8.5 What Engenders Loyalty?

Loyalty is a bond that develops, characterised by trust and belief in the dependability of the other (e.g. Bowlby 1980; Granovetter 1985). Trust between two people is important as it leads to reciprocal support or exchange (Blau 1964) in terms of what is trying to be achieved, how to go about it as well as the personal character displayed across diverse situations (Chen and Blanchard-Fields 2000).

When a person is confident not only in their world view but their self-view, they are liberated to trust others.

In a mentoring relationship, when the mentee verifies through good mentoring their self-view and this is acknowledged by the mentor, trust between them is triggered. Mentees seek to confirm their self-views, often by looking at the responses and views of mentors (Swann 1990). When the mentor acknowledges the mentee, loyalty to the mentoring relationship begins to develop. The instigation of loyalty is based on some form of identifying with each other, although not necessarily equal. Loyalty is important because it helps to determine responsibilities (Culbertson et al. 2010; Wu et al. 2012).

Having a significant other, like a mentor, verify one's views means that the mentee's sense of self is confirmed. In turn, the mentee starts to view the mentor as trustworthy and begins to open up to explore the questions and concerns that they wish to address. This process cannot be rushed and may unfold over a number of meetings.

What happens in mentoring is that the mentee's sense of self is bolstered as well as their regard for others as they begin to perceive the world differently. It is only in revealing the self to others that others respond differently to the mentee and see them in a different light. A social exchange is activated when there are significant and reciprocal interpersonal interactions.

For the mentee, this may result in being included as part of the desired group. This membership serves also to bolster further a sense of self for the newly included member and confidence is increased further, so the benefits are wider than the actual membership. Both are valued by the mentee and serve to enhance their self-esteem and ultimately, self-efficacy. A person's emotions are intensified, providing an aura of positivity i.e. feels at ease with their place in the world. This elation affects all aspects of their demeanor and actions. Resilience is also an outcome especially if the mentee gains the confidence to deal with exploitative loyalty in the workplace (Sloan et al. 2010; van Heugten 2010).

Are people disloyal? The answer is they can be but it is not usual. Disloyalty is often judged as an act of relationship betrayal rather than one based on position, professional or client requirements. In regard to the latter, the betrayal is often viewed as a failure of duty of care. In circumstances where there is disloyalty, lack of acknowledgement of effort or contribution or a lack of opportunity to experience loyal relationships, disbenefits for the person occur. For example, when people are not positively reinforced for their loyalty not only is there a risk they "exit" the relationship but also it will impact their selfhood as outlined above. The exit may not result in physical departure. It may occur by becoming silent, preoccupied or compliant.

## 8.6 Conclusion

Trust is crucial for loyalty so is acknowledgement for a good job done. Many mentees feel a sense of not being acknowledged for their efforts and contribution. If this feeling is prolonged, they look to move on. This is a matter of survival and career development rather than disloyalty although many interpret leaving as disloyalty. Mentoring can assist mentees to articulate their expectations. This is a reciprocal process of give and take which occurs in any relationship anywhere. When people voice, they have a sense of control and freedom and contribute so much more.

## References


Baron, J., Ritov, I., & Greene, J. D. (2013). The duty to support nationalistic policies. *Journal of Behavioural Decision Making, 26*, 128–138.

Bartholomew, K., & Horowitz, L. M. (1991). Attachment styles among young adults: A test of a four-category model. *Journal of Personality and Social Psychology, 61*(2), 226–244.

Blau, P. M. (1964). *Exchange and power in social life*. New York: Wiley.

Bowlby, J. (1973). *Attachment and loss: Separation*. New York: Basic Books.

Bowlby, J. (1980). *Attachment and loss: Sadness and depression*. New York: Basic Books.

Burke, P. J., & Tully, J. (1977). The measurement of role/identity. *Social Forces, 55*, 881–997.

Carstensen, L. L., Turan, B., Scheibe, S., Ram, N., Ersner-Hersfield, H., Samanez-Larkin, G. R., et al. (2011). Emotional experience improves with age: Evidence based on over 10 years of experience. *Psychology and Aging, 26*(1), 21–33.

Chen, Y., & Blanchard-Fields, F. (2000). Unwanted thought: age differences in teh correction of social judgments. *Psychology and Ageing, 15*:475–482.

Collins, N. L., & Feeney, B. C. (2000). A safe haven: An attachment theory perspective on support seeking and caregiving in intimate relationships. *Journal of Personality and Social Psychology, 78*(6), 1053–1073.

Consedine, N. S., & Magai, C. (2006). Emotional development in adulthood: A developmental functionalist review and critique. In C. Hoare (Ed.), *Handbook of adult development and learning* (pp. 123–148). New York: Oxford University Press.

Culbertson, S. S., Huffman, A. H., & Alden-Anderson, R. (2010). Leader-member exchange and work-family interactions: The mediating role of self-reported challenge—And hindrance-related stress. *Journal of Psychology, 144*(1), 15–36.

Durkheim, E. (1965). *The elementary forms of the religious life*. New York: Free Press.

Festinger, L. (1957). A theory of cognitive dissonance. Stanford: Stanford University Press.

Foster, D. J., Kernis, H. M., & Goldman, M. B. (2007). Linking adult attachment of self-esteem stability. *Self and Identity, 6*(1), 64–73.

Granovetter, M. (1985). Economic action and social structure: The problem of embeddedness. *American Journal of Sociology, 91*, 481–510.

Hennig-Thurau, T., Gwinner, K. P., & Gremler, D. D. (2002). Understanding relationship marketing outcomes: An integration of relational benefits and relationship quality. *Journal of Service Research, 4*(3), 230–247.

Hill, R. (2003). The compassionate organisation in the 21st century. *Organisational Dynamics, 32* (4), 331–341.

Hirschman, A. O. (1970). *Exit, voice, and loyalty: Responses to decline in firms, organizations, and states*. Harvard University Press.

Howard, D. J., & Gengler, C. (2001). Emotional contagion effects on product attitudes. *Journal of Consumer Research, 28*(2), 189–201.

Ingram, G. P. D., & Bering, J. M. (2010). Children's tattling: The reporting of everyday norm violations in preschool settings. *Child Development, 81*, 945–957.

Laan, A. J., Marcel, A. L. M., & Vingerhoets, J. J. M. (2012). Individual differences in adult crying: The role of attachment styles. *Social Behaviour and Personality an International Journal, 40*(3), 453–471.

Magai, C. (2008). Attachment in middle and later life. In J. Cassidy & P. R. Shaver (Eds.), *Handbook of attachment: Theory, research, and clinical applications* (2nd ed., pp. 532–551). New York: Guilford.

Merz, E. M., & Consedine, N. S. (2012). Ethnic group moderates the association between attachment and well-being in later life. *Cultural Diversity and Ethnic Minority Psychology, 18* (4), 404–415.

Merz, E. M., Consedine, N. S., Schulze, H. J., & Schuengel, C. (2009). Wellbeing of adult children and ageing parents: Associations with intergenerational support and relationship quality. *Ageing and Society, 29*(5), 783–802.

Mikulincer, M., & Shaver, P. R. (2007). *Attachment in adulthood.* New York: Guilford.

Pierce, T., & Lydon, J. E. (2001). Global and specific models in the experience of social interactions. *Journal of Personality and Social Psychology, 80*, 613–631.

Rai, T. S., & Fiske, A. P. (2011). Moral psychology is relationship regulation: Moral motives for unity, hierarchy, equality, and proportionality. *Psychological Review, 118*, 57–75.

Sexton, T. L., & Whiston, S. C. (1994). The status of the counselling relationship: An empirical review, theoretical implications, and research directions. *The Counselling Psychologist, 22*(1), 6–78.

Shaw, A., DeScioli, P., & Olson, K. R. (2012). Fairness versus favouritism in children. *Evolution and Human Behaviour, 33*, 736–745.

Sloan, L. M., Matyók, T., & Schmitz, C. L. (2010). A story to tell: Bullying and mobbing in the workplace. *International Journal of Business and Social Science, 1*(3), 87–97.

Sluss, D. M., & Ashforth, B. E. (2008). How relational and organizational identification converge: Processes and conditions. *Organisation Science, 19*(6), 807–823.

Sluss, D. M., Ashforth, B. E., & Gibson, K. R. (2012). The search for meaning in (new) work: Task significance and newcomer plasticity. *Journal of Vocational Behavior*, 81(2):199–208.

Swann, W. B. (1990). To be adored or to be known? The interplay of self-enhancement and self-verification. In E. T. Higgins & R. M. Sorrentino. (Eds). *Handbook of motivation and cognition* (pp. 408–450). New York: Guilford.

van Heugten, K. (2010). Bullying of social workers: Outcomes of a grounded study into impacts and interventions. *British Journal of Social Work, 40*(2), 638–655.

Wu, T., Hu, C., & Jiang, D. (2012). Is subordinate's loyalty a precondition of supervisor's benevolent leadership? The moderating effects of supervisor's altruistic personality and perceived organizational support. *Asian Journal of Social Psychology, 15*(3), 145–155.

Yim, C. K., Tse, D. K., & Chan, K. W. (2008). Strengthening customer loyalty through intimacy and passion: Roles of customer-firm affection and customer-staff relationships in services. *Journal of Marketing Research, 45*, 741–756.

# Chapter 9
# Mentoring for All Seasons

*"I could nor would rule my King. But there's a little ... little, area ... where I must rule myself."*
*Act one, scene seven A Man for all Seasons*

**Abstract** This chapter contains a series of vignettes to demonstrate the positive outcomes of reciprocal feedback used across organisational settings and in workplaces. The approach is similar to that used in one–on-one mentoring albeit in a more structured way between management and staff, especially when it is embedded within other 'normal' procedures. In the same way that businesses invite feedback from customers and clients, a similar principle is relevant to staff, with value not only for staff but also for the organisation as a whole. These cases demonstrate how groups benefit by delivering mutual feedback. It is reciprocal in that it provides support for staff and creates less uncertainty. Feedback is a core part of all staff development as well as mentoring.

## 9.1 Introduction

This chapter reveals a series of case examples of how mentoring has been used in organisations that demonstrate a range of diverse and positive outcomes. It is as the quotation above suggests about doing things that people believe in and because they do what they know is right. Mentoring helps people to discover how to achieve things for others without foregoing what is important. Strategies and programs for staff development based on feedback such as an enterprise-wide mentoring program not only provide feedback to participants but also modify the workplace culture such that feedback becomes embedded as a norm in all the processes of an organisation. Changing organisational norms and values is another example of the wider effects associated with, and which occur beyond mentoring. In the same way that management in these organisations invited feedback from customers and clients, they applied a similar principle and access to their staff with some significant benefits not only for staff but also for the organisation as a whole. These cases demonstrate how management ensured that by delivering mutual feedback in the

 
A.M. Brewer, *Mentoring from a Positive Psychology Perspective*,
DOI 10.1007/978-3-319-40983-2_9

organisation and providing support for acting on this feedback and taking a stand on the quality of feedback, it became a core part of all staff development programs. It also had far-reaching effects on other processes beyond these.

Why is feedback important? Most people desire feedback in some form either to understand how they are going in the course of their work; how well a project went or what the impact of their influence is. The issue in most organisations is that feedback is often delivered when something is going wrong. Many staff are not given feedback frequently when all goes to plan. Human beings tend to comment on what can be improved when something does not work well rather than remark why when it does. To demonstrate this point, think of the last time you experienced a poor service or a faulty product. How many people did you tell about it? By contrast how many people do you tell when a service or product works as expected? This pattern of communication is reflected in organisations with staff too. Managers tend to either provide no feedback or if they do, it is negative and usually about a staff member's poor performance. Even in the latter situation, managers often avoid having a difficult conversation and so staff often are not aware when their performance falls short of management's expectations. More importantly, if feedback is provided it is delivered in a way that serves little to improve the situation; and sometimes it is so weak in meaning that a staff member does not understand the significance or implication of an issue or problem. Consequently, they are left unsure as to how to respond.

This chapter focuses firstly on the ways mentoring can be utilised in a range of organisational and professional settings with managers and staff, especially before, during and after change; whether this change is for financial restructuring, streamlining processes, cultural diversity, succession planning and so on. Specifically, the aim is to demonstrate the importance of feedback and how mentoring is used to serve that purpose not only in one-on-one situations but also through enterprise-wide strategies. A second purpose is to show how mentoring enhances staff capability, both individually and collectively. Finally, the chapter explores challenges that staff face and highlights the elements of how and effective mentoring development program can support them and instil best practice. By introducing a coherent mentoring program at all levels within an organisation, large or small, this can return significant value not only to the organisation as a whole but also to both mentees and mentors as this chapter demonstrates. Mentoring not only assists capable people understand their strengths but also where improvements can be made even in situations where everything seems to be heading in the wrong or right direction. It is particularly effective where people need to develop their capability and self-efficacy and without additional support, may otherwise fail.

Mentoring is a process of exploring and discovering opportunities together for the benefit of the mentee and their profession, organisation or both. The relationship is important because it both encompasses and uncovers the tangible and unobservable elements within organisations through the eyes of the staff. Managers are not always aware of this except tacitly (Schneider et al. 2013). Through mentoring, mentees learn how to uncover issues, deal with them and implement outcomes arising from this process. They, in turn, become self-efficacious (based on Chell 2008) in the following ways:

a. Goal directed;
b. Develop responsibility for self-directed learning;
c. Identify choices;
d. Evaluate the options (risks) associated with each;
e. Explore opportunities arising from the option generation process;
f. Action-orientated;
g. Develop a perception of their own effectiveness, real and potential;
h. Social capability; and
i. Develop a vision for future possibilities.

To identify, attract, appoint and retain staff effectively, every organisation needs a strategic development program focused on staff needs including their career plans as well as a workforce succession strategy. This is not to overlook the importance of good recruitment and selection in the first place—something that is often not viewed against workforce and succession planning.

Succession planning is vital for the future growth of the workforce in terms of its capability. The impending retirement of the baby boom generation has heightened the need for the development of staff and succession planning. In Australia for example, at the turn of the last century (1901), older people constituted 4.0 % of Australia's population. Between 1971 and 2011, the proportion of Australia's population aged 65 years and over increased to 14 %. For those aged 85 years and over it more than tripled, from 0.5 to 1.8 %. In 2011, women aged 65 years and over formed 15 % of the total population of women, while older men constituted a smaller proportion of all men, 13 %. This pattern is similar in all developed western nations (ABS 2012).

Management is facing two major challenges in finding and developing the next generation of leaders. They need to identify qualified candidates to fill current and future leadership roles, and they need to develop a comprehensive leadership program to cultivate and develop the leaders of tomorrow. All of this is occurring as technology changes and businesses are restructured, presenting a scenario where no one really knows what skills will be at the forefront for future leaders.

Mentoring has a special place in this process not only in terms of staff development but also in regard to enhancing workforce capability and preparing staff for succession. In any case, mentoring benefits both the mentee and mentor. In a structured program, prospective mentees are more likely to be selected and matched more effectively leading to improved outcomes for the mentee. In informal mentoring programs, it is left up to the individual's discretion in terms of offering and delivering mentoring and up to a mentee to seek it. Moreover, if a staff member has had the benefit of being well-mentored, they will have experienced first-hand some people understanding the benefits and more likely wanting to contribute and reciprocate the advantage to others. There are corresponding benefits for mentors. In acting as a mentor, people have the opportunity to develop further their own skills and knowledge.

This value is more likely to occur within a structured mentoring program rather than an ad hoc one, where it can be factored into the equation. In the past, staff development was focused on a few, select individuals, usually midway and above in the management hierarchy of an organisation. Even though globalisation of markets has reshaped products and services, the focus of most businesses in developing staff is still individual-focused leading to silos of specialist skill domains rather than integrated ones.

Mentoring offers one such integrated framework. Mentoring is also deep engagement for staff where moral purpose and ethics can be further developed not only in the mentee but also the mentors. An enterprise-wide mentoring strategy allows management to implement an approach which integrates ways of assessing and selecting staff, aligned with specific programs for example for aspiring leaders to develop skills in this direction while assuring the measurement of the success of outcomes for individuals, groups and organisations. This can be done by using a combination of strategies, for example, mentoring or coaching with 360° feedback. This provides evidence to staff and management about their progress. As already mentioned throughout this book, there are many and varied reasons for offering and seeking mentoring including career development, succession planning for capability and promotional purposes, leadership, retention of highly capable staff, developing a shared mindset that influences the cultural and strategic directions of the organisation as well as addressing diversity and capability gaps and challenges that staff may be experiencing in dealing with client service relationships, diversity issues and conflict to cite a few. This chapter will focus on these issues as well as making a case for an organisational-wide mentoring program, regardless of the nature and size of the business even if it is family-owned and managed. Further, it points to how technology can be deployed to extend these practices across the enterprise providing easy access for all staff wherever they are located.

## 9.2 Mentoring Is a Diversity Initiative

Business prospers from workforce, diversity initiatives, and cross-cultural mentoring programs is a good example of this. The workforce includes the aging workforce whereby an increasing percentage of staff cannot afford to retire early or on time or just don't want to. Staff are increasingly exposed to the diversity of business practices by virtue of their employer's position in a global supply chain. Further, women are playing a stronger role in management and a growing number of culturally diverse employees are entering the workforces in all countries. Through mentoring, diversity is explored, better understood and actioned. Given the diversity of cultures that are represented in the workplace today, this is pivotal. Increasingly management and boards understand that both communication and positive workplace interactions are the cornerstone of professional relationships, whether communicating with customers or within the organisations, vertically and horizontally. The question is how best to achieve this.

In this example of leadership development, senior management of a company understood the benefits of mentoring and used the building and expanding of customer and internal relationships across the various divisions of the organisation. The latter was their primary intention. While there had been a lot of informal mentoring, it had not necessarily captured the staff that could potentially benefit most from it. None of the mentoring to date had been part of a structured program. Most mentoring was "ad hoc" primarily among white male staff. Based on an internal staff survey following their decision to initiate a mentoring program, the review of staff feedback showed that there was a low incidence of female and culturally diverse staff accessing any form of staff development, and none had participated in mentoring.

Management wanted to develop and implement a formal mentoring program that would engage all staff. They established a 'mentoring advisory board' for line managers to steer the program so that it could align with both the divisional and enterprise strategies as well as address individual needs. Their challenge was to implement the program within a six month period while the survey feedback remained fresh in people's minds. Line managers were asked to sponsor staff in each of their divisions. They, in turn, requested team leaders to nominate names to fulfil roles for both mentors and mentees. Once this was process was completed, management invested in bringing in a mentoring specialist to work with the board to create a formal mentoring program that had a strong focus on staff diversity. Management undertook a base line measure of staff diversity at the commencement of the program with the intention to reassess this every three years. One suggestion for improving the board would be to ensure that its composition represented the diverse group of mentees targeted for this program.

The approach used was to canvass and audit the needs of prospective mentees. The challenge was how to encourage participation amongst those who would benefit most to maximise the potential and impact. Based on staff consultation over a few weeks, lead mentors were appointed, selected and approved by the advisory board, who then worked with the consultant to develop a strategy. This process led to a charter of development needs of potential mentees. Senior management followed this process with a search conference of line managers including those from diverse backgrounds to see how this would be best communicated to all staff in the organisation as well as ideas for promoting it to other staff in a range of geographical locations.

The mentoring board decided that a small pilot mentoring program with a focus on diversity would be the best approach initially, since positive outcomes from the pilot program would help achieve participation and sponsorship from line management from the whole organisation, management and staff. The pilot program was the forerunner to the organisational-wide roll out. For the pilot, volunteers were invited to become mentoring champions to encourage mentors to volunteer and for mentees to identify themselves and participate. Confidentiality and privacy were assured for the mentees. Training for mentors was the first step provided by the mentoring consultant followed by the matching program conducted online with potential for referrals.

The Mentoring Program was inaugurated with the Head of one of the divisions, key line managers and HR Director present to show their support and endorse the program's legitimacy. A further specialist was hired to monitor and evaluate the program and was able to observe all parts: from the mentoring board's deliberations through to the way staff diversity was being assessed. While it is too early to record in this book its outcomes, by all account, the mentoring program was judged well by staff, based on the feedback from mentors and mentees who both valued shared experiences, management's understanding about diversity's contribution to the organisation, and that every participant recorded found a safe forum to discuss pertinent issues.

## 9.3 Mentoring Is the First Step in Succession Planning

After reviewing the rate of growth for their company the Board of a national organisation focusing on health needed to institute an internal succession plan. Its unprecedented growth due to high client demand meant that more and more agencies were being opened requiring a manager to administer each one. The company had a talented workforce and people needed to be identified within it to take up lead-manager roles as well as recruit from outside the organisation. It was decided that the HR team develop a set of core competencies for all Lead Agency positions as well as additional competencies specific to each role. The CEO engaged an HR expert to assess potential candidates to evaluate their viability as candidates and created development plans to ensure their readiness. Each potential lead- manager received a detailed report and individual feedback from the HR team to help prepare for the development planning process. At the same time, it was decided to introduce a mentoring program to support newly appointed lead-managers and aspirants to these positions. This process is still being rolled out. Staff feedback showed almost unanimous support for mentoring support.

## 9.4 Mentoring for Developing Leadership

A large Australian international logistics company needed to bolster their leadership capacity and build greater organisational effectiveness during a period of significant, accelerated growth for its workforce especially in dealing with its suppliers.

A mentoring program was developed together with the logistics Directors who acted as the internal champions. The plan was sponsored by the CEO and the leadership team. The mentors were identified by divisional heads and requested to participate in a leadership development program based on leadership principles and tools designed for the front line, middle and senior management. This approach provided a coherent leadership strategy and systems across the three tiers of leadership in this organisation. The programs included critical engagement between participants and senior leaders on current leadership and organisational challenges by way of mentoring conversations. From here mentees were identified based on the performance reviews over the last three (3) years. There has been a significant shift in the leadership culture of the organisation to a values-based leadership approach based on feedback from participants and management.

## 9.5 Mentoring Managers and Staff for Organisational Change

In order to maintain its leading position in a competitive marketplace, a global beverages distributor needed a flexible, specialised workforce to facilitate a large-scale change strategy for more streamlined delivery aligning this to their state of the art technology as well as staff development.

Consultation kicked off the process, and peer mentoring was introduced via Skype between global managers in each country. Each site benefited from speaking with a similar manager who either had completed the change, in the middle of it or preparing for its introduction. Peers who matched by role and markets. Mentoring helped develop managers and staff to understand the changes and prepare them for new skill requirements and expectations within their own teams. Peer mentoring introduces a more collaborative problem-solving element and less confronting then with peers in the same location.

Managers acting as mentors for mentees in other divisions assisted with cross-fertilisation of ideas and helped managers understand some of the change leadership. Managers joined a mentoring circle to assist them in overseeing career decision conversations and co-ordinate outcomes with their direct reports.

Mentors also worked with mentees to assist them in navigating change and managing their careers, leveraging the benefits of mentoring as well as other critical decisions. Staff feedback surveys identified issue around expectations of change by managers and staff and whether these were adequately addressed through mentoring.

## 9.6 Group Mentoring to Align Workforce with Changes to Organisational and Business Strategy

Another organisation, while undergoing change due to market fluctuations, decided to instigate panel discussions, selected using vertical slices of staff to ensure reporting relationship from within the organisation (maximum of 10 members) with professional mentors, external to the organisation.

Mentors facilitated group sessions that enabled participants to identify, prioritise and align initiatives specific to achieving the new business strategy. The mentor analysed these examples with each panel of staff. Intact work groups, who relied on each other, worked together to reach a common understanding of their responsibilities for managing change so that pinpoint the new skills that team leaders would need to address within their teams. Individuals were requested to self-identify if they required one on one mentoring. The CEO found the process so valuable that mentoring was expanded and rolled out more widely in the organisation as an ongoing program. Additional mentors from within the organisation were trained for participating within the mentoring panels.

## 9.7 Mentoring for Redeploying Staff

In this next example, a formal mentoring program assisted management of a small, medium sized enterprise to identify and facilitate career transition for staff who wanted to develop their skills and experience. This program had several outcomes including:

a. Identifying inefficiencies in recruitment
b. Instigate and enhance value through a more targeted re-employment process.

Mentoring assisted managers, and HR staff to discover a better fit between people, context, career stage and aspirations. They re-designed their staff deployment process which had been seen previously in a negative light. The program will now continue on an ongoing basis.

## 9.8 Mentoring Assisted in Enhancing Staff Retention, Re-engagement and Career Planning

A large, merchant bank was experiencing growing retention problems in their workforce in one of its largest divisions. Staff who were exiting were highly qualified and had been in the same role for approximately two years. Recent downsizing at the top and bottom levels of the organisation had resulted in an exceptional increase in staff moving sideways across the organisation. A state of uncertainty had descended upon the organisation. Young, educated staff were looking for new opportunities. Management became concerned that they would lose staff prematurely and find it difficult to replace them in the short term. An internal staff survey showed continuing low staff willingness to envisage a career path within the bank.

A mentoring program was introduced as a way for staff to think about and plan their career development. Each staff member was requested to complete a staff profile on line, a self-review of their performance before they engaged in one to one mentoring for about 10 weeks. A follow up survey showed staff attitudes were positive about management facilitating this career planning process.

## 9.9 Mentoring Lessons from the Case Studies

In each of the cases above, management chose which strategy and parallel-process they wished to use. All programs contained some form of feedback through mentoring or a mentoring-type program. Whatever the reason for mentoring, it is a source of feedback which can be more formalised while still protecting the confidentiality and privacy of mentees.

## 9.10 A Mentoring Responsive Culture

The effect of mentoring on an enterprise culture is profound. As individual staff participate in mentoring, feedback is viewed as increasingly the norm, and staff become more feedback-responsive. These examples show how mentoring is not only an investment in individual staff but also there is an investment in cultural development, both immediate and beyond the mentoring experience leading to a form of social or mentoring capital.

## 9.11 Mentoring Capital

Mentoring capital, which includes understanding how to engage in the workplace and professional spheres, plays a crucial part the ongoing development of staff. Where an enterprise culture is responsive to feedback this will lead to higher numbers of staff seeking mentors and, therefore, higher levels of feedback overall. Staff will be more inclined to request mentoring; with positive spin offs such as taking risks within the relationship when they feel that this is well received by all in their workplace and by their supervisor (Tan 2013).

A feedback responsive culture develops and strengthens trust and a "psychologically safe" context to discuss how things are done; whether they are done well or not so well which reinforces meaningful feedback (Nyhan 2000). For example, mentors, especially in enterprise-wide programs, are trained to foster trust so as to establish a feedback culture. A psychologically, safe environment is related to the receptivity of feedback as it assures that negative feedback is not transformed into relational conflict and moreover that the levels of feedback-seeking activity increases among staff. Trust also enhances the meaningfulness of feedback because it promotes openness and encourages staff to receive feedback mindfully. To build a trusting and safe environment, staff and managers engage in problem-solving communication which is a more equitable form to find a common understanding and ground between them. Informal and mutual feedback between supervisors, staff and amongst co-workers deepens trust and uncovers ambiguities (Rosen et al. 2006). Feedback occurring in this way is more likely to be timely, relevant, and, therefore, acted upon.

## 9.12 Safe Learning Culture and Dialogue

Feedback-responsiveness leads to action orientated learning and ultimately, a safe learning culture. Once this culture is assured, additional endeavours can be geared towards creating dialogue—meaningful free-flowing conversations that occur in a diverse range of communication channels. This is more likely a highly favourable outcome of feedback-responsive cultures. Dialogue is made of any number of conversations between participants such as a CEO maintaining a dialogue with staff (a community-wide dialogue); team leaders with their teams, a supervisor with a staff member and so on. The form that the dialogue takes will vary from co-operative to conflictual; according to the dynamics of when the conversations occur, the complementarity between the participants, and the context. All dialogue requires a degree of coordination as well as an understanding amongst the participants about what is at stake, and a degree of latitude for refuting each other. "Communication means to bring others and oneself together with others, into such being-in-the-world and to dwell in it" (Heidegger 2011, p.23). Dialogue is non-threatening and emerges intentionally from parties that feel a sense of goodwill towards each other. Managers need to model dialogue at every level of the organisation.

Feedback is essential for creating a sense of management and staff being responsive to each other. Feedback does not exist in isolation of real attempts to create this. A mentoring strategy implemented throughout the organisation shapes the norms and expectations that relating to each other is important; that support is available and that the organisation is listening to staff. This approach directs attention to the way in which members constitute mutual understanding in and through interaction while also lending meaning to their everyday experiences (Colombo and Senatore 2005). It follows that individual and collective actions carried out in relation to shared representations also contribute to the (re)construction of the organisational milieu. Organisations become 'community-in-the-mind' is no less important than materialistic conceptions of the community (Pahl 2005, p. 621). The strength of the culture, its meaning and its reality exist in staff's minds and everyday working lives. And, by virtue of residing in the minds of multiple actors, as a shared symbolic referent, a feedback-responsive culture has the potential of collective transformation.

The process of entering into dialogue with others has the potential to generate a relational sphere in which diverse ways of thinking and acting can emerge. Through a relational approach, staff are more likely to become engaged with each other in a coordinated sense (McNamee 2004). Communication and dialogue give expression to the multiple discourses that together contribute to the ongoing development of the culture, jointly constructed meanings, and collective actions (McNamee 2004).

Dialogue and culture are beyond the personal and extends to the self in relation to others the continued transformation of the organisation (Grossen and Salazar Orvig 2011, p. 497). Organisations for staff are formed on the how staff interrelate with others. Dialogue assists in the formation of communal ties and practice.

Particularly, efforts to reduce formality and careful word selection may also incite communication and the sharing of information. Engaging in strategic dialogue with staff is risky as meaning and understanding is highly uncertain. Communicating feedback in an informal setting with staff prevents some potential biases (but not all), although it reduces discomfort for either the feedback provider or receiver. Something as simple as the feedback location can affect the tone of the message. In addition, feedback providers should remain cognizant about the choice of words during dialogue exchanges.

Dialogue suggests that communication is mechanical and based on transmission via channels and that these channels are open. Communication whether as feedback or not, flows in all directions; and this exchange of information is rarely embraced throughout the organisation or indeed listened to. Listening is not mutual. So creating meaningful dialogue has to be learnt as both management and staff feel concerned about communicating freely and with others other than their supervisor and co-workers (Kudisch et al. 2006). The major issue that staff experience with communications in their workplaces is a lack of clear expectations and an absence of information to assist their learning for performance. If the information is not forthcoming, distrust takes hold, and staff begin to feel uncertain and anxious. As such, the expectations and perceptions need to be co-ordinated to assure that communication happens across the organisation so as to minimise conflicting messages.

### *9.12.1 How to Achieve a Feedback Responsive Culture Suitable for Mentoring*

Open communication needs to at the centre of management priorities. Modelling open communication will happen and expand if every level of management sees this as a strategic priority and values it within their teams and workplaces. Managers need to engage in genuine communication amongst themselves and with their teams in everyday organisational life. In modelling the behaviour and in expecting it from their direct reporting staff, staff will follow suit and see open communication as a norm for performance. They will mirror the behaviour and sooner or later embrace a similar approach, hence establishing a flow-on effect. In that sense, dialogue becomes a cultural standard aligned to all strategic goals. An increasing number of organisations now include dialogue as a key performance indicator.

In addition to the role and responsibilities of higher management, a third recommendation focuses on employee empowerment. Employees contribute immensely to the development of dialogue and feedback-responsive cultures. They too have to endorse the feedback culture and take a participative role in promoting and honouring these novel culture goals. It is important to bear in mind that higher management not only owns the responsibility of authorising and encouraging empowerment, but also staff are expected to show courage and step up to progress in their roles (Chaleff 2009). In essence, mobilising followership action will empower staff in an organisation. The more staff engage, the more encouraged they will become to take initiative, solve problems and voluntarily participate in desired projects. The more open the communication is with management; the more staff are willing to be open and share their opinions and ideas, and this will be reciprocated by management. Mentoring is a way to learn this process either one-on-one or in small groups. Staff feedback is usually welcomed in organisations. It is critical for management to learn what is going on and assists them to understand the inevitable changes in the workplace, enhance divergent thinking, discover new resources, and help individuals to adjust to change (Reid 2013). Emphasising dialogue then, motivates staff to take initiative and seek feedback because such an orientation diminishes vertical relations and simultaneously promotes horizontal relations (i.e., promotes communication between all levels).

Interestingly, research from survey Feedback and similar shows that individuals' personal image within the organisation affects their decision to seek and provide feedback (Northcraft and Ashford 1990). By thoughtfully acknowledging an employee's contribution to the organisation, this may actually increase the sense of belonging and engagement, thus feeding into the employee's personal image and leading to more feedback seeking behaviours. What is more, feedback seeking has been found to occur most frequently among employees who believe that this behaviour is the norm across the organisation (Morrison 2002). The key point is that the culture of a workplace establishes the norms in regards to feedback, and it reinforces desired behaviours (Chatman and Cha 2003; Reid 2013) benefiting everyone. Accordingly, employee empowerment, attributes of the receiver, provisions of feedback, and stigma around feedback are all volatile and sensitive components to take into account when focusing on dialogue and building a feedback-responsive culture.

Communication and feedback system need to be used to monitor and evaluate the strategies in place. The use of feedback surveys or open-ended questions to capture the change, barriers, and value are encouraged. This type of an approach will also reinforce the central message of open dialogue. Multiple channels of communication with open access increase levels of meaningful feedback from staff and management. With the commitment and involvement of all leaders and followers, as well as the implementation of each of the bus ness and HR processes, alluded to earlier, an organisation will develop and reinforce a key performance driver, the feedback-responsive culture (Reid 2013).

In order to tackle most organisational issues or to introduce staff development, a deep understanding of the culture needs to occur. From the outset and throughout this book, commencing most prominently in Sect. 1.2.1, the importance of culture has been emphasised: a critical part of mentoring mindedness is preparing mentees for cultural experiences, whatever and how diverse these may be.

There are three significant lessons from these case studies bringing culture and mentoring together. The culture of an organisation overall needs to be open to sharing and integrating all staff i.e. a diversity culture. Secondly, management in particular but also staff need to be open to learning continually, expanding their capacity to achieve goals, especially where innovative thinking is required, and staff have been recruited with this in mind. Organisational learning is essentially a collaborative process (Senge 1990). Thirdly, management and staff need to trust each other. If these cultural dimensions are strong, an organisational-wide mentoring strategy will work more effectively.

In these cases, mentoring provided facilitative (i.e., continuous feedback) and directive (i.e., appraisals) feedback which not only may boost learning among associates, but also feedback that aids learning and shows interest in staff, is truly valuable for the organisation (Archer 2010). Feedback is best when embedded in a sequential process to help employees truly understand the meaning and significance of their progress over time (Archer 2010). In other words, the provision of feedback and the influence of feedback on the receiver are most efficient when it is offered in a structured, timely manner and builds off the preceding series of feedback. Feedback needs to be also interpreted as active information in order to become a pedagogic activity, and this is most attainable when it is provided sensibly, specifically, and when it is rooted in a greater organisational goal. The notion of creating a culture which embraces active feedback provided over continuous learning stages is the most effective way to advance organisations as this would create an environment where employees desire and strive for learning opportunities.

Mentoring assists mentee's attitudes about perceived problems. They learn to accept that mistakes are foreseeable depending on the context. Through mentoring they are prepared to cope with the unpredictably of this by identifying patterns and signposts alerting them to this (van der Rijt et al. 2012). They learn to accept that mistakes happen, unavoidably, and that can learn from this by dealing with problems rather than evading them. Mentoring not only encourages providing meaningful and reliable feedback but it also promotes and shapes positive attitudes for mentees. As well, the mentoring relationship, which facilitates this learning (i.e., translating positive critique into action), occurs in a feedback and learning-oriented relationship (Tayfur 2012). Mentoring is immediate: a problem is discussed followed by immediate feedback, so a direct link is made between the problem and learning. When feedback is not provided or not associated with the specific issue, it is not appreciated and is not translated into action (Bindal et al. 2011). If feedback is not immediate and delivered in a supportive way, it will be ignored. Mentoring creates a learning continuum for the mentee and not only is it useful for them it is something they can emulate with their colleagues.

Mentors aim to cultivate a learning environment in order to implement a feedback-friendly culture. Feedback will not only be perceived as providing supportive suggestions, but it will also be delivered in a timely manner that would guarantee the transfer of learning (Rummler and Brache 2012). There are three specific learnings from the case studies here:

1. Mentoring is a continuum, and, therefore, each session needs to promote it
2. Encourage the mentee to engage in creating learning opportunities by bringing questions and issues to be considered
3. Challenging mentees in their own thinking and analysis by getting to face novel situations and receive new information. This approach keeps mentees focused and involved.

These three learnings are critical to mentoring mindedness.

Where a mentoring strategy and program have been implemented in an organisation for the wider benefit of staff, it is seen as a resource and a benefit. The advantages are many including instrumental e.g. skill and knowledge based associated with performance as well as social, cultural and symbolic value or capital (based on Bourdieu's (1994) concept of cultural capital). Instrumental capital is important primarily because it is so significantly associated with the other benefits. For example, if performance is poor than accessing other resources is not likely to occur.

Mentoring provides a social advantage as mentees can begin to access other professional networks that may have been denied them in the past. It also describes the extent to which individuals can extract such resources in attaining professional and personal goals. Thus, social capital is concerned not only with widening their network but also deepening it with contacts who can assist them either in terms of their status, whom they know and so on. A snowball effect takes place.

Mentoring opens the doorway to cultural capital. The very notion of capital denotes a range of resources such understanding how things are perceived and done in this situation as well as from the perspective of wider professional networks working within the same organisation. Cultural capital includes the accoutrements of the workplace and professional cultures. A person's network is often expressed by whom they know, what circles they work and socialised in and whom they can call upon for assistance e.g. act as a referee or a sponsor for a future role. In order to tap into these resources, mentees need to culturally aware and resourceful.

Mentoring within a profession fosters a trusting climate and dialogue amongst novices and experienced staff. If done well, it can assist in creating positive feedback and building a culture to develop and reinforce this especially for novice professionals. This process may cut across professional lines, for example, an experienced nurse with a novice physician. Continuous learning processes, inquiry and dialogue, require a trusting relationship between groups and individuals (i.e., organisational, environmental and individual) so as to be efficient (Marsick and Watkins 2003). Certainly communication across any domain within an organisation requires trust in order to be understood and received well by each end (Avolio and Reichard 2008).

How does this work? A "trust-based" model (Nyhan 2000, p. 102) suggests that organisational culture is the fluid for good communication to be transmitted and transform the nutrients of communication into well-functioning groups and members. Mentoring provides an organisational-level feedback strategy which targets both individual staff and organisational development incorporating mutual exchanges to promote trust (Grenier et al. 2012). Negative feedback leads to task and relational conflict. However, staff working in a trusting culture responded better to criticism than those who did not and further were more likely to act on it. Staff who perceived trust in the workplace acknowledged that negative feedback still holds value and meaning rather than unconstructive implications (Peterson and Behfarb 2003).

Mentoring also provides access to "a form of power that is not perceived as power but as legitimate demands for recognition, deference, obedience, or the services of others" (Swartz 1997, p. 90). It is both personal influence and position status that is important. For example, resources are used by specialist groups and others to exercise their influence. Dominant social groups establish social hierarchies. An example of this is where some professional groups (medicos, lawyers, accountants) may discuss their non-work activities and resources alongside other staff (e.g. clerical) as a way of further elevating their status above them. Others do this by discussing activities such as playing tennis, cycling, mountain climbing, etc. demonstrating particular prowess and strengths outside of work thereby distancing themselves from others who cannot join in such activities and discussion. People converse in this way either intentionally or insensitively drawing on social and symbolic capital as a way to limit access to others who feel left out and marginalised. The often marginalised unconsciously accept this without questioning it (Schubert 2008, pp. 183–198). Others seek points of entry so they can bask in the symbolic culture and enjoy the spoils too.

Mentoring is viewed as a field of learning (Bourdieu 1986) and action, both in an interpersonal and organisational wide sense. The field is a conceptual space for mentees and mentors to share perceptions, to discern and discover new insights. Active participation in the process of the engagement between the mentee and the mentor and where such engagement has transformative effects including developing self-efficacy, amplifying personal well-being and strengthening learning. If mentoring is established as a program whereby all staff can access it either as mentors or mentees, it becomes an important part of staff development and feedback. If mentoring is effective within an organisational setting, it will be valued by all.

Mentoring will become part of the norm and form an essential dimension of the cultural life of the organisation. The parameters of the mentoring program at a policy level and the relations between the mentees and mentors set the terms on which mentoring occurs, defining the value and the credibility that the program is perceived to have for individuals and the organisation. These perceptions in turn shape the sustainability of mentoring. As mentees increase their confidence through mentoring by overcoming uncertainties, they develop distinct forms of knowledge through learning about self and others, about professional and organisational life, about dealing with tricky situations with colleagues and clients. These new found (or rediscovered) competences form mentoring capital.

Mentoring capital essentially seeks to address the gap in the otherwise unequal distribution of knowledge and power in an organisational setting. It provides access for people who are positioned in the lower reaches of the management hierarchy to engage with others (not their direct supervisors) with greater power and elevated status to assist them to develop competences that will benefit them in their own and other organisations. Mentoring capital is not merely a social resource that is used for skill development, completing a project but also an important element of an individual's status in the hierarchy (Bourdieu 1986). Mentoring capital also includes the sum of a person's subjective dispositions including self-image and actions as well as their internalisation of social and cultural norms, social structures and relationships—referred to as 'habitus' (Browitt 2004). An internalised habitus guides the mentee about what is appropriate or inappropriate (sometimes becoming an inner critic see Chap. 8), available or unavailable for them to access or draw upon and also what is possible or impossible for individuals of different standings in a given social situation. Habitus is both encouraging and self-limiting. In regard to its positive effects, it guides mentees' preferences, choices and their relationships within groups and sub-cultures. Habitus captures the manner in which individuals' dispositions are structured by deep socio-historical conditioning (Widick 2004). As such, it is an expression of individuals' social status as well as historical position within a given context. Some examples of this include historically, a nurse, female; low status; CEO male; high status. Habitus is also self-limiting in that it can result in fixed assumptions about how the person perceives themselves especially in relation to others. The longer such beliefs or assumptions go unchallenged, the more likely that incidents especially negative ones reinforce the faulty conviction and prevent the person from seeing anything to the contrary. Habitus, whether positive or negative creates a self-fulfilling prophesy as mentees act according to their fixed assumptions and beliefs. The longer this pattern goes unaddressed, the harder it is to unravel. This is where mentoring is significantly effective and builds 'capital' for the mentee to draw upon in the future assisting them to be more flexible not only their thinking but also their actions. Mentoring capital helps the mentee build a positive mind set.

Understanding mentoring capital is inextricably linked to workplaces, professional milieus and other social spaces where individuals' assumptions, beliefs, values and actions are played out in interaction with each other (based on Bourdieu's 1984 notion of 'field'). Individuals hold their own position and implement their own strategies to engage and contend with other players for various outcomes including maintaining or improving their status. If the latter they amass personal resources in its various forms (Thomson 2008, p. 69). Multiple fields exist in society, and each field has its own history, rules, and social orders and people learn to navigate their way through these sometimes with the assistance of mentors and the like.

## 9.13 Conclusion

There are a number of lessons to be learnt. Mentoring is a powerful resource for staff and continues to be cited as an important strategy. As can be seen from the case examples above there are many different viewpoints and techniques for determining the most appropriate mentoring strategy and approach for organisations. There is no one right approach to mentoring pertaining to all organisations. For example, mentoring required by a leader transitioning to the executive suite is very different from someone who is progressing to the positions of supervisor or team leader. Identifying the best possible mentoring approach for an organisation includes identification of the type of work e.g. service delivery, operations, marketing, finance, professional or creative services, the complexity of the organisation, and the knowledge and professionalisation of the workforce. The optimal approach is determined by assessing the organisational context, its strategy, culture and leadership. It also depends on the internal resources already in place that staff can access such as succession planning, career development programs, and the like.

A well-designed mentoring program is a key to identifying, attracting, filling, and retaining corporate mentoring. The elements of the program should include a strategy and execution of the process outlined at the outset of this chapter.

Mentoring and mentoring development are a critical aspect of attaining optimum output from organisational talent management and requires the effective execution of many talent management practices. Flexible online applications provide an enabling e-learning platform, including capability assessments, succession and career planning and development programs. The benefits of an optimised mentoring program include

a. A pipeline of capability and mentoring talent
b. Talent aligned with corporate goals
c. Improved engagement
d. Increased retention
e. Improved know how and know to do
f. Consistent measurement through development and performance management.

All organisations need strong leadership. Practices to develop the workforce and individual staff assist in building this capacity.

## References

ABS 2071.0—*Reflecting a nation: Stories from the 2011 census*, 2012–2013. (2012 June). Released at 11:30 AM (Canberra time).

Archer, J. (2010). State of the science in health professional education: Effective feedback. *Medical Education, 44*(1), 101–108.

Avolio, B. J., & Reichard, R. J. (2008). The rise of authentic followership. In R. E. Riggio, I. Chaleff, & J. Lipman-Blumen (Eds.), *The art of followership* (pp. 325–337). San Francisco, CA, USA: Jossey-Bass.

Bindal, T., Wall, D., & Goodyear, H. (2011). Trainee doctors' views on workplace-based assessments: Are they just a tick box exercise? *Medical Teacher, 33*(11), 919–927.

Bourdieu, P. (1984). *Distinction: A social critique of the judgment of taste* (R. Nice, Trans.). Cambridge, MA: Harvard University Press.

Bourdieu, P. (1986). The forms of capital. In J. G. Richardson (Ed.), *Handbook of theory and research for the sociology of education New York* (pp. 241–258). NY: Greenwood.

Bourdieu, P. (1994). *Practical reason: On the theory of action*. Cambridge, UK: Polity Press.

Browitt, J. (2004). Pierre Bourdieu: Homo sociologicus. In J. Browitt & B. Nelson (Eds.), *Practising theory: Pierre Bourdieu and the field of cultural production* (pp. 1–12). Newark, DE: University of Delaware Press.

Chaleff, I. (2009). *The courageous follower*. San Francisco, CA: Berett-Koehler Publishers.

Chatman, J. A., & Cha, S. E. (2003). Leading by leveraging culture. *California Management Review, 45*(4), 20–34.

Chell, E. (2008). *The entrepreneurial personality: A social construction* (Vol. 2). London: Routledge.

Colombo, M., & Senatore, A. (2005). The discursive construction of community identity. *Journal of Community and Applied Social Psychology, 15*, 48–62.

Grenier, S., Chiocchio, F., & Beaulieu, G. (2012). Performance appraisal and motivation at work: Research proposals for feedback on the performance that promotes the satisfaction of psychological needs. *Management International, 16*(4), 169–179.

Grossen, M., & Salazar Orvig, A. (2011). Dialogism and dialogicality in the study of the self. *Culture and Psychology, 17*, 491–509.

Heidegger, M. (2011). *The concept of time* (I. Farin, Trans., 2nd ed.). New York; Continuum.

Kudisch, J. D., Fortunato, V. J., & Smith, A. F. R. (2006). Contextual and individual difference factors predicting individuals' desire to provide upward feedback. *Group and Organization Management, 31*(4), 503–529.

Marsick, V. J., & Watkins, K. E. (2003). Demonstrating the value of an organization's learning culture: The dimensions of the learning organization questionnaire. *Advances in Developing Human Resources, 5*, 132–151.

McNamee, S. (2004). Commentary—Imagine Chicago: A methodology for cultivating community social construction in practice. *Journal of Community and Applied Social Psychology, 14*, 406–409.

Morrison, E. (2002). Newcomers' relationships: The role of social network ties during socialisation. *The Academy of Management Journal, 45*(6), 1149–1160.

Northcraft, G. B., & Ashford, S. J. (1990). The preservation of self in everyday life: The effects of performance expectations and feedback context on feedback inquiry. *Organisational Behaviour and Human Decision Processes, 47*(1), 310–334.

Nyhan, R. C. (2000). Changing the paradigm: Trust and its role in public sector organisations. *American Review of Public Administration, 30*(1), 87–109.

Pahl, R. (2005). Are all communities, communities in the mind? *The Sociological Review, 53*, 621–640.

Peterson, R. S., & Behfarb, K. J. (2003). The dynamic relationship between performance feedback, trust, and conflict in groups: A longitudinal study. *Organisational Behaviour and Human Decision Processes, 92*, 102–112.

Reid, A. (2013). Environmental education research: Towards and beyond passionate, scholarly conversation. *Environmental Education Research, 19*(2), 147–153.

Rosen, C. C., Levy, P. E., & Hall, R. J. (2006). Placing perceptions of politics in the context of the feedback environment, employee attitudes, and job performance. *Journal Applied Psychology, 91*(1), 211–220.

Rummler, G. A., & Brache, A. P. (2012). *Improving performance: How to manage the white space on the organizational chart* (3rd ed.). San Francisco, CA, USA: Jossey-Bass.

Schneider, B., Ehrhart, M., & Macey, W. (2013). Organisational climate and culture. *Annual Review of Psychology, 64*, 361–388.

Schubert, J. D. (2008). Suffering/symbolic violence. In M. Grenfell (Ed.), *Pierre Bourdieu: Key concepts Durham*. Acumen: England.

Senge, P. (1990). *The fifth discipline: The art and practice of the learning organisation*. Transworld.

Swartz, D. (1997). *Culture and power: The sociology of Pierre Bourdieu*. Chicago, IL: University of Chicago Press.

Tan, C. (2013). *Learning from Shanghai: Lessons on achieving educational success*. Dordrecht: Springer.

Tayfur, O. (2012). Antecedents of feedback seeking behaviours: Review of the feedback seeking literature. *American International Journal of Contemporary Research, 2*, 92–101.

Thomson, P. (2008). Field. In M. Grenfell (Ed.), *Pierre Bourdieu: Key concepts* (pp. 67–84). Durham, England: Acumen.

van der Rijt, J., Segers, M., Van den Bossche, P., Gijselaers, W., & van de Wiel, M. (2012). The role of individual and organisational characteristics in feedback seeking behaviour in the initial career stage. *Human resource development international, 15*(2), 233–257.

Widick, R. (2004). Flesh and the free market: On taking Bourdieu to the options exchange. In D. L. Swartz & V. L. Zolberg (Eds.), *After Bourdieu: Influence, critique, elaboration* (pp. 193–238). Boston, MA: Kluwer Academic Publishers.

# Chapter 10
# Mentoring for Resilience and Sustainability

*And it ought to be remembered that there is nothing more difficult to take in hand, more perilous to conduct, or more uncertain in its success, than to take the lead in the introduction of a new order of things.*

Machiavelli The Prince (1992 Chapter VI)

**Abstract** The final chapter reinforces the power of mentoring as a process of building support and ultimately resilience for the mentee. Ideally, it engenders within the mentee, deep learning to sustain them well beyond their mentoring experience. Processes to ensure the sustainability of mentoring from the strategic to the personal are discussed. The outcome is that the mentee uses mentoring as a springboard to enhance their personal and professional power to make a difference in their life.

## 10.1 Introduction

Mentees and mentors are taking things in hand, taking the lead to question the old order of things so that the foundations for the future can be laid down firmly. It is a perilous journey as many have discovered.

The focus of this chapter is on both mentoring for resilience and ensuring its sustainability. What it means in terms of being a worthwhile professional pursuit with real value for mentees. Sustainability is always open to interpretation. Given this, how sustainable is mentoring, in the sense that it viable, workable and maintainable especially in workplaces? From the outset of this book, it was stated that conceptualising mentoring is not straightforward as it crosses over into coaching, sponsoring and even counselling in terms of the processes it employs and the skills that it draws upon.



A.M. Brewer, *Mentoring from a Positive Psychology Perspective*,
DOI 10.1007/978-3-319-40983-2_10

## 10.2 Resilient Mentoring

Resilience, as stated in Chap. 8, is the capability to adjust to "adversity, maintain equilibrium, retain some sense of control over their environment, and continue to move on in a positive manner" (Jackson et al. 2007, p. 3).

Resilient mentoring assists mentees get on the front foot; provide or restore their voice, build their confidence leading to an enhanced feeling of positivity. For resilience to be sustained mentoring needs to occur so that learning and benefits are able to be implemented and improved once mentoring has ceased. In this sense mentoring is a form of participatory action learning and action research which lead to outcomes both personally and professionally. Through participation with the mentor, mentees learn how to detect and correct the impacts of their own actions which can be applied in their lives beyond mentoring. Moreover, for the capacity to detect and correct to become sustainable, actions need to be performed within a broader participatory framework that compels mentees to be attentive through questioning to discover what is impeding their progress or to pull themselves up, when they may fall back into routine habits of thinking and doing (Argyris 1993, 2000). It is through this process that mentees can see the value of adjusting their approach and continue to do so.

Resilient mentoring assumes that learning is at its core especially when the mentee needs to address and challenge situations. What generally happens in most situations is this: an issue, question or problem initiates the process. It may not present formally as this. For example, the mentee may be called to a meeting. During the meeting, an issue is discussed which requires a decision. At this point members proffer suggestions, others disagree. People will take sides, emotions may become charged as people persuade others to their way of thinking. As this situation develops, the conflicts and the emotions impede deep and thoughtful learning. Surface learning often leads to decisions being made which are unactionable due to low commitment, lack of understanding or simply little follow through to implementation. In other words, decisions are made for the sake of arriving at a decision point without considering the consequences and longer term impacts. Without deeper, critically reflective learning to override these automatic, taken-for-granted, habitual responses by mentees, then nothing changes.

It is important for mentees to know how to engage in critical learning so they can override and create opportunities to solve issues for themselves. A challenge addressed this way is a learning opportunity for a process that is potentially repeatable and sustained.

Resilient mentoring is a logical, critical learning process that is learnt within the mentoring context and can be readily applied outside it. By assisting mentees identify their current patterns of thinking and doing and what options they have to modify especially if their present ones are not working well for them. Applied to mentoring, the double loop learning perspective helps mentees identify any defensiveness on theirs and other's parts, which is important in coming to terms with complex issues in often complicated scenarios. By understanding the frameworks, it intensifies their capacity to learn and reason productively. This new reasoning process would replace the former one which may be limiting options and action choices available to mentees, leading them to use more protective, habitual strategies consistent with their taken-for-granted world view.

The basis of resilient mentoring is twofold:

(a) communicative learning: 'Through communicative learning a person constructs an inter-subjective understanding of a situation with others, which becomes especially relevant in the context of wicked problems where there is no clear knowledge, or perhaps there is conflicting knowledge, available about the situation or the best solution' (Muro and Jeffrey 2008, p. 3). Transformative learning describes a process where people gradually change their views on the world and themselves. Such a transformation often occurs in response to an external 'trigger', when faced with a disorienting dilemma. These dilemmas or anomalies cannot be explained by old ways of knowing and eventually lead to critical reflection and perspective transformations (Muro and Jeffrey 2008, p. 3).

(b) double loop learning: Argyris (1977) distinguishes between two forms of learning: 'single-loop learning' (SLL) and 'double-loop learning' (DLL) as follows:

'Single-loop learning' refers to the non-reflective, non-critical type of learning that people tend to adopt when dealing with complex problem solving. As a result, they fail to engage in processes of detecting errors and adjusting existing strategies to meet new requirements. SLL is non-reflective and non-critical because it 'does not solve the most basic problem of why these problems existed in the first place' (Argyris 1990, p. 92). When people 'deal with issues that are embarrassing or threatening, their reasoning and action conform to a type of theory-in-use I call Model I' (Argyris 2004, p. 62), which they implement to protect and defend themselves against fundamental, disruptive change; 'almost uniformly, we deal with difficult situations by not dealing with them. We find ways to pretend to engage and in fact manage to avoid engaging and keep what we are doing hidden from ourselves' (Argyris 2010, p. 22, emphasis in original). Thus, when negotiators are on the defensive due to the threats and potential embarrassments triggered by difficult conflicts, they are likely to rely, with speed and automaticity, on the non-reflective, non-critical single loop learning pattern. The SLL pattern is often characterised by learners saying one thing and doing another, denying or becoming unaware of the gap, making the denial undiscussible, then making the undiscussibility of the denial itself undiscussible and closing the matter to themselves and others, thus whirling into a self-sealing, anti-learning loop. This loop explains the axiom that people who are on the defensive tend to learn very little, if at all; they are usually busy shielding themselves from potential threats and embarrassment. In fact, data collected under defensive conditions (about the self, the conflict, and the negotiating party) are usually marred by bias and are typically used to build counterattacks (Malhorta and Murnighan 2008).

The unconscious and automatic defensiveness triggers the automatic and taken-for-granted master plan of Model I action strategies, which 'tells individuals to craft their positions, evaluations, and attributions in ways that inhibit inquiry into them and tests of them with others' logic. The consequences of these Model I strategies are likely to be defensiveness, misunderstanding, and self-fulfilling and self-sealing processes' (Argyris 1993, p. 52). It is worth mentioning here that SLL can be appropriate in some conflict situations, for example in simple or routine contexts (Argyris 1993, 2004). Argyris (2004, p. 11) suggests that 'Model I produces actions that are skilful yet incompetent because they produce consequences that the actors do not intend. The actors are unaware of their skilful incompetence while producing it', and they do it with speed and automaticity because the very action required to be skilful produces unawareness. Once people become skilled, they forget much of what they went through to become skilful. Skilful actions are those that work, that appear effortless, that are automatic, and usually tacit, and that are taken for granted.

Accordingly, SLL and its anti-learning patterns are likely to trigger negotiators to summon their respective habitual conflict-handling strategies—for example, fleeing the conflict for an avoider, giving up the store for a yielder, competing viciously for a win-lose negotiator. Alternatively, when low defensiveness reduces the chances of adopting non-reflective SLL, a negotiator may find it possible to shift slightly, temporarily, and only instrumentally from one habitual negotiation style to another (e.g. an avoider trying the yielding style), but the move will not be of the type that requires questioning rooted assumptions, frames of reference, and governing values that inform actions. Finally, it is worth noting that while conditions exist where any of these habitual styles may be appropriate to handle the conflict at hand (e.g. Lewicki et al. 2010), the emphasis here is on habitual responses versus thoughtful and critical reflection on the conflict at hand.

'Double-loop learning', by contrast, refers to a more profound process of learning, where 'underlying organisational policies and objectives' (Argyris 1977, p. 116). This process requires deeper thinking, and challenges underlying assumptions which are questioned and changed. It militates against skimming the surface in problem analysis and encourages people to investigate, identify options and weigh these up, which can lead to further modification. In this way, outcomes and results are not superficially compared with the supporting factors or strategies. In double loop learning the factors that govern the context, especially those that are not obvious, are closely examined. A key component of double loop learning is a reflection.

This effect is attributed to the low experience of failure by many leaders up until the point where they are leading complex situations. Part of the defensiveness comes from their heightened visibility due to the roles they have assumed in their professional life. Moreover, people fear failure and when they do not achieve their aspirations they experience an "inappropriately high sense of despondency, or even despair" (Argyris 1991, p. 104). This fear of failure is detrimental to maintaining a sense of self-control, confidence and building self-efficacy. Often the training, the

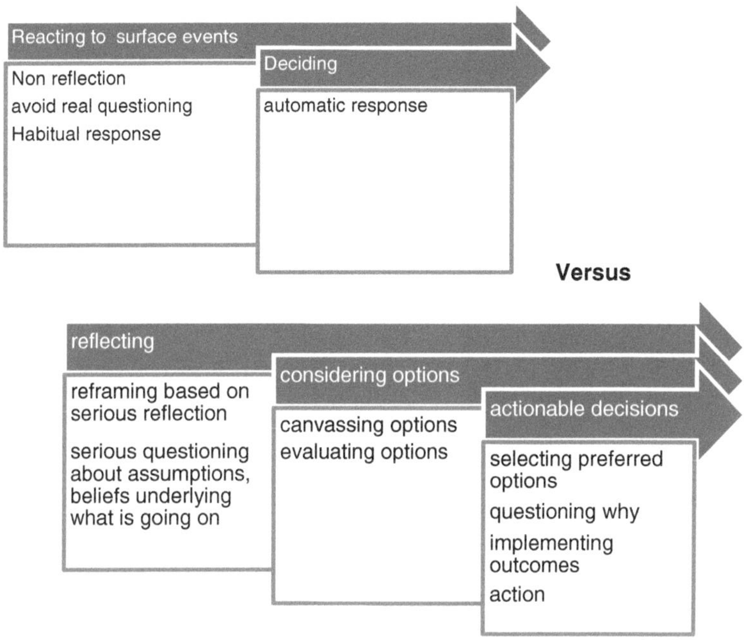


**Fig. 10.1** Single loop learning versus double loop learning

socialisation and the very nature of the work that leaders have done does not always provide the best preparation for leadership.

Dealing with double-loop problems necessitates understanding human defences especially where people may feel embarrassed or threatened. In these instances, double-loop learning comes to the fore. Mentees are often sitting on problems that are difficult to discuss e.g. harassment, diversity issues. The difficulty in finding the courage to raise these issues is according to Agyris (1970) a double-loop problem. Issues that mentees continue to experience are likely to have double-loop issues embedded in them. For example, a mentee might be sent to training, due to their attitude/behaviour and yet the real issue lies within their relationship with their supervisor. Both the mentee and the supervisor know this. The supervisor will not address it and is likely to deny it, so the mentee goes along with the pretence, effectively covering up the issue. The problem remains unsolved (Fig. 10.1).

Most issues and situations that cause people concern have elements of self-protection within them. For example, mentees may be concerned about what it will mean for them, their role, position, relationships if they uncover the real issues of concern. In any situation whether there are conflicts, internal or external i.e., whether they reside in the situation implicitly or explicitly, people move to one or other point of view and engage in some sort of protective behaviour, to defend their position. The more critical the issue, the more overt this becomes as well as the rise in emotions. People may disagree without anyone's knowledge as they may not have declared their position. Hence conflict may be overt or covert. If taking a particular position leads to a decision that changes the current situation, some people will see themselves as winners and others as losers. Attempts to maintain or change the situation or policy leads to conflict and even resistance because one or more people disapprove of what is happening, why it is occurring, the person responsible and the process itself, or its likely outcomes (Lewicki et al. 2010). Change for many people evokes feelings of anxiety, fear, and being threatened due to heightened uncertainty. Such feelings trigger and exacerbate protective behaviours Argyris (1993). This situation becomes layered by the complexity of responses including emotional responses to the original suggestion. Once this spiral takes hold, people start to agitate and compete for their preferred option: aim, process, person, outcome (Kets de Vries 2004). Any form of violence mimics this process as emotions fuel automatic responses to the situation (Feldman et al. 2007).

Resilient mentoring assists mentees to become more aware, own up and deliberate on their responses directing them to purposeful outcomes through

a. awareness of the influence or at least the possibility of influence by others; intentionally or otherwise,
b. capability to exert the control through being prepared with evidence, and
c. focused attention to become purposive.

How?

Through critical thinking defined as "the intellectually disciplined process of actively and skilfully conceptualising, applying, analysing, synthesising and/or evaluation information gathered from, or generated by observation, experience, reflection, reasoning or communication as a guide to belief and action" (Scriven and Paul 2008 cited in Mulnix 2012, p. 465).

Mentoring mindedness is essentially critical thinking rather than descriptive questioning by the mentor and descriptive recall by the mentee—a process that typically characterises conventional mentoring. An example of a critical question to a mentee is 'what are some of the changes you could make about …?' This question requires the mentee accessing their understanding and some analysis of the situation under focus. It demands heightened perception and evaluation and invites the mentee to consider actions. The next stage following this, once fully explored delves into limitations to potential action. However, this would not occur until limitations to current thinking are explored. Most critical questioning needs to be neutral in judgement. An example of a critical question to explore this would be 'why do you think this?' The mentee's response requires evaluating, creating a reason based on judgement and being able to blend various factors into a newly constructed viewpoint. The mentor develops critical thinking through questioning the mentee's own circumstances, moving from the abstract to the concrete, from the 'what if' to the 'given' context. In this way, the mentee starts to feel empowered.

| Aim | How to break it down | Approach |
|---|---|---|
| 1. **Understanding**: the mentor encourages the mentee to understand and express meaning about their experiences. | Describing what they mean | The mentee self-directs their thinking without judgement. |
| | Interpreting meaning | The mentee explains what it means for them; appreciates non-verbal behaviour and how this contributes to their situation. |
| | Explaining meaning | The mentee restates or the mentor reflects so as to reaffirm what they said; all the while preserving their original meaning or correcting what they intended to say. Help iron out ambiguities. |
| 2. **Investigate**: the mentor assists the mentee identify the intended and actual inferences within their statements, questions, descriptions, beliefs, judgments about others or events; their experiences, reasons for thinking in a particular way, and their opinions. | Examining ideas | The mentee compares their statements throughout their conversation and from one to the next with the mentor's assistance. |
| | Determining reasons | The mentee reviews their claims; opinion versus evidence. |
| | Considering their conclusions | The mentee states (a) their intended conclusion, (b) the grounds for and reasons underlying this, (c) any extraneous factors which may be impacting the situations, (d) and with the mentor's assistance any tacit reasoning, (e) focuses on the intended line of reasoning, and then they (f) check for non-verbal meaning which either accords or contradicts their stated expressions. |
| 3. **Appraise**: together the mentor assists the mentee assess what they are saying against what they believe or perceive, their experiences, situations, judgments, beliefs, or opinions; as well as inferences. | Weighing up their statements | The mentee states what factors are relevant here to assist them to make their own judgements. |
| | Assessing statements | The mentee focuses on their reasoning and emotional relationship: what they are feeling, thinking is it aligned with what they are saying? What is the likelihood of their thinking relevant to the situations they encounter at work? How much more information do they need? |

(continued)

(continued)

| Aim | How to break it down | Approach |
|---|---|---|
| 4. **Inference**: the mentor using a reflective question approach assists the mentee reach a way forward. | Further questioning | To work out what information is required; to determine plausible ways for acquiring that information; to develop a persuasive argument to support one's opinion, to evaluate contextual information. |
| | Proposing options | The mentee formulates multiple alternatives for resolving a problem, develops 2–3 options for addressing and resolving the given problem; works out their priorities, considers any further difficulties and the benefits which are likely to result if they make a decision on this basis. |
| | Resolving | The mentee expresses an intent to want to understand and resolve their internal or external conflicts. |
| 5. **Elucidation**: the mentor assists the mentee to clarify and explain ideas taking into account context; history, key stakeholders and relationships. | Asserting and affirming what is known | The mentees state reasons for holding a given view. |
| | Modifying choices | The mentee weighs up each option by examining the pros and cons of each. |
| | Stating preferred option | The mentee explains the reasons and how they evaluated the situation to arrive at their preferred option. |
| 6. **Focusing on what is important**: the mentor assists the mentee monitor thinking and ideas, the elements contributing to those thoughts, and the outcomes. The mentor uses questioning, confirming, validating, or checking the mentee's reasoning and outcomes. | Focusing on self | The mentee examines their views sensitive to personal bias; self-interest; to identify and review evidence of situation, experience, opinions or assumptions in coming to a given point of view; to identify and assess reasons and reasoning processes in coming to a given conclusion. |
| | Making relevant amendments | The mentee revises their viewpoint and then work out if the revisions warrant changes in any other aspects. |

If the mentor does not have a critical thinking approach in that it is not understood, then all questioning strategies are haphazard with little consistency in regard to internal logic. The mentee can become lost along the way as will the mentor.

Understanding the distinctions between critical questions, opposing questions and descriptive questions assists mentors examine their current practices and avoid confusion in the mentoring conversation. It also helps create a baseline of understanding. Mentoring conversations can lead to more meaningful goals and strategies for action. This understanding has the power to move mentoring to a new significance.

Mentoring would look noticeably different. Depending on the mentor, changes could occur in the way they interact with mentees, the focus may be shifted, the learning outcomes may change. Due to the complex and frequently messy conversations between mentors and mentees, the critical questioning helps construct distinct themes for each meeting. This process leads to follow up on from one meeting to the next.

Mentoring would change as mentors infused conversations with critical learning, inviting the voice of the mentee and encouraging them to be critical. Critical mentoring begs mentors to examine "uncritical acceptance of and obedience" to governing norms and values, and taken-for-granted rituals and repertoires that mentees have bought into unwittingly or unwillingly. For mentoring to be satisfyingly effective for mentees, they need to feel that the issues have been tackled well by the mentor; and likewise for the mentor. It assists mentees to learn not to avoid challenging issues in their work or professional contexts. Most contexts are filled with an array of challenging concerns that need to be dealt with which either effect work outcomes, personal ones or both for the mentee. Mentoring mindedness is about learning, replacing or supplementing habits of the mind as fundamental to gaining wisdom and resilience. Time in mentoring needs to be balanced between building new knowledge and skills in regard to thinking and practising these in relation to future action and empowerment. Mentoring is a huge investment by individuals and organisations. It can rely on skimming the surface, or dealing with trivial issues. Its aim is to face the big questions that mentees bring to it providing the invitation to open up on these is there.

## 10.3 Moving to Sustainability

The next step is to embed this process encouraging the mentee to bring together their perceptions, reasoning, emotions and aligning this to their goals. This in itself can pose a trap (Kets de Vries and Korotov 2007) for mentees if they have not integrated a critical learning approach to their complex problem solving situations. If they have not, then the outcome is nothing better than surface learning characterised by double loop learning where they become puzzled and wedged between different viewpoints, assumptions and conflict. Things become "undiscussible" (that is not up for discussion either implicitly or explicitly) enforcing one or other to suppress their voice, to silence them and to feel intimidated. The mentor through the mentoring process assists mentees question their repeated thoughts and actions so that they can untangle themselves from this self-defeating spiral. Avoiding or ignoring it will not resolve this problem. A dynamic, reflective process between the mentee and mentor establishes a framework for deep learning, assisting the mentee to make sense of their challenges, which ultimately provides greater insights regarding their intra and interpersonal conflicts.

Resilient mentoring is aimed at critical and flexible learning and is an advantage for mentees in that it provides them with a process for delving into issues and problems that they encounter. The process allows mentees to foster within them an approach to change their everyday learning processes. It assists them demystify complexity, clarify ambiguity, question assumptions which means they return not to the "site" where they encounter the issue but to reflect on the governing values that surround and contribute to it (see Argyris' 1993, 2004) perspective, Cunliffe's 2009) 'complexifying' concept). This process of learning is sustainable. While sustainability may be considered a platitude by some (Jamali 2006); its continued use suggests the salience of the experience for mentees, a state or a process that can be maintained for the foreseeable future to meet the demand of those seeking to change the order of things.

How does this sustainability align with mentoring? Building and sustaining learning from mentoring is a challenging effort for both the mentee and mentor. Sustainable mentoring is potentially integrating all the dimensions of an issue and putting them on the table rather than seeing them as individual (i.e. the mentee's) issues. Sustainable mentoring is a process that is measured on a continuous scale where the store of learning is increased throughout the mentoring relationship for both parties.

It refers to its endurance for its beneficiaries, current and future. If these important processes are to be sustained, they need to be done in a way that does not deplete the resources or become resource draining including human effort and willingness.

The concepts of mentoring and sustainability together are novel. It is important to ask the following questions:

a. What aspects of communication patterns in a community assist in creating a sustainable future or what characteristics are necessary for a sustainable learning community over time?
b. What are the necessary conditions for a sustainable community learning process?

In addressing these issues, the focus needs to be on aspects of a sustainable learning processes as well as community characteristics e.g. community engagement, ties which are essential for collaboration, co-operation and social problem solving.

From an economic perspective, sustainability and capital go hand in hand. While capital in an economic sense suggests a transformation of resources into products or services for financial exchange, here it refers to the transformation of human attributes and resources. Learning sustainability is linked to learning capital (based on Jeffries and Rogers 2007). This form of capital is built up over time to improve people's problem solving, gaining knowledge, know-how and wisdom as well as their learning relationships.

Just as economic capital means having a ready supply and demand of resources so too is it relevant for learning capital relying on effective opportunities for learning and mentoring, developing interpersonal trust, opportune social links, a climate for the differences in values and opinions. Three questions are posed here:

1. What aspects of the learning capital are important for a community to sustain itself?
2. What would make this sustainable?
3. What policies are needed for this process to occur? For example:

a. A climate of communication
b. A commitment to community and community action
c. Need for knowledge and know how, problem solving and exchange of wisdom
d. Managed diversity
e. Level of public activity
f. Utilisation of current resources
g. Organisational involvement
h. Institutional trust
i. A speedy and efficient diffusion pattern of information, news and events
j. Access to pertinent expertise through open communication channels
k. Established channels connecting community leaders with participants.

Mentoring is founded on a conversation between a mentee and a mentor. Through a series of conversations, stories and experiences are shared through multiple processes of listening, inquiry, reflection, purposeful questioning and action-"orienteering" (i.e. the mentee works and the mentor to find a way forward) to highlight a few of these. When mentoring works effectively, it is a powerful learning journey to create a new future for the mentee (Senge et al. 2005), which requires some degree of transformational change on their part, particularly strength in terms of emotions and resolution as outlined as follows. A great deal of research on organisational development and change shows that most are briefly effective, without long-lasting impact. These programs quickly erode. Failure is likely when change requires behaviours not supported elsewhere or by management in the case of organisations. The learning and lasting effects of mentoring could easily follow a similar route.

It is important to consider: What must be done to ensure that the value of the mentoring journey: its relationship and learnings are not wasted? How can professions and employers develop a far-reaching capability to ensure that the mentee's new learning is translatable into actions for the wider benefit of others?

## 10.4 The Potentially Sustainable Effects of Mentoring

Mentoring is associated with 'social capital' and 'social cohesion', concepts that encompass social networks, reciprocity and features of social organisation such as the integration of resulting social action. With this in mind, the sustainability of mentoring has a number of dimensions:

| Mentoring dimensions | Skills developed and enhanced through mentoring |
|---|---|
| Situation | Understanding limitations, change orientation: working around them for flexible and responsive change; balance shorter-term with longer-term needs |
| Mindedness | Self-efficacy; reflection, learning from mistakes; the ability of mentees to continue their learning and to attain an acceptable level of professional function and development |
| Professionalism | The quality and professionalism (does not mean qualifications rather how they conduct themselves) of the mentor |
| Endurance | Tenacity, fortitude, patience; persuasive energy |
| Collaboration | Teamwork, partnership, co-operation; trust |
| Innovation | Translating ideas into implementable actions |
| Mutuality | Empathy, support, affinity with the profession, the organisation, the team; organising people and networks |

Based on Senge (2008), Lueneburger and Goleman (2010)

## 10.5 Processes to Ensure Sustainability of Mentoring

For mentoring to become sustainable, it requires some form of evaluation post-mentoring, especially if instituted as part of a formal program in the workplace. The form of the evaluation is again a three-way conversation between the mentee, mentor and the "assessor" (e.g. a senior practitioner from the profession or the organisation). A 360° process might also be an important part of this assessment to provide feedback as a baseline prior to mentoring and then again say 12 months down the track. The focus of the assessment is about improvement at professional, organisational and personal levels. Another form of assessment could be an action oriented project with a supervisor (other than the current mentor) to assess the application of the mentee's learning in an operational context.

The sustainability of mentoring involves the extent that the mentee can socially interact with colleagues, navigate their professional networks; participate in local, formal and informal; levels of trust with a positive sense of identification with, and pride in, the chosen profession.

The sustainable view of mentorship is based on the notion that all mentees are members of organisations, professions, groups and networks. The idea that mentoring creates value for the mentee in that it is knowledge based, knowledge creating and generates confidence by bringing together strategies to ensure that individual performance combines a concern for both the collective world that the mentee belongs in and interacts with.

### 10.5.1 Board and Management Support

Boards need to be focused on the triple bottom line: financial, environmental and social. The latter includes social impact of its people: customers, staff and key stakeholders. In this book, our focus is on staff and how the organisation is dealing with the issues that their staff have to learn and handle which includes customer and stakeholder relationships as well as the development of staff.

Mentoring alone is not enough. It requires other processes and systems to support it including how decisions are made including resource allocation, developing staff and leaders, blind recruitment and promotion (where the candidate's demographic characteristics are unknown to the decision makers); and flexible work processes.

### 10.5.2 Shared Influence

Few organisations, despite their organisational charts, truly function through centralised power given that they rely on global online networks 24/7. In other words, management rely on staff at various levels of authority, to make decisions. Protocols are in place, and highly trained staff at all levels are required. All staff are able to persuade, influence and decide without necessarily being in a position of high authority.

### 10.5.3 A Capability Strategy

A capability strategy involves change and refreshment in line with changing needs of the professions, organisations, consumers as well as other social trends including technological change.

Mentoring is an important driver of capability development: it is focused on individuals, outcomes are relatively immediate, and it can be followed up especially through a formal evaluation process, post-mentoring.

It is important to continue a dialogue in mentoring about its critical approach to thinking, finding ways to emphasise critical reflection, questioning of governing norms and other constraints including systems thinking. This approach can be challenging to implement and achieve. However, it has the power to render mentoring more relevant and meaningful it needs to be seriously considered.

## 10.6 Conclusion

After centuries of practice and decades of research, mentoring remains the backbone of support for novices, people making career and life transitions. Mentoring itself has gone through transitions, and this will continue as organisations and career pathways change. The primary purpose of this book was to take a deep dive into mentoring to answer the following questions: why, what, with whom, when, where and how. In addition, examining the social and organisational influences in the broader context that continue to shape mentoring is essential. This knowledge will assist both mentees and mentors to bring about positive outcomes in their relationships and lives.

## References


Argyris, C. (1990). *Overcoming organisational defenses: Facilitating organisational learning*. Boston, MA: Allyn and Bacon.

Argyris, C. (1991). *Teaching smart people how to learn* (pp. 99–109). Harvard Business Review (May–June).

Argyris, C. (1993). *Knowledge for action: A guide to overcoming barriers to organisational change*. San Francisco, CA: Jossey-Bass.

Argyris, C. (2000). *Flawed advice and the management trap*. Oxford: Oxford University Press.

Argyris, C. (2004). *Reasons and rationalisations*. Oxford: Oxford University Press.

Argyris, C. (2010). *Organisational traps: Leadership, culture, organizational design*. Oxford: Oxford University Press.

Cunliffe, A. L. (2009). The philosopher leader: On relationalism, ethics and reflexivity : a critical perspective to teaching leadership. *Management Learning, 40*(1), 87–101.

Feldman, L.B., Lindquist, K., & Gendron, M. (2007) Language as context for the perception of emotion. *Trends in Cognitive Sciences, 11*(8), 327–332.

Jackson, D., Firtko, A., & Edenborough, M. (2007). Personal resilience as a strategy for surviving and thriving in the face of workplace adversity: A literature review. *Journal of Advanced Nursing, 60*(1), 1–9.

Jamali, D. (2006). Insights into integration from a learning organization perspective. *Business Process Management Journal, 12*(6), 809–821.

Jeffries, P., & Rogers, K. (2007). Evaluating simulations. In P. Jeffries (Ed.) *Simulation in Nursing Education*. New York: Lawrence Erlbaum.

Kets de Vries, M. (2004). Organizations on the couch: A clinical perspective on organizational dynamics. *European Management Journal, 22*(2), 183–200.

Kets de Vries, M., & Korotov, K. (2007). Creating transformational executive education programs. *Academy of Management Learning and Education, 6*(3), 375–387.

Lewicki, R., Barry, B., & Saunders, D. (2010). *Negotiation* (6th ed.). Boston: McGraw Hill.

Lueneburger, C., & Goleman, D. (2010). The change leadership sustainability demands. *MIT Sloan Management Review, 51*(4).

Machiavelli, N. (1992). *The prince* (R. M. Adams, Trans.). New York: Norton (A revised translation).

Malhorta, D., & Murnigham, J. (2008). *When winning is everything* (pp. 78–86). Harvard Business Review (May).

Muro, M., & Jeffrey, P. (2008). A critical review of the theory and application of social learning in participatory natural resource management processes. *Journal of Environmental Planning and Management, 51*(3), 325–344.

Scriven, M., & Paul, R. (2008). In J. Mulnix (2012) (eds.), Thinking critically about critical thinking. *Educational Philosophy and Theory, 44*(5): 464–477 (Number 7).

Senge, P. M. (2008). *The necessary revolution: How individuals and organisations are working together to create a sustainable world.* New York: Doubleday.

Senge, P. M., Jaworski, J., Scharmer, C. O., & Flowers, B. S. (2005). *Presence: Exploring profound change in people, organisations and society.* New York: DoubleDay.

# Index





A.M. Brewer, *Mentoring from a Positive Psychology Perspective*,
DOI 10.1007/978-3-319-40983-2

FSC
www.fsc.org
MIX
Papier | Fördert
gute Waldnutzung
FSC® C083411

Kolibri 360 GmbH
Ferdinand-Jühlke-Straße 7
99095 Erfurt, Deutschland
produktsicherheit@kolibri360.de